HISTORY OF MATERIALISM AND CRITICISM OF ITS PRESENT IMPORTANCE • VOLUME 1 • FRIEDRICH ALBERT LANGE

Publisher's Note

The book descriptions we ask booksellers to display prominently warn that this is an historic book with numerous typos, missing text, images and indexes.

We scanned this book using character recognition software that includes an automated spell check. Our software is 99 percent accurate if the book is in good condition. However, we do understand that even one percent can be a very annoying number of typos! And sometimes all or part of a page is missing from our copy of a book. Or the paper may be so discolored from age that you can no longer read the type. Please accept our sincere apologies.

After we re-typeset and design a book, the page numbers change so the old index and table of contents no longer work. Therefore, we often remove them.

We would like to manually proof read and fix the typos and indexes, manually scan and add any illustrations, and track down another copy of the book to add any missing text. But our books sell so few copies, you would have to pay up to a thousand dollars for the book as a result.

Therefore, whenever possible, we let our customers download a free copy of the original typo-free scanned book. Simply enter the barcode number from the back cover of the paperback in the Free Book form at www.general-books.net. You may also qualify for a free trial membership in our book club to download up to four books for free. Simply enter the barcode number from the back cover onto the membership form on the same page. The book club entitles you to select from more than a million books at no additional charge. Simply enter the title or subject onto the search form to find the books.

If you have any questions, could you please be so kind as to consult our Frequently Asked Questions page at www.general-books.net/faqs.cfm? You are also welcome to contact us there.

General Books LLC™, Memphis, USA, 2012. ISBN: 9780217223553.

Grad. R. *R i THE ENGLISH AND FOREIGN PHILOSOPHICAL LIBRARY.*

Philosophical Inquiry is essentially the chief intellectual study of our age. It is proposed to produce, under the title of "The English And Foreign Philosophical Library," a series of works of the highest class connected with that study.

The English contributions to the series consist of original works, and of occasional new editions of such productions as have already attained a permanent rank among the philosophical writings of the day.

Beyond the productions of English writers, there are many recent publications in German and French which are not readily accessible to English readers, unless they are competent German and French scholars. Of these foreign writings, the translations have been entrusted to gentlemen whose names will be a guarantee for their critical fidelity.

"The English And Foreign Philosophical Library" claims to be free from all bias, and thus fairly to represent all developments of Philosophy, from Spinoza to Hartmann, from Leibnitz to Lotze. Each original work is produced under the inspection of its author, from his manuscript, without intermediate suggestions or alterations. As corollaries, works showing the results of Positive Science, occasionally, though seldom, find a place in the series.

The series is elegantly printed in octavo, and the price regulated by the extent of each volume. The volumes will follow in succession, at no fixed periods, but as early as is consistent with the necessary care in their production.

THE FOLLOWING HAVE ALREADY APPEARED:—

Vols. I.-III. Second Edition. Vol. I., post 8vo, pp.350, cloth, price 10s. 61.

A HISTORY OF MATERIALISM.

By Professor P. A. LANGE.

Authorised Translation from the German by Ernest C. Thomas.

(Vols. II. and III. in the press.)

"This is ft work which has long and impatiently been expected by a large circle of readers. It has been well praised by two eminent scientists, and their words have created for it. as regards its appearance in our English tongue, a sort of ante-natd reputation. The reputation is in many respects well deserved. The book is marked throughout by singular ability, abounds in striking and suggestive reflections, subtle and profound discussions, felicitous and graphic descriptions of mental aud social movements, both in themselves and in their mutual relations."—*Scotsman.*

"Although it is only a few years sinco Longc's book was originally published, it already ranks as a classic in the philosophical literature of Germany. He was not only *t* man of vat learning, but had a very rare power both of analysis and generalisation; and li is style Is singularly clear, strong, and graceful. Nominally only a history of materialiHm, It is in reality very much more. It takes in the whole development of philosophical opinion, but with especial reference to materialism. So far as he lias proceeded, Mr. Thomas bas done his work with great spirit and intelligence. We have tested the translation at different points, and have always found that, it reflects the original freely and accurately."—*Pall Mall Gazette.* ' Every section of Dr. Lunge's work is followed by a copious body of notes, abounding In references to authorities, and bearing ample testimony to the extensive reading of tbe t, author."—*Saturday Review.*

"We see no reason for not endorsing the translator's judgment that is ' raised far above tuo level of ordinary-controversial writing by its thoroughness, coinprohensivoife&s, and imi»artiality.

"—*Contemporary Review.*

"The English and Foreign Philosophical Library could not be more worthily inaugurated than by a translation of Langc's great work."—*Mind.*

Vol. IV. Post 8vo, pp. xii.—362, cloth, price ios. 6rl.

NATURAL LAW: An Essay in Ethics.

By EDITH BIMCOX.

Second Edition.

"Miss Sirocox deserves cordial recognition for the excellent v-ork she has done in vindication of naturalism, and especially for the high nobility of her ethical purpose."— *JtJtena-um.*

"A book which for the rest Is a mine of suggestion."—*Academy.*

"The writer's highest skill is seen in bringing together aspects of ideas which limit one another, and even seem to conflict, in elucidating the paradoxical side of accepted pr, positions, and embodying acute perceptions in elaborate epigrammatic periods."— *Examiner.*

"This thought hil and able work is in many respects the moat important contribution yet made to the ethics of the evolution theory."—*Mind.*

Vols. V. VI. In Two Volumes, post 8vo, pp. 268 and 288, cloth, price 15a.

THE CREED OF CHRISTENDOM: ITS FOUNDATIONS CONTRASTED WITH ITS SUPERSTRUCTURE,

By W. R. GREG.

Sixth Edition, with a New Introduction.

"Professional reproaches against a book so manly and modest, so evidently truthloving, Fo high-minded and devout, as this of Mr. Greg's, are but a melancholy imbecility..... No candid reader of the 'Creed of Christendom ' can close the book without the secret acknowledgment that it is a model of honest Investigation and clear exposition, conceived in the true spirit of serious and faithful research."— *Westminster Review.*

"This work remains a monument of his industry, his high literary power, his clear intellect. and his resolute desire to arrive at the truth. In its present shape, with its new introduction, it will be still more widely read, and more warmly welcomed by those who believe that in a contest between Truth and Error, Truth never can be worsted."— *Scotsman.*

Vol. VII. In post 8vo, pp. xix.—249, cloth, price 7s. 6d.

OUTLINES OF THE HISTORY OF RELIGION TO THE SPREAD OF THE UNIVERSAL RELIGIONS. By O. P. TIELB,

Dr. Theol., Professor of the History of Religions in the University of Leiden. Translated from the Duteh by J. Estlin Carpenter, M.A.

"Few books of its size contain the result of so much wide thinking, able and laborious) s' udy, or enable tbe reader to gidn a better bird's-eye view of the latest results of investigations into the religious history of nations. As Professor Tiele modestly says, 'In this liitle book are outlines—pencil isketches, I might say—nothing more.' But there are some men whoso sketches from a thumb-nail are of far more worth than an enormous canvan covered with the crude painting of others, and it Ih easy to sec that these pages, full of Information, these sentences, cut and perhaps alto dry, short and clear, condense the fruit of long and thorough research."—*Scotsman.*

"To us the value of the book seems to consist in the condensed statement of what is certainly known of all the chief religions of tho world up to the rise of Buddhism, Christianity, Islam, which arc qualified as universal religions; and the opportunity which it thus affords to the student of making original and more minute investigation from a starting-point of unquestioned fact."—*Theological Review.* *THE ENGLISH AND FOREIGN PHILOSOPHICAL LIBRARY.* or,. VIIL In post 8vo, pp. 276, cloth, 7a. 61.

RELIGION IN CHINA:

Containing a Brief Account of the Three Religions of the Chinese, with (Observations on the Prospects of Christian Conversion amongst that People.

By JOSEPH ED KINS. D.D., Peking.

"We confidently recommend a careful perusal of the present work to all interested n this great subject."—*London and China Express.* "Dr. Edkins has been most careful in noting the varied and often complex phases of opinion, so as to give an account of considerabie value of the subject.—*Scotsman.*

Vol. IX. In post 8vo, pp. 216, cloth, *jg.* 6d.

A CANDID EXAMINATION OF THEISM.

By PHYSIOTJS.

An essay of marked ability that does not belie its title."—*Mind.*

"On the whole a candid, acute. an-i honest attempt to work out a problem which is of vast and perpetual interest."—*Scotsman.* It is impossible to *go* through this work without forming a very high opinion of his speculative and argumentative power, and a sincere respect for his temperance of statement and his diiigent endeavour to make out the best case ho can for the views he rejects." — *Academy.* This is a telling contribution to the question of questions. The author has pushed a step further than any one before him the bearing of modern science on the doctrine of Theism."—*Examiner.* *PREPARING FOR PRESS.*

In Two Volumes, post 8vo, about 400 pages each.

ORIENTAL RELIGIONS, AND THEIR RELATION TO UNIVERSAL RELIGION.

By SAMUEL JOHNSON.

I.—INDIA.

In post *8vo,* THE PHILOSOPHY OP MUSIC.

A Popular Exposition of the General Theory of the Art, aa based on the researches of Helmholtz. Being the Substance of a Course of Lectures delivered at the Royal Institution of Great Britain, in February and March 1877.

By WILLIAM FOLK, Must Doc. Oxon. Fellow of the RoyiU Societies of London and Edinburgh.

The great and justly celebrated work recently published by Professor Helmholtz, of Berlin, "The Doctrine of the Perception of Musical Sounds, considered as a Physiological Basis for the Theory of Music," consists of two parts, which may be called the Physical and the Musical Parts respectively. The former, containing the author's novel investigations and discoveries in the domains of Acoustics, has been already made familiar in this country by popular illustrative works; but the latter portion, which is the mure interesting to the musical pubhc, as containing the philosophical application of these investigations and discoveries to the Science of Music, has received, as yet, but littie attention, and can only be studied in the elaborate form 111 which it exists in the author's treatise.

The object of the present publication is to explain the Philosophical Theory of Music, as based on Helmhoitz's investigations, in a way which, it is hoped, will be intelligible to practical musicians, and to such of the general pubiic as take an interest in the art. And it is thought that such an introduction to the subject may be particularly useful at the present time, when the Universities are beginning to insist on theoretical knowledge as an indispensabie qualification for the musical honours granted by them.

In tht yrus. In post 8vo, about 300 pages, THE COLOUR SENSE: Its Origin and Development. AN ESSAY IN COMPARATIVE PSYCHOLOGY.

By GRANT ALLEN, B.A., Author of "Psychological Pathetics"

I. Aether Waves and their Varieties.

II. The Earliest Form of Vision.

III. The Colour Sense in Insects.

IV. The Colour Sense in Vertebrates.

V. The Colour Sense in Han.

VI. The Aesthetic Value of Colour.

VII. Tho Growth of the Colour Vocabulary.

VIII. Colour in Printing.

IX. Summary and Recapitulation.

In preparation. EXTRA SERIES.

Two Volumes, post 8vo, pp. 348 and 374, with Portrait, cloth, price 218. LESSING: His Life and Writings.

By JAME3 SIME, M.A.

' It is to Lessing that an Englishman would turn with readiest affection. We cannot but wonder that more of this man is not known amongst us."—Thomas Carlylk.

"But to Mr. James Sime has been reserved the honour of presenting to the English public a full-length portrait of Lessing, in which no portion of the canvas is uncovered, and in which there is hardly a touch but tells. He has studied his subject with that patient care which only reverence and sympathy can support; he has attained the true proportion which can alone be gained by penetration and clear insight into motive and purposes. We can say that a clearer or more compact piece of biographic criticism has tiot been produced in England for many a day."— *Westmnutter Review.*

"An account of Lessings life and work on the scale which he deserves is now for the first time offered to English readers. Mr. Sime hat performed his task with industry, knowledge, and sympathy; qualities which must concur to make a successful biographor."—*Pall Mall Oatette.*

"This is an admirable book. It lacks no quality that a biography might to have. Its method is excellent. its theme is profoundly interesting: its tone is the happiest mixture of sympathy and discrimination: its style is clear, masculine, free from effort or affectati«,n, yet eloquent by its very sincerity. It is not a page too long; and though the reader closes it with regret, the critic must own that it is not a page too short."—*Standard.*

"He has given a life of Leasing clear, interesting, and full, while hu has given a study of his writings which bears distinct marks of an intimate acquaintance with his subject. and of a solid and appreciative judgment."—*Scotsman.*

"Vor allem erweist sich der Verfawer als ein Maim vom freiem, unbefangenem Geiste, von vielseitiger ernster Bildung."—*Im neuen Reich.*

"Sich or wird dieses Buch, das mit solcher Liebe und eingehenden Crundlichkeit sich an die Schilderung des Lebons eines so bedeutsamen Geistes unsrer Vcrgangeuhcit macht, und diese hohe schone Aufgube in einer so vortrefflichen Weise lost. sich nicht Moss in des Verfassers Heimathslande, sonderu auch in der Heimath des Dichters liube und vicle Freunde erwerben."—*Weter Zeitung.* "Diessmal ist es cin Englander. welcher den Unsterblichen in der verbreitetsten Bpraebe dor civilisirten Welt einfuhrt. und siehe da, der englischo Leasing hat fur uns kaum ein fremdes Hoar, kaum eine fremde Nuance odor Zuthat. Soin lebensgrosses Bild strahlt aus dera von der Liebe polirten und hingehalteuen Spiegel rein und voll r.uruck. Die loidige Kritmernation' hat wieder cin ma! gezeigt. dass sic vollkommen auf der HOhe des ' urcigonen Geistes' zu stehen vermag, dtiss sic im Stande ist in dio feinsten Faltendea kritisch-philosophischen Gewebes hincinzuschanen und das Ratuscl dialectiseher Analyse virtue *zi* lojen."—*Augsburger Allgemeine Zeitung.*

Vol. I., post 8vo, pp. 264, cloth, price 7s. 6d.

AN ACCOUNT OF THE POLYNESIAN RACE: ITS ORIGIN AND MIGRATIONS, AND THE ANCIENT HISTORY OP THE HAWAIIAN PEOPLE TO THE TIMES OF KAMEHAMEHA I.

By ABRAHAM FORNANDER, Circuit Judge of the Island of Maui, H.I.

"Mr. Fornander has evidently enjoyed excellent opportunities for promoting the study which has producod this work. Unlike most foreign residents in Polynesia, he has acquired a good knowledgo of the language spokon by the people among whom he dwelt.

Thm has enabled him, during his thirty-four years residence in the Hawaiian Inlands, to collect material which could be obtained only by a person possessing such an advantage

It is so seldom that a private settlor in the Polynesian Islands takes an intelligent interest in local ethnology and archreology, and makes use of the advantage he possesses, that we feel especially thankful to Mr. Fornander for his labours in this comparatively little known field of research."—*Academy.*

Vol. II. in preparation. LONDON: TRUBNER & CO., LUDGATE HILL.

TRANSLATOR'S PREFACE.

The " History of Materialism " was hailed, upon its original publication in Germany, as a work likely to excite considerable interest. In this country, Professor Huxley suggested, in the "Lay Sermons, Lectures, and Addresses" (published in 1870), that a translation of the book would be "a great service to philosophy in England." Soon afterwards there was published a second—thoroughly remodelled and re-written—edition of the work. And then, in the autumn of 1874, attention was again specially directed to it by Professor Tyndall's acknowledgment of his indebtedness "to the spirit and to the letter" of the work in his memorable address as President of the British Association at Belfast.

It was shortly after this that, seeing with regret that the book had so long awaited a translator, I ventured to apply to the author for his authority to undertake the task. The causes that have delayed its completion, since they are personal to myself, it would be an impertinence to trouble the reader with. The only one that is not so, is to be deplored on other grounds besides that of mere delay. The lamented death of the author, in November 1875, deprived me of the hoped-for opportunity of submitting my rendering to his friendly criticism.

The impatience expressed in many quarters has decided us to defer publication no longer; and accordingly the reader has now before him the first instalment, to be speedily followed by two other volumes, which will complete the work. The division into three volumes instead of two—which in some respects might have been preferable—has been dictated by practical considerations.

The difficulties attending the translation of a philosophical German work into English are notorious. It would be absurd to suppose that I have always succeeded in meeting or eluding these difficulties; but I have endeavoured everywhere to translate as literally as was consistent with English idiom.

It may serve also to explain possible obscurities to remember that the book is written with continual reference to the problems and questions under discussion in Germany, and to the forms of speculation current there. It has been treated, indeed, by Von Hartmann as a polemic, 'eine durch geschichtliche Studien angeschwollene Tendenzschrift.' And as an assertion of the Materialistic standpoint against the philosophy of mere 'Notions' (' intuitionless conceptions,' in Coleridge's phrase), and of the Kantian or Neo-Kantian standpoint against both, no doubt it is a polemic; but it is, at the same time, raised far above the level of ordinary controversial writing by its thoroughness, its comprehensiveness, and its impartiality.

E. C. T.

2 South Squabb, Gray's Inn. See Eduard von Hartmann: Neukantianinmus, Schopenhanerianismn» und Hegelianismus in ihrer Stellung zu den philosophischen Aufgaben der Gegenwart. Berlin, 1877. *FREDERICK ALBERT LANGE:*

BIOGRAPHICAL NOTES.

Frederick Albert Lange was born at Wald near Solingen, in the district of Diisseldorf, on the 28th of September 1828. He was the son of the well-known Bible Commentator, Dr. J. P. Lange, now Professor in Bonn, who has also shown himself possessed of special capacities by rising from the position of a carter and labourer to be one of the leading Evangelical theologians of Europe.

The boy's early life was spent in Duisburg; but at the age of twelve, his father having received a call as Professor to Zurich, Switzerland became his second 'Fatherland,' and until the last he retained a strong love for the Republic and a keen interest in its politics. Already in his earlier years this interest must have been excited, for in that stirring period political passions extended even to the boys at school.

In 1848, having already attended the University of Zurich for two sessions, he followed the German custom of migrating from university to university, and went to Bonn to attend lectures on philology. His journey had to be made through a country shaken by the storms of that revolutionary period; and he wore for his protection while travelling a cockade of black gold and red. This he, with the patriot Arndt, was one of the last in Bonn to lay aside. All the struggles and activities of the time he followed with interest and enthusiasm. In a letter written in May 1849, he asks, "Should it not be clear to every reasonable man that civilised Europe must enter into one great political community?" Unfortunately, twenty-eight years have done little to bring us nearer to this ideal. Another of his aspirations, expressed somewhat later, was destined to be realised. Germania was to wake up, like the heromaiden in Schiller's poem, and cry, " Give me my helm!"

Having taken his degree of Doctor, he became an assistant-master in the ' Gymnasium,' or grammar-school, at Cologne; and in the following year he married.

But in 1855 he returned to Bonn as 'Privat-docent' of philosophy, lecturing on the History and Theory of Education, on the Schools of the Sixteenth Century, on Psychology, on Moral Statistics, and finally, in the summer of 1857, upon the History of Materialism. At the same time he was studying natural science, attending the lectures of Helmholtz upon physiology, and profiting by intimate intercourse with Frederick Ueberweg, the author of the well-known "System of Logic," and the "History of Philosophy."

In 1858, however, he was fain to take a mastership once more, this time at the Gymnasium at Duisburg; and there he continued until political considerations caused him to resign in 1861. He had now devoted himself to social and economic questions and to political agitation; and, amongst numerous other offices, filled the position of secretary to the Chamber of Commerce at Duisburg. In this post he gave evidence of a genius for finance which astonished and delighted the merchants and manufacturers of Duisburg. He was still, moreover, steadily working at his "History of Materialism," and was at the time delivering privntely courses of lectures on the History of Modern Philosophy. From 1862 until 1866 he was one of the editors of the daily newspaper the "Ehein- und Euhrzeitung," and maintained the principles of freedom and progress against the onslaught of reactionary government. His occupations were still further multiplied by his becoming a partner in a publishing and printing business, in which he undertook the direction of the printing establishment. He was anxious for the spread of information amongst the people. Among the various works which he published at this period were his "Arbeiterfrage"

(Labour Question), 1865, third edition 1874; and "John Stuart Mill's Ansichten fiber die Sociale Frage und die angebliche Umwalzung der Socialwissenschaft durch Carey," 1866 (Mill's views on the social question and the asserted revolution worked in social science by Carey). He founded also a newspaper to represent the interests of labour in the Rhenish and Westphalian provinces, but the attempt was continued for nine months only.

His own position was meanwhile becoming very difficult. His bold and independent treatment of the social question, which was then in the full tide of the agitation led by Ferdinand Lassalle, caused some coldness between Lange and his political friends. At the same time he was harassed by the press prosecutions which German Governments seem unable to avoid, and which the German people still continue to endure. Under these circumstances, he accepted overtures of partnership made to him by an old schoolfellow, who was proprietor of the well-known democratic newspaper, the " Landbote" of Winterthur, then, as now, a paper of great influence. To Winterthur, accordingly, he removed with his wife and family in November 1866; and he was speedily engaged to fill as many municipal and public offices as he had already held at Duisburg.

But the love of teaching, which had always been strong within him, led him to join the University of Zurich as a 'Privat-docent,' although he continued to live in Winterthur, until, in 1870, he was called to Zurich as Professor of Philosophy. For two years he worked zealously here, and declined a call to Konigsberg. But much as he loved Switzerland, yet Germany was his true home, and a feeling of home-sickness (as he says) came over him when, in 1872, he was again invited by the Minister Falk to become Professor at Marburg. He accepted the invitation, and once more removed.

His work at Marburg was destined to be of short duration. The disease which ultimately proved fatal had some time before declared itself. He had undergone a serious operation, though with little prospect of advantage, at Tubingen, from which place he wrote to his wife:—

"Yesterday, in the Botanical Garden, I read 'Die Kiinstler' once more. I could not help applying a little to myself the splendid lines which have always been favourites with me—

'At peace with Fate, serenely goes his race—
Here guides the Muse, and there supports the Grace;
The stern Necessity, to others dim
With Night and Terror, wears no frown for him:
Calm and serene, he fronts the threatened dart,
Invites the gentle bow, and bares the fearless heart.'

"Can one express the Christian idea of resignation more beautifully or philosophically? And yet with such true poetry!"

For two years, however, he laboured with great energy and eminent success, lecturing before large classes upon various subjects connected with philosophy. These embraced logic and psychology, as a matter of course, but they were by no means limited to these. In one session, for instance, he lectured on the History of Modern Education, on the Theory of Voting, and on Schiller's Philosophical Poems.

It has been already mentioned that the " History of Materialism" had originally formed the subject of a course of lectures at the University of Bonn. By the side of such a list, indeed, the lecture-lists of the professors at our great English universities look very jejune and meagre. And it will be long, perhaps, before an Oxford professor lectures upon any subject so *real* as the 'Present Significance of Materialism.' But then, as we all know, our English universities are the proper homes of dead languages, and not of living ones; of extinct systems, and not of living, breathing thought. At Oxford, philosophy begins with Plato and ends with Aristotle; unless, perhaps, as some concession to two thousand years, we throw in a few aphorisms of Bacon, or a ' strayed scholastic' like Mr. Mill.

I have used the translation of Lord Lytton, Knebworth edition of his "Translations from Schiller," p. 220. The original lines are— "Mit dem Geschick in hoher Einigkeit Gelasscn hingestutzt auf Grazien und Musen, Empfangt er das Geschoss, das ihn bedriiut, Mit freundlich dargebotenem Busen, Vom sauften Bogen der Nothwendigkeit."

Meanwhile his disease continued its painful progress; but, undismayed by the approach of death, he busied himself, in addition to his professorial duties, with the preparation of the second edition of the " History of Materialism. " The preface to the first volume of this substantially new work is dated June 1873; to the second, the' end of January 1875.' After February of this same year, 1875, he was unable to leave the house again. Until three weeks before his death, and while his voice could scarcely rise above a whisper, he continued to work at his "Logical Studies," which have since been published. He died on the 21st of November.

With him, in the words of one of his old colleagues at Duisburg, there went to the grave "a light of science, a standard-bearer of freedom and progress, and a character of spotless purity."

Lange's restless activity and many-sidedness may be readily seen from the facts here put together. The distinguishing features of his mind and character are sufficiently illustrated in his great work, now presented to the reader. But two points that may be specially mentioned were, his intense belief in the 'reality of ideals;' and the way in which he connects the theories of science with ethical ideas. His heart beat for the lot of the masses, and he felt that the question of labour would be the great problem of the coming time, as it was the question that decided the fall of the ancient world. The core of this problem he believed to be 'the struggle against the struggle for existence,' which is identified with man's spiritual destiny. And so we can understand the anxiety with which he looked forward to the great revolution which, in common with many thoughtful men, he believed to be impending upon modern society. But all that he could do to warn his fellow-men of the 'rocks' that were 'ahead,' and of the way in which they might be avoided, he did, not discouraged although he were little heeded. In his own words: "Never, indeed, will our efforts be wholly in vain. The truth, though too late, yet comes soon enough; for mankind will not die just yet. Fortunate natures hit the right moment; tut never has the thoughtful observer the right to be silent, merely because he knows Jiat for the present there are tut few who listen to him." AUTHOR'S PREFACE TO THE SECOND AND LATER EDITIONS.

The changed form in which the "History of Materialism" appears in this second edition is partly a necessary consequence of the original plan of the book, but partly also a result of the reception it has met with.

As I incidentally explained in the first edition, my intention was rather to exercise an immediate influence; and I should have been quite content if my book had, in the course of five years, been again forgotten. Instead of this, however, and despite a number of very friendly reviews, it required almost five years for it to become thoroughly known, and it was never in greater demand than at the moment when it went out of print, and, as I felt, was already in many parts out of date. This was especially so with regard to the second portion of the work, which will receive at least as thorough a revision and remodelling as this present volume. The Books, the Persons, and the Special Questions around which turns the strife of opinions are partially changed. In particular, the rapid progress of the natural sciences required an entire renewal of the matter of some sections, even although the line of thought and the results might remain essentially unaltered.

The first edition, indeed, was the fruit of the labours of many years, but it was in point of form almost extemporised. Many defects incident to this mode of origin have been removed; but, on the other hand, some of the merits of the first edition may have at the same time disappeared. I wished, on the one hand, to do justice to the higher standard which its readers, contrary to my original intention, have applied to the book; while, on the other, the original character of the work could not be wholly destroyed. I am very far then from claiming for the earlier portion, in its new form, the character of a normal historical monograph. I could not, and indeed I did not, wish to discard the predominant didactic and expository tone, that from the outset labours for and prepares the way for the final results of the Second Book, and sacrifices to this effort the placid evenness of a purely objective treatment. But as I everywhere appealed to the sources, and gave abundant vouchers in the notes, I hoped in this way to supply to a great extent the want of a proper monograph, without prejudice to the essential purpose of the book. This purpose consists now, as before, in the *exposition of principles,* and I am not over-eager to justify myself if some slight objection is therefore made to the appropriateness of my title. This has now its historical justification, at all events, and may remain. The two parts, however, form to me now, as before, an inseparable whole; but my right expires as soon as I lay down the pen, and I must be content if all my readers, even those who can use for their purposes only particular portions of the whole, will give due weight to the consideration of the difficulty of my task.

A. LANGE. Mabbubg, *June* 1873.

FIRST SECTION. MATERIALISM IN ANTIQUITY. CHAPTER I. THE EARLY ATOMISTS—ESPECIALLY DEMOKKITOS.

Materialism is as old as philosophy, but not older. The physical conception of nature which dominates the earliest periods of the history of thought remains ever entangled in the contradictions of Dualism and the fantasies of personification. The first attempts to escape from these contradictions, to conceive the world as a unity, and to rise above the vulgar errors of the senses, lead directly into the sphere of philosophy, and amongst these first attempts Materialism has its place.

With the beginning, however, of consecutive thinking there arises also a struggle against the traditional assumptions of religion. Keligion has its roots in the earliest crudely-inconsistent notions, which are ever being created afresh in indestructible strength by the ignorant masses. An immanent revelation, vaguely felt rather than clearly realised, lends it a deep content, while the rich embellishments of mythology and the venerable antiquity of tradition endear it to the people. The cosmogonies of the East and of Greek antiquity present us with ideas that are as little spiritual as they are material. They do not try to explain the world by means of a single principle, but offer us anthropomorphic divinities, primal beings half sensuous half spiritual, a chaotic reign of matter and forces in manifold changeful struggle and activity. In the presence of this tissue of imaginative ideas awakening thought calls for order and unity, and hence every system of philosophy entered upon an inevitable struggle with the theology of its time, which was conducted, according to circumstances, with more or less open animosity.

My first sentence, which has been sometimes misunderstood, is directed, on the one hand, against the despisers of Materialism, who find in this view of the universe an absolute contradiction of all philosophical thought, and deny it the possession of any scientific importance; and. on the other hand, against those Materialists who, in their turn, despise all philosophy, and imagine that their views are in no way a prsduct of philosophical speculation, but are a pure result of expe rience, of sound common sense, and of the physical sciences. It might, perhaps, have been more simply maintained that the first attempt at a philosophy at all amongst the Ionic physicists was Materialism; but the consideration of a loDg period of development, reaching from the first hesitatingand imperfect systemsdowu to the rigidly consistent and calmly reasoned Materialism of Demokritos, shows us that Materialism can only be numbered "amongst the earliest attempts." Indeed, unless we iden-between the soul-atoms and the warm tify it with Hylozoism and Pantiie-air of Diogenes of Apollonia, despite ism, Materialism only becomes a com-all their superficial similarity, is of plete system when matter is *conceived* quite fundamental importance. The *at purely material*—that is, when its latter is an absolute Reason-stuff constituent particles are not a sort of *(Vernunftttoff);* it is capable in itself *thinking matter,* but physical bodies, of sensation, and its movements, such which are moved in obedience to as they are, are due to its rationality, merely physical principles, and being Demokritos' soul-atoms move, like all in themselves without sensations, pro-other atoms, according to purely mete sensation and thought by parti-chanical principles, and produce the cularform-sof their combinations. And phenomenon of thinking beings only thorough-going Materialism seems in a special combination mechanically always necessarily to be Atomism, brought about. And so, again, the since it is scarcely possible to explain "animated magnet" of Thales harwhatever happens out of matter monises exactly with the expression clearly and without any mixture of *tcivra.* irXiJpij *$t&v,* and yet is at bot-supersensuous qualities and forces, tom clearly to be distinguished from unless we resolve matter into small the way in which the Atomists atatoms and empty space for them to tempt to explain the attraction of move in. The distinction, in fact, iron by the magnet.

It is a mistake to overlook the presence, and indeed the momentous influence, of this struggle in Greek antiquity, although it is easy to see the origin of the mistake. If the generations of a distant future had to judge of the whole thought of our own time solely from the fragments of a Goethe and a Schelling, a Herder or a Leasing, they would scarcely observe the deep gulfs, the sharp distinctions of opposite tendencies that mark our age. It is characteristic of the greatest men of every epoch that they have reconciled within themselves the antagonisms of their time. So is it with Plato and Sophokles in antiquity; and the greatest man often exhibits in his works the slightest traces of the struggles which stirred the multitude in his day, and which he also, in some shape or other, must have passed through.

The mythology which meets us in the serene and easy 7 dress due to the Greek and Eoman poets was neither the / religion of the common people nor that of the scientifically educated, but a neutral territory on which both parties could meet.

The people had far less belief in the whole poeticallypeopled Olympus than in the individual town or country deities whose statues were honoured in the temple with special reverence. Not the lovely creations of famed artists enthralled the suppliant crowd, but the old-fashioned, rough-hewn, yet honoured figures consecrated by tradition. Amongst the Greeks, moreover, there was an obstinate and fanatical orthodoxy, which rested as well on the interests of a haughty priesthood as on the belief of a crowd in need ofhelp.2

This might have been wholly forgotten if Sokrates had not had to drink the cup of poison; but Aristotle also fled from Athens that the city might not a second time commit sacrilege against philosophy. Protagoras also had to flee, and his work upon the gods was publicly burnt. Anaxagoras was arrested, and obliged to flee. Theodorus, " the atheist," and probably also Diogenes of Apollonia, were prosecuted as deniers of the gods. And all this happened in humane and enlightened Athens.

In view of the completely opposite variety of development than the conaccount of Zeller (Phil. d. Griechen, stitutions of the individual cities and i. S-44 ff. 3 Aufl.), it may be proper countries. It was natural that the to remark, that we may assent to the thoroughly local character of their proposition, "The Greeks had no cultus, in conjunction with an increashierarchy, and no infallible system of ing friendly intercourse, should lend dogmas," without needing to modify to a toleration and liberality which the representation in the text. "The was inconceivable amongst highly creGreeks," we must remember, had no dulous and at the s.'ime time cenpolitical unity in which these could tralised peoples. And yet, of all the have been developed. Their system Greek efforts towards unity, those of a of faiths exhibited an even greater hierarchic and theocratical tendency were perhaps the most important; and we may certainly consider, for example, the position of the priesthood of Delphi as no insignificant exception to the rule that the priestly office conferred "incomparably more veneration than power." (Comp. Curtius, Griech. Gesch. , i. p. 451; Hist. of Gr., E. T., ii. 12, in connection with the elucidations of Gerhard, Stephani, Welcker, and others as to the share of the theologians of Delphi in the extension of Bacchus-worship and the mysteries.) If there was in Greece no priestly caste, and no exclusive priestly order, there were at least priestly families, whose hereditary rights were preserved with the most inviolable legitimism, and which belonged, as a rule, to the highest aristocracy, and were able to maintain their position for centuries. How great was the importance of the Eleusinian mysteries at Athens, and how closely were these connected with the families of the Eumolpidre, the Kerykes, the Phyllidre, and so on! (Comp. Hermann, Gottesd. Alterth., S. 31, A. 2r; Schomann, Griech. Alterth., ii. S. 340, n. f. 2 Anfl.) As to the *political* influence of these families, the fall of Alkibiades affords the clearest elucidation, although in trials which bring into play high-church and aristocratic influences in connection with the religions fervour of the masses, the individual threads of the network are apt to escape observation. As to orthodoxy, this must indeed not be taken to imply a scholastio and organised system of doctrines. Such a system might perhaps have arisen if the Theocrasy of the Delphic theologians and of tho mysteries had not come *too late* to prevent the spread of philosophic rationalism amongst the aristocratic and educated classes. And so men remained content with the mystery-worships, which allowed every man on all other points to think as he pleased. But all the more inviolable remained the general belief in the sanctity and importance of these particular gods, these forms of worship, these particular sacred words and usages, so that here nothing was left to the individual, and all doubt, all attempts at unauthorised changes, all casual discussion, remained forbidden. There was, however, without doubt, even with regard to the mythical traditions, a great difference between the freedom of the poets and the strictness of the local priestly tradition, which was closely connected with the cnltus. A people which met with different gods iu every city, possessed of different attributes, as well as a different genealogy and mythology, without having its belief in its own sacred traditions shaken thereby, must with proportionate ease have permitted its poets to deal at their own pleasure with the common mythical material of the national literature; and yet, if liberties thus taken appeared in the least to contain a direct or indirect attack upon the traditions of the local divinities, the poet, no less than the philosopher, ran into danger. The series of philosophers named in the text as having been persecuted in Athens alone might easily be enlarged; for example, by Stilpo and Theophrastos (Meier u. Schomann, Att. Prozess, S. 303, n. f.). There might be added poets like Diagorasof Melos, on whose head a price was set; Aeschylos, who incurred the risk of his life for an alleged violation of the mysteries, and was only acquitted by the Areopagus

From the standpoint of the multitude, every philosopher, even the most ideal, might be prosecuted as a denier of the gods; for no one' of them pictured the gods to himself as the priestly tradition prescribed.

If we cast a glance to the shores of Asia Minor in the centuries that immediately precede the brilliant period of Hellenic intellectual life, the colonies of the Ionians, with their numerous important cities, are distinguished for wealth and material prosperity, as well as for artistic sensibility and refinement of life. Trade and political alliances, and the increasing eagerness for knowledge, led the inhabitants of Miletos and Ephesos to take long journeys, brought them into manifold intercourse with foreign feelings and opinions, and furthered the elevation of a free-thinking aristocracy above the standpoint of the narrower masses. A similar early prosperity was enjoyed by the Doric colonies of Sicily and Magna Graecia. Under these circumstances, we may safely assume that, long before the appearance of the philosophers, a freer and more enlightened conception of the universe had spread amongst the higher ranks of society.

in consideration of his great services; Euripides, who was threatened with an indictment for atheism, and others. How closely tolerance and intolerance bordered upon each other in the minds of the Athenians is best seen in a passage from the speech against Andokides (which, according to Blass, Att. Beredsamkeit, S. 566 ff., is not really by Lysios, although it is a genuine speech in those proceedings). There it is urged that Diagoras of Melos had only outraged (as a foreigner) the religion of strangers, but Andokides had insulted that of his own city; and we must, of course, be more angry with our fellow-countrymen than with strangers, because the latter have not transgressed against their own gods. This subjective excuse must have issued in an objective acquittal, unless the sacrilege was especially directed against the Athenian, and not against a foreign religion. From the same speech we see further, that the family of the Eumolpidae was authorised, under certain circumstances, to pass judgment against religious offenders according to a secret code whose author was entirely unknown. (That this happened under the presidency of the King Archon— comp. Meier u. Schomann, S. 117, u. f.—is for our purpose unimportant.) That the thoroughly conservative Aristophanes could make a jest of the gods, and even direct the bitterest mockery against the growing superstition, rests upon entirely different grounds; and that Kpikuros was never persecuted is of course explained sim ply by his decided participation in all the external religious ceremonies. The political tendency of many of these accusations establishes rather than disproves their foundation in religious fanaticism. If the reproach of dirSfia was one of the most effectual means of overthrowing even popular statesmen, not the letter of the law only, but the passionate religious zeal of the masses must obviously have existed; and accordingly we must regard as inadequate the view of the relation of church and state in Schomann, Griech. Alterth., i. S. 117, 3 Aufl., as well as many of the points in Zeller's treatment of the question above referred to. And that the persecutions were not always in connection with ceremonies, but often had direct reference to doctrine and belief, appears to be quite clearly proved by the majority of the accusations against the philosophers. But if we reflect upon the by no means small number of cases of which we hear in a single city and in a comparatively short space of time, and upon the extreme peril which they involved, it will scarcely appear right to say that philosophy was attacked "in a few only of its representatives." We have still rather seriously to inquire, as again in the modern philosophy of the seventeenth, eighteenth (and nineteenth?) centuries, How far the influence of conscious or unconscious accommodation to popular beliefs beneath the pressure of threatening persecution has left its mark upon the svstems themselves?

It was in these circles of men, wealthy, distinguished, with a wide experience gained from travel, that philosophy arose. Thales, Anaximander, Herakleitos, Empedokles took a prominent position amongst their fellow-citizens, and it is not to be wondered at that no one thought of bringing them to account for their opinions. This ordeal, it is true, they had to undergo, though much later; for in the last century the question of the atheism of Thales was eagerly handled in special monographs. If we compare, in this respect, the Ionic pliilosophers of the sixth century with the Athenians of th fifth and fourth, we shall at once be reminded of the contrast between the English sceptical movement of the seventeenth and the French of the eighteenth century., In the one case, nobody thought of drawing the people into the war of opinions; in the other, the movement was *d* weapon with which fanaticism was to be assaulted. i Comp. Zeller, L S. 176, Anm. 2, reason," especially in the Stoical 3 Au(I., and the works quoted in sense, refers merely to an immanent, Marbach, Gesch. d. Phil. , S. 53, not anthropomorphic, and therefore which, and that by no mere coincialso not a personal God. Even dence, appeared at the period of the though the Stoic tradition may rest Materialist controversy of the last upon a mere interpretation of an older century. With regard to the state-tradition in the sense of their own ment of Zeller, who seems to me to system, yet it does not follow from rate Thales too low, I may observe, this that this interpretation (apart that the passage in Cicero, De Nat. from the genuineness of the *words)* is Deorum, i. x. 23, formerly employed also false. Judging from the conto prove the theism of Thales, with miction, the probably genuine expresCicero's characteristic shallowness, sion that all things are full of gods by the expression '' fingere ex," in-may very likely be the origin of the dicates a Demiurgus standing *outside* notion—an expression which even the world-stuff, while God, as " world-Aristotle (De An., i. 5, 17) obviously interprets *tymholically; no* that the doubt indicated by *tawt* rsfers (and rightly) to his own interpretation only, which is, in fact, much more perverse and improbable than that of the Stoics. To refute (Zeller, i. 173) the view of the latter by Aristotle (Met., i. 3) is unsafe, because Aristotle is undoubtedly there bringing out the element in Anaxag1?ras which was related to his own philosophy, that is, the *tepa-ration* of ihe worldforming Reason, as of the cause of Becoming, from the matter upon which it works. That he i' not content with this very element lu Anaxagoras, as is shown by the very next chapter, because the trans cendentil principle appears only ocl asionally, and is not consistently ca fried out, is a necessary consequenc of the transitional and by no men ns wholly

Hand in hand with this intellectual movement proceeded among the Ionians the study of mathematics and natural science. Thales, Auaximander, and Anaximenes busied themselves with special problems of astronomy, as well as with the explanation of the universe; and Pythagoras transplanted the taste for mathematical and physical inquiry to the westward colonies of the Doric stock. The fact that, in the eastern portion of the Greek world, where the intercourse with Egypt, Phoenicia, Persia, was most active, the scientific movement began, speaks more decidedly for the influence of the East upon Greek culture than the fabulous traditions of the travels and studies of Greek philosophers. The idea of an absolute originality of Hellenic culture may be justified if by this we mean originality of form, and argue the hiddlen character of its roots from the perfection of the flower. It becomes, however, delusive if we insist upon the negative results of the criticism of special traditions, and reject those connections and influences which, although the ustial sources of history fail us, are obviously suggested by a View of the circumstances. Political relations, and, aUove all, commerce, must necessarily have caused knowledge, inventions, and ideas to flow in many ways from people to people; and if Schiller's saying, "Euch ihr Gotter gehoret der Kaufmann" (" To you, 0 gods, belongs the merchant"), is genuinely human, and therefore valid for all tim, many an intercommunication will have, been later connected by mythology with some famous names, whose true bearers have for ever been lost to memory.

consistent position of Anaxngoras. So the way in which he speaks of his doubtful merit, as also the severe censure of his inconsistency, are in Aristotle only the continuation of the fanatical zeal with which the Platonic Sokrates, in the *Phaedo,* c. 46, handles the same point. Comp. Buckle, History of Civilization, i. 497 sqq. Compare the lengthy refutation of the views as to the rise of Greek philosophy from Oriental speculation in Zeller, i. S. 20 ff., 3 Aufl. , and the concise but very careful discussion of the same question in Ueberweg, i., 4 Aufl., S. 32, E. T. 31. The criticism of Zeller and others has for ever displaced the cruder views that the East taught philosophy to the Greeks; on the other hand, the remarks of Zeller (S. 23 ff.) as to the influence of the common Indo-Germanio descent, and the continual influence of neighbourhood, may well gain an increased significance with the progress of Oriental studies. Especially with regard to *philosophy,* we may observe that Zeller—as a result of his Hegelian standpoint — obviously undervalues its connection with the general history of thought, and isolates too much the "speculative" ideas. If our view of the very intimate connection of speculation with religious rationalism, and with the beginning of scientific thought, is at all correct, then the stimulus to this changed mode of thought may have come from the East, but may in Greece, thanks to the more favourable soil, have matured more noble fruits. Compare the observation of Lewes, Hist. of Phil., i. p. 3: "It is a suggestive fact that the dawn of scientific speculation in Greece should be coincident

Certain it is that the East, in the sphere of astronomy and the measurement of time, was ahead of the Greeks. The people of the East, too, possessed mathematical knowledge and skill at a time when no one thought of such things as yet in Greece; although it was in this very sphere of mathematics that the Greeks were destined to outrun all the nations of antiquity.

with a great religious movement in the East." Conversely, also, it is quite possible that particular philosophical ideas may have come from the East to Greece, and there have been developed just because suitable intellectual circumstances had been prepared by the Greeks' own development. The historians will also have to adopt scientific theories. The crude opposition of originality and tradition qan no longer be employed. Ideas, Uksj organic germs, fly far and wide, but the right ground alone brings thelru to perfection, and often gives thehi higher forms. And in this case, of course, the possibility of the origin of Greek philosophy *without* such Stimulus is not excluded, although, of course, the question of originalit; r bears quite a new aspect. The true independence of Hellenic culture r sts in its *perfection,* not in its beginn;ngs.

With the freedom and boldness of the Hellenic mind was united an innate ability to draw inferences, to enunciate clearly and sharply general propositions, to hold firmly and surely to the premisses of an inquiry, and to arrange the results clearly and luminously; in a word, the gift of scientific deduction.

It has in our days become the fashion, especially amongst the English since Bacon, to depreciate the value of deduction. Whewell, in his well-known "History of the Inductive Sciences," is constantly unjust to the Greek philosophers, and notably to the Aristotelian school. He discusses in a special chapter the causes of what he regards as their failure, continually applying to them the standard of our own time and of our modern scientific position. We must, however, insist that a great work had to be done before the uncritical accumulation of observations and traditions could be transformed into our fruitful method of experiment. A school ojL vigorous thinking must first arise, in which men were/'cbntent to dispense with premisses for the attainment of their immediate end. This school was founded by the Greeks, and it was they who gave us, at length, the most essential basis of deductive processes, the elements of mathematics and the principles of formal logic. The apparent inversion of the natural Although the modern Aristo- Notion, and frequently, indeed, con telians are so far right that the cssen-tradict it. Much, however, as it muy tial feature of the Aristotelian Logic, now be the fashion to despise Formal from its author's standpoint, is not Logic, and to over-estimate the meta the Formal Logic, but the logico-meta-physical doctrine of the Notion, yet physical Theory of Knowledge. At a calm consideration establishes be the same time he has also left us cer-yond question that the fundamental tain elements of Formal Logic, of principles of Formal Logic are alone course only collected and developed demonstrated strictly as the prin by him, which, as I hope to show in ciples of Mathematics, and these only a later work, have a merely external so far as they are not (asis the-doctrine connection with the principle of his of the conclusions from modal judgments) adulterated and corrupted by Vera. Einl., especially the passage iii.

order, in the fact that mankind learnt to *deduce* correctly before they learnt to find correct *starting-points* from which to reason, can he seen to he really natural only from a psychological survey of the whole history of thought.

Of course, speculation upon the universe and its inter-relations was not, like mathematical inquiry, able to reach results of permanent value: innumerable vain attempts must first shake the confidence with which men ventured upon this ocean before philosophic criticism could succeed in showing how what was apparently the same method brought about in the one case sure progress, and in the other mere blind beating about the bush? And yet, even in the last few centuries, nothing so much contributed to lead philosophy, which had just broken off the Scholastic yoke, into new metaphysical adventures, as the intoxication caused by the astonishing advances of mathematics in the seventeenth century. Here also, indeed,' the error furthered again the progress of culture; for the systems of Descartes, Spinoza, and Leibniz, not only brought with them numerous incitements to thought and inquiry, but it was these systems that first really displaced the Scholasticism already doomed by the sentence of criticism, and thereby made way for a sounder conception of the world.

But in Greece, men had to succeed for once in freeing the vision from the mist of wonder, and in transferring their study of the world from the dazzling fable-land of religious and poetical ideas to the sphere of reason and of sober theory. This, however, could, in the first place, only be accomplished by means of Materialism; for external things lie nearer to the natural consciousness than the "Ego," and even the Ego, in the ideas of primitive peoples, is connected rather with the body than with the shadowy the Aristotelian Metaphysic. S. 38, Hartenstein. A full discussion Compare the formulation of the of the questions of method will be

Eame problem in Kant, Kritik d. rein, found in the Second Book.

Soul, the product of sleeping and of waking dreams, that they supposed to inhabit the body.8

The proposition admitted by Voltaire, bitter opponent as he otherwise was of Materialism, "I am a body, and I think," would have met with the assent also of the earlier Greek philosophers. When men began to admire the design in the universe and its component parts, especially in the organic sphere, it was a late representative of the Ionic natural philosophy, Diogenes of Apollonia, who identified the reason that regulated the world with the original substance, Air.

If this substance had been conceived as sentient, and its sensations supposed to become thoughts by means ot the growing complexity and motion of the substance, a vigorous Materialism might have been developed in this direction; perhaps a more durable one than that of the Atomists. But the reason-matter of Diogenes is omniscient; and so the last puzzle of the world of appearances is again at the outset hopelessly confused.

The Atomists broke through the circle of this *petitio principii* in fixing the essence of matter. Amongst all the properties of things, they assigned to matter only the V' simplest, and those indispensable for the presentation of something in time and space, and endeavoured from these alone to develop the whole aggregate of phenomena. In / Comp. the article "Seelenlehre" tellectual life of man from a series in the Encyc. des Ges. Erziehungs-of sentient conditions in his corpo und Unterrichtswescns, Bd. viii. real atoms, we strike upon the same

S. 594. rock as the Atomism of Demokritos, s Comp. Note 1. Details as to when he builds up, *e.g.,* a sound or a

Diogenes of Apollonia in Zeller, i. colour from the mere grouping of 218 ff. The possibility here sug-atoms in themselves neither lumin gested of an equally consequent Ma-ous nor sounding; while, if we trans terialism without Atomism will be fer again the whole contents of human considered in the Second Book, when consciousness, as an internal condi we discuss the views of TJeberweg. tion, to a single atom—a theory which

Now we will only observe that a recurs in modern philosophy in the third possibility, which also was most various modifications, though it never developed in antiquity, lies in was so far from the mind of the an the theory of sentient atoms; but cients—then Materialism is trans here, as soon as wo build up the informed into a mechanical Idealism.

this respect the Eleatics, it may be, had prepared the way for them, that they distinguished the persistent matter that is known in thought alone as the only real existence from the deceitful change of sense-appearances; and the referring of all sense qualities to the manner of combination of the atoms may have been prepared for by the Pythagoreans, who recognised the essence of things in number, that is, originally in the numerically fixed relations of form in bodies. At all events, the Atomists sup- plied the first perfectly clear conception of what is to be. understood by matter as the substratum of all phenomena! With the introduction of this notion, Materialism stood complete as the first perfectly clear and consequent theory of all phenomena.

This step was as bold and courageous as it was methodically correct; for so long as men started at all from the external objects of the phenomenal world, this was the only way of explaining the enigmatical from the plain, the complex from the simple, and the unknown from the known; and even the insufficiency of every mechanical theory of the world could appear only in this way, because this was the only way in which a thorough explanation could be reached at all.

'With few great men of antiquity can history have dealt so despitefully as with Demokritos. In the distorted picture of unscientific tradition, almost nothing appears of him except the name of the "laughing philosopher," while figures of incomparably less importance extend themselves at full length. So much the more must we admire the tact with which Bacon, ordinarily no great hero in historical learning, chose exactly Demokritos out of all the philosophers of antiquity, and awarded him the premium for true investigation, whilst he considers Aristotle, the philosophical idol of the Middle Ages, only as the originator of an injurious appearance of knowledge, falsely so called, and of an empty philosophy of words. Bacon may have been unfair to Aristotle, because he was lacking in that historical sense which, even amidst gross errors, recognises the inevitable transition to a deeper comprehension of the truth. In Demokritos he found a kindred spirit, and judged him, across the chasm of two thousand years, much as a man of his own age. In fact, shortly after Bacon, and in the very shape which Epikuros had given it, Atomism became the foundation of modern natural science.

Demokritos was a citizen of the Ionian colony of Abdera on the Thracian coast. The "Abderites " had not as yet earned the reputation of "Gothamites," which they enjoyed in the later classical times. The prosperous commercial city was wealthy and cultivated: Demokritos' father was a man of unusual wealth; there is scarcely room to doubt that the highly-gifted son enjoyed an excellent education, even if there is no historical foundation for the story that he was brought up by Persian Magi. It must not he supposed from this that I concur entirely in a kind of criticism employed with regard to this tradition hy Mnllach, Zeller, and others. It is not right to reject immediately the whole story of the stay of Xerxes in Abdera, merely because of the ridiculous exaggeration of Valerius Maximus. and the inaccuracy of a passage in Diogenes. We know from Herodotus that Xerxes made a halt in Abdera, and was very much pleased with his stay there (viii. 120; probably the passage which Diogenes had in his mind). That upon this occasion the king and his court would quarter themselves upon the richest citizens of the place is a matter of course; and that Xerxes had his most learned Magi in his train is again historical. But we are so far from being justifled, therefore, in supposing even an early stimulating influence to have been exercised by these Persians upon the mind of an inquisitive boy, that we might rather argue the contrary, since the great internal probability might only the more easily enable the germ of these stories to develop itself, from mere conjectures and combinations, into a factitious tradition, while the late appearance of the story, in untrustworthy authors, makes its external evidence very slight. As to the associated question of the age of Demokritos, in spite of all the acuteness spent in its treatment (comp. Frei, Qusestiones Protagoreoe, Bonnie, 1845, Zeller, j. S. 684 sqq., Anm. 2, and 783 sqq., Anm. 2), a successful answer in defence of the view of K. F. Hermann, which we followed in the ist edition, is by no means rendered impossible. Internal evidence (comp. Lewes, Hist. Phil., i. 97) declares, however, rather for placing Demokritos later. The view, indeed, of Aristotle, who makes Demokritos the originator of the Definitions, continued by Sokrates and his contemporaries (comp. Zeller, i. S. 686 Anm.), must not be too hastily adopted, since Demokritos, at all events, only began to develop his doctrines when he had reached mature age. If, then, we place this work of So; krates at the height of his intercourse

Demokritos appears to have spent his whole patrimony in the "grand tour" which his zeal for knowledge induced him to make. Returning in poverty, he was supported by his brother, but soon, by his successful predictions in the sphere of natural philosophy, he gained the reputation of being a wise and heaven-inspired man. Finally, he wrote his great work, the "Diakosmos,"—the public reading of which was rewarded by his native city with a gift of one hundred, according to others, five hundred talents, and with the erection of commemorative statues.

The year of Demokritos' death is uncertain, but there is a general admission that he reached a very advanced age, and died cheerfully and painlessly.

A great number of sayings and anecdotes are connected with his name, though the greater portion of them have no particular import for the character of the man to whom they relate. Especially is this so of those which sharply contrast him as the "laughing" with Herakleitos as the "weeping" philosopher, since they see nothing in him but the merry jester over the follies of the world, and the holder of a philosophy which, without losing itself in profundities, regards everything from the good side. As little pertinent are the stories that represent him merely as a *Polyhistor,* or even as the possessor of mystic and secret doctrines. What in the crowd of contradictory reports as to his person is most certain is, that his whole life was devoted to scientific investigations, which were as serious and logical as they were extensive. The collector of the scattered fragments which are all that remain to us of his numerous works, regards him as occupying the first place for genius and knowledge amongst all the philosophers before Aristotle, and goes so far as to conjecture that the Stagirite has largely to thank a study of the works of Demokritos for the fulness of knowledge which we admire in him. with the Sophists, about 425, Demo- Mullach, Fragm. Phil. Graec., Par.

kritos could, at all events, be as old 1869, p. 338: "Fait ille quamqunm as Sokrates, but, of course, not have in cseteris dissimilis, in hoc axjuabili been born as late as 460. omnium artium studio simillinjus

It is significant that a man of such extensive attainments has said that "we should strive not after fulness of knowledge, but fulness of understanding;" and where he speaks, with pardonable complacence, of his achievements, he dwells not upon the number and variety of his writings, but he boasts of his personal observation, of his intercourse with other learned men, and of his mathematical method. "Among all my contemporaries," he says, "I have travelled over the largest portion of the earth in search of things the most remote, and have seen the most climates and countries, heard the largest number of thinkers, and no one has excelled me in geometric construction and demonstration—not even the geometers of the Egyptians, with whom I spent in all five years as a guest." 13

Amongst the circumstances which have caused Demokritos to fall into oblivion, ought not to be left unmentioned his want of ambition and distaste for dialectic discussion. He is said to have been in Athens without making himself known to one of its philosophers. Amongst his moral aphorisms we find the following: "He who is fond of contradiction and makes many words is incapable of learning anything that is right."

Such a disposition suited little with the city of the Sophists, and certainly not with the acquaintance of a Sokrates or a Plato, whose whole philosophy was developed in dialectic word-play. Demokritos founded no school.

His words were, it appears, more eagerly copied from than copied out; and his whole philosophy was finally absorbed by Epikuros. Aristotle mentions him frequently

Aristotelis. Atque hand scio an Stamark that it shows "that Demo girites illam quareliquos philosophos kritos in this respect had little to superat eruditionem aliqua ex parte learn from foreigners," goes much too

Democriti librorum lectioni debu-far. It is not even certain from De erit." mokritos's observation that he was Zeller, i. S. 746, Mullach, Fr. superior to the "Harpedonnptae"

Phil., p. 349, Fr. 140-142. *on hit arrival in* Egypt; but even if Fragm. Varii Arg. 6, in Mullach, he were, he might, it is obvious, still

Fragm. Phil., pp. 370 sqq.; comp. learn much from them.

Zeller, i. 688, Anm., where the re-

VOL. I. B 4, 18 *MATERIALISM IN ANTIQUITY.* with respect; but he cites him, for the most part, only when he attacks him, and this he by no means always does with a fitting objectivity and fairness. How often he has borrowed from him without naming him we do not know. Plato speaks of him nowhere, though it is a matter of dispute whether, in some places, he has not controverted his opinions without mention of his name. Hence arose, it may be, the story that Plato in fanatical zeal would have liked to buy up and burn all the works of Demokritos.'

In modern times Patter, in his " History of Philosophy," emptied much antimaterialistic rancour upon Demokritos's memory; and we may therefore rejoice the more at the quiet recognition of Brandis and the brilliant and convincing defence of Zeller; for Demokritos must, in 1/truth, amongst the great thinkers of antiquity, be num *r* bered with the very greatest.

As to the doctrines of Demokritos, we are, indeed, better informed than we are as to the views of many a philosopher whose writings have come to us in greater fulness. This may be ascribed to the clearness and consecutiveness . of his theory of the world, which permits us to add with the *j* greatest ease the smallest fragment to the whole. Its core is Atomism, which, though not of course invented by him, through him certainly first reached its full development. We shall prove in the course of our history of Materialism that the modern atomic theory has been gradually developed from the Atomism of Demokritos. We may consider the following propositions as the essential foundations of Demokritos's metaphysic.

Cum p., *e.g.,* the way in which nomenon as such. See Zeller, L

Aristotle, De Anima, i. 3, attempts to 74c u. f.

render ridiculous the doctrine of De-- However incredible such fanati mokritos as to the movement of tho cism may appear to us, it is quite con body by the Soui; further, the inter-sonant with the character of Plato; polation of *chance* as a cause of move-and as Diogenes' authority for this ment, which is gently censured by statement is no less a person than

Zeller, i. 710, 711, with Anm. 1, and Aristoxenos, it may be that we have the statement that Demokritos had here something more than a " story." attributed truth to the sensible phe-Cf. Ueberweg, i. 4 Aufl., S. 73, K T. 63. See the proofs in Zeller, L 691, Aom. 2.

I. *Out of nothing arises nothing; nothing that is can be destroyed. All change is only combination and separation of atomsM* This proposition, which contains in principle the two great doctrines of modern physics—the theory of the indestructibility of matter, and that of the persistence of force (the conservation of energy)—appears essentially in Kant as the first "analogy of experience:" "In all changes of phenomena matter is permanent, and the quantity thereof in nature is neither increased nor diminished." Kant finds that in all times, not merely the philosopher, but even common sense, has presupposed the permanence of matter. The doctrine claims an axiomatic validity as. a necessary presupposition of any regulated experience at all, and yet it has its history! In reality, to the natural man, in whom fancy still overrides logical thought, nothing is more familiar than the idea of origin and disappearance, and the creation "out of nothing" in the Christian dogma is scarcely ever the first stumbling-block for awakening scepticism.

With philosophy the axiom of the indestructibility of matter comes, of course, to the front, although at first it may be a little veiled. The "Infinite" *(aTretpov)* of Anaximander, from which everything proceeds, the divine primitive fire of Herakleitos, into which the changing world returns, to proceed from it anew, are incarnations of persistent matter. Parmenides of Elea was the first to deny all becoming and perishing. The really existent is to the Eleatics the only "All," a perfectly rounded sphere, in which there is no change nor motion; all alteration is only phenomenal. But here arose a contradiction between appearance and being, in face of which philosophy could not be maintained. The one-sided maintenance of the one axiom injured another: "Nothing is without cause." How, then, from such unchanging existence could the phenomenal arise? To this was added the absurd denial of motion, which, of course, led to innumerable logomachies, and so furthered the development of Dialectic. Empedokles and Anaxagoras drop this absurdity, inasmuch as they refer all becoming and perishing to combination and separation. Only first by means of Atomism was this thought fully represented, and made the corner-stone of a strictly mechanical theory of the universe; and it was further necessary to bring into connection the axiom of the necessity of everything that happens. and that he attributed more weight to reflection with regard to knowledge than to immediate perception. His reflection dealt with notions that kept close to the perceptions of sense, and were for that very reason suited to explain nature. From the one-sidedness of those whose hypotheses are mere deductions from notions Demokritos was saved by this, that he constantly tested his theory of the atomic movements by picturing it to himself in the forms of sense.

II. *"Nothing Jiappens by chance, but everything through a cause and of necessity."*

This proposition, already, according to a doubtful tradition, held by Leukippos, must be regarded as a decided negation of all teleology, for the "cause" (X0709) is nothing but the mathematico-mechanical law followed by the atoms in their motion through an unconditional necessity. Hence Aristotle complains repeatedly that Demokritos, leaving aside teleological causes, had explained everything by a necessity of nature. This is exactly what Bacon praises most strongly in his book on the "Advancement of Learning," in which, in other respects, he prudently manages to restrain his dislike of the Aristotelian system (lib. iii. c. 4).

This genuinely materialistic denial of final causes had thus, we see, led, in the case of Demokritos, to the same misunderstandings that, in our own day, Materialism finds almost everywhere predominant—to the reproach that he believed in a blind chance. Although no confusion is more common, nothing can be more completely opposite than chance and necessity; and the explanation lies in this, that the notion of necessity is entirely definite and absolute, while that of chance is relative and fluctuating.

When a tile falls upon a man's head while he is walking 17 Fingm. Phys., 41, Mullach, p. &XXA *T&vto. k 6yov rt Koll ir in*365: *"oiUv XPW P&np ytixrai iymis."* down the street, this is regarded as an accident; and yet no one doubts that the direction of the wind, the law of gravitation, and other natural circumstances, fully determined the event, so that it followed from a physical necessity, and also from a physical necessity must, in fact, strike any head that at the particular moment happened to be on the particular spot.

This example clearly shows that the assumption of chance is only a partial denial of final cause. The falling of the stone, in our view, could have had no reasonable cause if we call it an accident.

If, however, we assume, with the philosophy of the Christian religion, an absolute predestination, we have as completely excluded chance as by the assumption of absolute causality. In this point the two most consequent theories entirely coincide, and both leave to the notion of chance only an arbitrary use, practically no use whatever. We call accidental anything the cause or object of which we do not know, merely for the sake of brevity, and therefore quite unphilosophically; or we start from a one-sided standpoint, and maintain, in the face of the teleologist, the accidental theory of events, in order to get rid of final causes, while we again quite abandon this same theory jf chance so soon as we have to deal with the principle of sufficient reason.

And rightly, so far as physical investigation or any exact science is concerned; for it is only from the side of efficient causes that the phenomenal world is accessible to inquiry, and all infusion of final causes, which are by way of supplement placed above or beside the nature forces subject to necessity—that is, those operating with the utmost regularity of ascertained laws—has no significance whatever, except as a partial negation of science, an arbitrary exclusion of a sphere not yet subjected to thorough investigation. 18 Of course, this is also true of the to set aside the fundamental principle most recent and the boldest attempt of all scientific thought— the 'Philosophy of the Uncoil scions!' We shall Book of returning to this late fruit have an opportunity in the Second of our speculative Romanticism. ' Fragm. Phys., i, Mullnch, p. 357.

An absolute teleology, however, Bacon was willing to admit, although his conception of it was not sufficiently clear. This notion of a design in the totality of nature, which in detail only gradually becomes intelligible to us by means of efficient causes, does not refer, of course, to any absolutely human design, and therefore not to a design intelligible to man in its details. And yet religions need an absolutely anthropomorphic design. This is, however, as great an antithesis to natural science as poetry is to historical truth, and can, therefore, like poetry, only maintain its position in an ideal view of things.

Hence the necessity of a rigorous elimination of final causes before any science at all can develop itself. If we ask, however, whether this was the impelling motive for Demokritos when he made an absolute necessity the foundation of all study of nature, we cannot here enter upon all the questions thus suggested; only of this there can be no doubt, that the chief point was there—a clear recognition of the postulate of the necessity of all things as a condition of any rational knowledge of nature. The origin of this view is, however, to be sought only in the study of mathematics, the influence of which in this direction has in later times also been very decided. IIL *Nothing exists but atoms and empty space: all else is only opinion.*

Here we have in the same proposition at once the strong and the weak side of all Atomism. The foundation of every rational explanation of nature, of every great discovery of modern times, has been the reduction of phenomena into the motion of the smallest particles; and undoubtedly even in classical ages the most important results might have been attained in this direction, if the reaction that took its rise in Athens against the devotion of philosophers to physical science had not so dis tinctly gained the upper hand. On the Atomic theory we explain to-day the laws of sound, of light, of heat, of chemical and physical changes in things in the widest sense, and yet Atomism is as little able to-day as in the time of Demokritos to explain even the simplest sensation of sound, light, heat, taste, and so on. In all the advances of science, in all the modifications of the notion of atoms, this chasm has remained unnarrowed, and it will be none the less when we are able to lay down a complete theory of the functions of the brain, and to *A/*

show clearly the mechanical motions, with their origin and their results, which correspond to sensation, or, in other words, which effect sensation. Science must not despair, by the means of this powerful weapon, of success in deriving even the most complicated processes and most significant motives of a hiving man, according to the laws of the persistence of force, from the impulses that are set free in his brain under the influence of the nervous stimuli; but she is for ever precluded from finding a bridge between what the simplest sound is as the sensation of a subject—

mine, for instance—and the processes of disintegration in the brain which science must assume in order to explain this particular sensation of sound as a fact in the objective world.

In the manner in which Demokritos cut this Gordian knot we may perhaps trace the influence of the Eleatic School. They explained motion and change in general as mere phenomena, and, in fact, non-existent phenomena. Demokritos limited this destructive criticism to sense qualities. "Only in opinion consists sweetness, bitterness, warmth, cold, colour; in truth, there is nothing but the atoms and empty space. "

Since to him, therefore, the Immediately Given—sensation—had something deceptive about it, it is easily intelligible that he complained that the truth lies deep hidden, "Mullach, 357: "*vbfuf ykvuli nal piv, vuu.w* x/io«i' *irty U &Ttip.a xal* IV. *The atoms are infinite in number, and of endless variety oj form. In the eternal fall through infinite space, the greater, which fall more quickly, strike against the lesser, and lateral movements and vortices that thus arise are the commencement of the formation of worlds. Innumerable worlds are formed and perish successively and simultaneously.*

The magnitude of this conception has often in antiquity been considered as something quite monstrous, and yet it stands much nearer to our modern ideas than that of Aristotle, who proved *a priori* that besides his self-contained world there could be no second. When we come to Epikuros and Lucretius, where we have fuller information, we shall discuss more thoroughly their cosmical theory. Here we will only mention that we have every reason to suppose that many features of the Epikurean Atomism, in cases where we are not told the contrary, are due to Demokritos. Epikuros made the atoms infinite in number, but not infinitely various in form. More important is his innovation in reference to the origin of the lateral motion.

The main features of Atomism we mast, in defect of authentic fragments, take in the main from Aristotle and Lucretius; and we may remark, that even in these accounts, far removed as they are from the ridiculous disfigurements and misunderstandings of a Cicero, yet the mathematical clearness of the premisses and the connection of the individual parts has probably suffered. We are, therefore, justified in completing the defective tradition, though always in the sense of that mathematico-physical theory on which Demokritos's whole system hangs. So the procedure of Zeller, *e.g.,* is undoubtedly quite right when treating the relation of size and weight

of the atoms (i. 698702); on the other hand, there is even here, in the doctrine of motion, still a remnant left of the want of clearness so persistent in all later accounts. Zeller observes (p. 714), that the idea that in infinite space there is no above and below, appears not to have forced itself upon the Atomista; that what
Epiknros, in Diogenes, x. 60, says on this point is too superficial and unscientific to be credited to Demokritos. But this judgment is too decided; for Epiknros by no means opposes, as Zeller (iii. i. 377, *kc.*) supposes, to the objection of there being no above and below in infinite space ocular evidence only; but he makes the quite correct, and therefore, it may be, quite Demokritean remark, that in spite of this relativity of "above" and "below" in infinite space, yet that the direction from head to foot is a definitely given notion, and that from foot to head may be regarded as the opposed notion, however much we may suppose the line on which these dimensions are measured to be prolonged. In this direction follow the general movement of the free atoms, and clearly only in the sense of the movement from the head to the foot of a man standing in the line, and this direction is that from above to below —the directly opposite one that from below upwards.

Here Demokritos gives us a thoroughly logical view, although one which cannot be maintained in face of our modern physics; but yet it shows that the Greek thinker carried out his speculations as far as was then possible in subjection to strictly physical principles. Starting from the erroneous view that greater bodies—the same density being assumed—fall quicker than smaller ones, he made greater atoms in their descent overtake and strike the smaller. But as the atoms are of various shapes, and the collision will not take place in the centre of the atoms, then, even according to the principles of modern mechanical science, revolutions of the atoms on their axes and lateral motions will be set up. When once set up, these lateral motions must ever become more and more complicated, and as the collision of constant new atoms with a layer of atoms already in lateral motion constantly imparts new forces, so we may suppose that the motion will continually increase.

From the lateral motions in connection with the rotation of the atoms are then easily produced cases of retrogressive movement. If now, in a layer of atoms so involved, the heavier — *i.e.,* the larger—atoms continually receive a stronger impetus downwards, they will finally be collected below, while the light ones will form the upper stratum. The basis of this whole theory, the doctrine of the quicker descent of the greater atoms, was attacked by Aristotle, and it appears that Epikuros was thus induced, whilst retaining the rest of the system, to introduce his fortuitous deviations of the atoms from the straight line. Aristotle, that is, taught that if there could be void space, which he thought impossible, then all bodies must necessarily fall with equal speed, since the difference in the rapidity of the descent is determined by the various densities of the medium—as, for example, water and air. Now void space not being a medium, there is no difference therefore in the descent of different bodies. Aristotle in this case was at one with our modern science, as also in his doctrine of gravitation towards the centre of the universe. His deduction, however, is only in places rational, and is mixed with subtleties of the same kind as those by which he seeks to demonstrate the impossibility of motion in empty space. Epikuros cut the matter short, and comes to this simple conclusion: because in empty space there is no resistance, all bodies must fall equally fast—apparently in entire agreement with modern physics; but only apparently, since the true theory of gravitation of descent was wholly wanting to the ancients.

Comp. Fragm. Phys., 2, Mullach, impact of the atoms rushing in from p. 358, and the admirable remark of without attain a rotatory motion.

Zeller, i. 717, Aiim. 1, 011 the purely The stars, according to Demokritos, mechanical nature of this aggregation are moved by the rotating covering of the homogeneous atoms. But it of the world. Epikuros, of course, is less certain whether the vortical who was, however, it is certain, a movement (the "Kreis-oder Wirbel-very weak mathematician as compared bewegung," Zeller, p. 715, and Anm. with Demokritos, in spite of his being 2) really played the part in Demo-later, thought it also possible that kritos's system attributed to it by the sun may maintain its continual later reporters. It seems much more revolution round the earth in conse likely that he made the vortical movequence of the impulse once received ment of the mass of atoms of which in the general movement of the uni the world was composed only de-verse; and if we consider how vague velop itself after the atoms, and espe-were the pre-Galilean ideas as to the oially those of the outer covering of nature of motion, we need not be sur thc universe, had formed a compact prised that even Demokritos should body held together by the hooks of have made a vortical motion be devel the atoms. Such a body might then oped out of the rectilinear impaot;

Tery easily, partly by the original but convincing proofs of this view are motion of its particles, partly by the entirely wanting.

It is not uninteresting to compare how Galilei, as soon as, after many painful efforts, he had reached the true law of fall, directly ventured *a priori* to the conclusion that in empty space all hodies will fall equally fast, a considerable period before this, by means of the air-pump, could be proved to be the fact. It is a question to be considered how far reminiscences of Aristotle or Lucretius may not have assisted Galilei to this conclusion.23

V. *The variety of all things is a consequence of the variety of their atoms in number, size, figure, and arrangement; there is no qualitative difference oj atoms. They have no "internal conditions;" and act on each other only by pressure or collision.*

We have already seen, in connection with the third proposition, that

Demokritos regarded the sense qualities, such as colour, sound, heat, and so on, as mere deceptive appearances, which is only to say that he entirely sacrificed the subjective side of phenomena, which is, nevertheless, all that is immediately given, in order to be able to carry out a more consequent objective explanation; and accordingly Demokritos engaged, in fact, in the most exhaustive investigations as to what must be, in the object, the substratum of the sensible qualities.

According, then, to the difference in the arranging of the atoms in a "schema "—which may remind us of the "schemata" or atoms of our chemists—are determined our subjective impressions.

Aristotle complains that Demokritos had reduced all kinds of sensation into the one sensation of touch—a reproach which, in our eyes, will rather be counted to his praise. The gist of the problem will lie, then, just in this sense of *touch.* Comp. Whewell, Hist, of the In-Noteworthy is the general principle duct. Sci. , ii. 34 (ed. 1837). in Fr. 24: "The schema is in *itself* Here again the authentio proofs *ica.0 avri,* the sweetness, however, are lacking; we have chiefly to rely and the sensible quality is only in upon reports of Aristotle, which are relation to another and in another." here, however, very full, and raise Here we have, too, the souice of the no suspicion of misunderstanding. Aristotelian opposition of substance

Fuller details in Zeller, i. 704 ff. and accident, just as Aristotle found Here we have tolerably full ex-the original of his apposition of tracts in Theophrastos; comp. Fragm. *iiva/us* and *Mpyeta* in Demokritos.

Fhys., 24-39, Mullach, p. 362 sqq (Fragm. Phys., 7, Mullach, p. 358).

We can, indeed, easily enough rise to the standpoint of regarding all sensations as modifications of touch, although there will still remain unsolved enigmas enough. But we cannot so naively dispose of the question how the simplest and most elementary of all sensations is related to the pressure or collision which occasions it. The sensation is not in the *individual* atom, and still less is it an aggregate of them; for how could it be brought into a focus through void space? It is produced and determined by means of a *Form* in which the atoms act in mutual co-operation. Materialism here borders closely on Formalism, as Aristotle has not forgotten to point out.26 Whilst he, however, made the forms transcendentally causes of motion, and thereby struck at the root of all natural science, Demokritos was careful not to follow up the formalistic side of his own theory, which would only lead him into the depths of metaphysic. Here we first find the need of the Kantian "Critick of Eeason " to throw the first weak ray of light into the depths of a mystery which, after all the progress of our knowledge of nature, is yet to-day as great as it was in the time of Demokritos.

VI. *The soul consists of fine, smooth, round atoms, like those of fire. These atoms are the most mobile, and by their motion, which permeates the whole body, the phenomena of life are produced.-'?*

Here then, also, is the soul, as with Diogenes of Apollonia, a particular kind of matter; and Demokritos believes, also, that this matter is distributed throughout the universe, and everywhere produces the phenomena of heat and of life. Demokritos therefore recognises a distinction between soul and body, which our modern Materialists would scarcely relish; and he knows how to utilise this distinction, for his ethical system, just as the Dualists had done. The soul is the really essential part of man; the body is only the vessel of the soul, and this must be our principal care. The soul is the seat of happiness; bodily beauty without reason is in its nature merely animal. To Demokritos, indeed, has been ascribed the doctrine of a divine world-soul, only that he means by this merely the universal diffusion of that mobile matter which he could very well describe figuratively as the divine element in the world, without attributing to it other than material properties and mechanical movements.

Ariat. Phya.Auso., ii. a, where it *fwcpbv yap n pJpos 'Eurc$oicij! xal* is explained that nature ia twofold, At/o/c/wtos Too *elSovs* ical Tod Tj *%v* consisting of form and matter: the *m.i fiJ/avro.* earlier philosopher had regarded mat-a? *Q* teller i. 728 ff. tar only, with the limitation — *txl*

Aristotle ridicules the view of Demokritos as to the manner in which the soul influences the body by making a comparison. Daedalos is said to have made a moving statue of Aphrodite: this the actor Philippos explained had been done probably by pouring quicksilver into the interior of the wooden figure. In the same way Aristotle thinks would Demokritos have man moved by the mobile atoms within him. The comparison is clearly inadequate, but it may nevertheless serve to explain two fundamentally different principles of regarding nature. Aristotle thinks that not thus, but through choice and reflection the soul moves man—as if this were not clear to the savage long before the very slenderest beginnings of science. Our whole " comprehension" is a referring of the particular in phenomena to the general laws of the phenomenal world. The last step of this endeavour is the including of the See note 14 above. To do justice own words are—" Nam quos hie nolo Demokritos's idea we need only mino spiritus nil nisi corpora sunt, et to compare how Descartes (DePass., aliam nullum proprietatem hahent art. x. , li.) represents the action of nisi quod sint corpora tenuissima et the material " animal spirits'' in the quae moventur celerime, instar parmoving of the body. Descartes' tiumflammaeexfaceexeuntis. "—Te. o processes of reason in this chain. Demokritos took this step: Aristotle misconceived its importance.

The doctrine of mind, says Zeller (i. 735), has not in the case of Demokritos proceeded from the general necessity of a " deeper principle" for the explanation of nature. Demokritos regarded mind not as "the world-building force," but only as one form of matter amongst others. Even Empedokles had regarded rationality as an internal property of the elements; Demokritos, on the contrary, only as a "phenomenon taking its origin from the mathematical constitution of certain atoms in their relation to the others." And this is just Demokritos's superiority; for every philosophy which seriously attempts to understand the phenomenal world must come back to this point. The special case of those processes we call "intellectual" must be explained from the universal laws of all motion, or we have no explanation at all. The weak point of all Materialism lies just in this, that with this explanation it stops short at the very point where the highest problems J of philosophy begin. But he who devises some bungling explanation of nature, including the rational actions of mankind, starting from mere conjectural *a priori* notions which it is impossible for the mind to picture intelligibly to itself, destroys the whole basis of science, no matter whether he be called Aristotle or Hegel.

Good old Kant would here undoubtedly in principle declare himself on the side of Demokritos and against Aristotle and Zeller. He declares empiricism as thoroughly justified, so far as it does not become dogmatic, but only opposes " temerity, and the presumption of reason mistaking its true destiny," which " talks largely of insight and knowledge where insight and knowledge can really do nothing," which confounds the practical and theoretical interests," in order, where its convenience is interfered with, to tear away the thread of physical investigations." 29 "KritikderVernunft, Elementarl., further the remarkable note oa p.

ii. 2, 2, 2, Eaupst., 3 Abschnitt, 335.

llartenatein, iii. 334 *11.* Comp.

This intellectual presumption in the face of experience, this unjustifiable tearing of the thread of physical inquiries, plays to-day also its part, as well as in Hellenic antiquity. We shall have much to say about it before we have done. It is ever the point at which a healthy philosophy cannot too sharply and energetically take Materialism into its protection.

With all its elevation of the mind above the body, the ethic of Demokritos is nevertheless at bottom a theory of Hedonism, standing quite in harmony with the materialistic cosmology. Amongst his moral utterances, which have been preserved in much greater number than the fragments of his physical philosophy, we find, it is true, many of those primitive doctrines of wisdom which might find their place in the most diverse systems, which Demokritos—together with counsels of prudence drawn from his own personal experiences—taught in a too practical and popular shape for them to be considered as having formed distinctive marks of his system; but we can, nevertheless, unite the whole into a consecutive series of thoughts resting upon a few simple principles.

Happiness consists in the cheerful calmness of spirit which man can attain only by securing the mastery over his desires. Temperance and purity of heart, united with culture of the emotions and development of the intelligence, supply every man with the means, in spite of all the vicissitudes of life, of reaching this goal. Sensual pleasure affords only a brief satisfaction; and he only who does good for the sake of its intrinsic merit, without being swayed by fear or hope, is sure of this inward reward.

Such an ethical system is indeed very far removed from the Hedonism of Epikuros, or from the system of a refined egotism which we find associated with the Materialism of the eighteenth century; but it is nevertheless lacking in the distinctive mark of all idealistic morality, a principle of conduct taken directly from the consciousness, and asserted independently of experience. The distinctions of good and evil, right and wrong, Demokritos appears to suppose to be known without inquiry; that cheerful serenity of soul is the most lasting good, and that it can only be attained by right thinking and acting, are results of experience; and the reason for striving after this harmonious inward condition lies exclusively in the happiness of the individual.

Of all the great principles underlying the Materialism of our time, one only is wanting in Demokritos; and that is the abolition of all teleology by the principle of the development of the *purposeful* from the unpurposeful. We cannot, in fact, dispense with such a principle as soon as we seriously undertake to carry out one kind of causality, that of the mechanical impact of atoms. It is not sufficient to show that it is the finest, most mobile, and smoothest atoms which produce the phenomena of the organic world; we must also show why, with the help of these atoms, instead of arbitrary, aimless objects, there are produced the exquisitely articulated bodies of plants and animals, with all their organs for the maintenance of the individual and the species. Only when we have demonstrated the possibility of this, then, in the full sense of tho word, can the *rational* movements be understood as a special form of the universal movement.

Demokritos extolled the adaptation of organic bodies, and especially of the human frame, with the admiration of a reflective observer of nature. We find in him no trace of that false teleology, which may be described as the hereditary foe of all science; but we discover nowhere an attempt to explain the origin of these adaptations from the blind sway of natural necessity. Whether this means that there was a gap in his system, or only that there has been a gap in the tradition, we do not know; but we do know that this last basis of all Materialism, crudely, it 1s true, but yet in fully intelligible clearness, sprung from tho philosophical thought of the Greeks. What Darwin, rolying upon a wide extent of positive knowledge, has achieved for our generation, Empedokles offered to the thinkers of antiquity—the simple and penetrating thought, that adaptations preponderate in nature just because it is their nature to perpetuate themselves, while what fails of adaptation has long since perished.

Hellenic intellectual life attained to an active development in Sicily and Lower Italy not much later than on the coasts of Asia Minor. Indeed,'Magna Graecia,' with its proud and wealthy cities, far outstripped the mothercountry, until at last the rays of philosophy were again concentrated, as in a focus, at Athens. The rapid development of these colonies must have been influenced by an element like that which caused Goethe's ejaculation—

"Amerika! du hast es besser,
Als unser Continent, das ulte,
Hast keine verfallenen SchlOsser
Und keine Basalte."

The greater freedom from tradition, removal from antique religious observances, and from the contact of the priestly families and their despotic, deeply-rooted authority, seem to have especially favoured the transition from the prejudices of religious faith to scientific inquiry and philosophical speculation. The Pythagorean brotherhood was, with all its austerity, still at the same time a religious revolution of a tolerably radical nature; and amongst the intellectual chiefs of this confederation there arose the most fruitful study of mathematics and natural science which Greece had known before the Alexandrian epoch. Xenophanes, who migrated from Asia Minor to Lower Italy, and there founded the school of Elea, is an eager Rationalist. He attacks the mythological representation of the gods, and substitutes a philosophical conception.

Empedokles of Agrigentum cannot be described as a Materialist, because with him force and matter are still fundamentally separated. He was probably the first Greek who divided matter into the four elements, which, by means of Aristotle, secured so long a tenure of life, that even

Vol. 1. c in the science of to-day we constantly come upon their traces. Besides these elements, Empedokles supposed that there were two ultimate forces—Love and Hate—which, in the formation and dissolution of the world, performed the functions of attraction and repulsion. Had Empedokles made these forces properties of the elements, we might quietly rank him as a Materialist; for not only did the picturesque language of his poems draw its illustrations from the feelings of the human heart, but he set the whole Olympos and the lower world in motion in order to give life to his conceptions, and to find occupation for the imagination as well as for the reason. But his forces are independent of matter. For immeasurable periods now the one preponderates, now the other. If love has attained a complete predominance, then all matter, collected into a great sphere, enjoys a blessed peace. If hate has reached the height of power, everything is thrown into confusion and dislocation. In each case no individual things exist. All terrestrial life is in connection with the circumstances of transition, which lead from the unity of the worldsphere, through the growing power of hatred, to absolute dissolution, or the contrary way, through the increasing power of love. This latter way is that of our world-epoch, in which we gather from the fundamental principles of the system we must clearly have an enormous extent of time behind us. The special features of his cosmogony interest us here only so far as it deals with the development of organisms, since here we are met by that principle which, in the hands of Epikuros and Lucretius, has subsequently exercised so great an influence.

The principles of 'hate' and 'love' do not operate according to a plan, or, at least, have no other plan than that of universal separation and reunion. Organisms arise through the fortuitous play of the elements and elementary forces. First were formed plants, and then animals. The animal organs were first developed by nature individually: eyes without faces, arms without bodies, and so on. Then there resulted, in the progress of the combining tendency, a confused play of bodies, now united in one way, and now in another. Nature tried all possible combinations simultaneously, until there resulted a creature capable of life, and finally of propagation. As soon as this is produced it perpetuates itself, whilst the previous products had perished as they were produced.

Ueberweg remarks as to this doctrine (Hist, of Phil., E. T. L 62, n.), that it may be compared with the physical philosophy of Schelling and Oken, and the theory of descent proposed by Lamarck and Darwin; yet that these find the explanation of progress rather in the successive differentiation of simpler forms, while the Empedoklean doctrine seeks it rather in the union of heterogeneous forms. The observation is very just; and we might add, that the later theory of descent is supported by the facts, while the doctrine of Empedokles, considered from our present scientific standpoint, is absurd and fantastic. It is worth while, however, to point out what links the two doctrines in the most distinct and united opposition to the views of Schelling and Oken, and that is the purely mechanical attainment of adaptations through the infinitely repeated play of production and annihilation, in which finally that alone survives which bears the guarantee of persistence in its relatively fortuitous constitution. And if, in regard to Empedokles, criticism must still doubt whether he really so understood the matter, yet this much is quite certain, that Epikuros so construes the Empedoklean theory, and has accordingly fused it with his Atomism, and with his doctrine of the realisation of all possibilities.

About the name of Empedokles, as about that of Demokritos, there has gathered a mass of myth and legend, much of which is due to a mastery of natural forces, which seemed very wonderful to his contemporaries. But while Demokritos must have earned this renown, in spite of the most sober simplicity and openness in his life and teaching, by merely practical achievements, Empedokles appears to have loved the nimbus of the wonder-worker, and to have utilised it for his reforming purposes. He also sought to spread purer ideas of the gods, though he did not reach the rationalism of Xenophanes, who discarded all anthropomorphism. Empedokles believed in the transmigration of souls, and forbade the offering of sacrifices as well as the eating of flesh. His earnest demeanour, his fiery eloquence, the fame of his works, imposed upon the people, who revered him as a god. Politically, he was a zealous partisan of democracy, and contributed to its victory in his native city. Yet he, too, must have experienced the fickleness of popular favour: he died in the Peloponnese, probably in exile. How his religious views were to be reconciled with his scientific theories we do not know. "How many theological doctrines," remarks Zeller, "have there not been believed by Christian philosophers, whose philosophical conclusions would be in complete antagonism with these doctrines!" CHAPTER IL THE SENSATIONALISM OF THE SOPHISTS AND ARISTIPPOSO ETHICAL MATERIALISM.

What stuff or matter is in the outer world of nature, sensation is in the inner life of man. If we believe that consciousness can exist without sensation, this is due to a subtle confusion. It is possible to have a very lively consciousness, which busies itself with the highest and most important things, and yet at the same time to have sensations of an evanescent sensuous strength. But sensations there always are; and from their relations, their harmony or want of harmony, are formed the contents and meaning of consciousness; just as the cathedral is built of the rough stone, or the significant drawing is composed of fine material lines, or the flower of organised matter. As, then, the Materialist, looking into external nature, follows out the forms of things from the materials of which they are composed, and with them lays the foundations of his philosophy, so the Sensationalist refers the whole of consciousness back to sensations. Sensationalism and Materialism, therefore, agree at bottom in laying stress on matter in opposition to form: the question then arises, how are their mutual relations to be explained?

Obviously not by a mere convention, which at once sets a man down as a Sensationalist in regard to the internal, and a Materialist in regard to the external world. Although this standpoint is the commonest in our inconsequent practice, it is anything but a philosophical one.

Much rather will the consequent Materialist deny that sensation exists independently of matter, and will accordingly, even in the facts of consciousness, find only effects of ordinary material changes, and regard these in the same light as the other material facts of the external world: the Sensationalist will, on the other hand, be obliged to deny that we know anything whatever of matter, or of the things of the external world in general, since we have only our own *perception* of the things, and cannot know how this stands related to the things in themselves. Sensation is to him not only the material *(Stoff)* of all the facts of consciousness, but also the only immediately given material, since we have and know the things of the external world only in our sensations. As a result of.the undeniable correctness of this proposition, which is at once an advance upon the ordinary consciousness, and already presupposes a conception of the world as a unity, Sensationalism must appear a natural development of Materialising This development was brought about among the Greeks through that very school which in general struck deepest into ancient life, alike in its constructive and destructive influences,—by means of the Sophists.

It was said in later antiquity that the sage Demokritos once saw a porter in his native town packing together in a very ingenious manner the wood blocks he had to carry. Demokritos talked to him, and was so surprised by his quickness that he took him as a pupil. This porter was the man who furnished the occasion for a great revolution in the position of philosophy: he became a teacher of wisdom for gold. He was Protagoras, the first of the Sophists. i Compare, in the modern history case of Hobbes and Demokritos. Fir of philosophy, the relation of Locke ther, we see easily that Sensationalism to Hobbes, or of Condillac tc La-is at bottom only a transition to mettrie. This does not, of course, Idealism — as, for example, Locke mean that we most always expect a stands on untenable ground between chronological series of this kind, and Hobbes and Berkeley; for so soon as yet it is the most natural, and there-the sense-perception is the strictly fore the most frequent. We must, given, not only will the quality of however, observe how the sensation-the object be uncertain, but its alistic elements are, as a rule, already very existence must appear doubtful, present in the deeper Materialists; And yet this step was not taken by and very expressly, in especial in the antiquity.

Hippias, Prodikos, Gorgiaa, and a long series of less famous men, chiefly known through Plato's writings, were soon travelling through the cities of Greece, teaching and disputing, and in some cases they made great fortunes. Everywhere the cleverest youths flocked to them; to partake of their instructions soon became the mark of fashion; their doctrines and speeches became the daily topics of the upper classes, and their fame spread with incredible rapidity.

This was a new thing in Greece, and the old Marathonian warriors, the veterans of the liberation struggle, were not the only conservatives who shook their heads. The supporters of the Sophists themselves held towards them, with all their admiration, much the same position as, in our own day, the patrons of an opera-singer: the majority would, in the midst of their admiration, have disdained to follow in their steps. Sokrates used to embarrass the pupils of the Sophists by blunt questions as to the object of their teacher's profession. From Pheidias we learn sculpture, from Hippokrates medicine—what, then, from Protagoras?

The porter story must probably be considered fabulous, although this is a case where the traces of some such tale reach very far back. Comp. Brandis.Gesch. d. griech. rom. Filos., i. 523 ff., and, on the other side, Zeller, i. 866, Anm. 1, where certainly too much stress is laid upon the "scurrility" of Epikuros. The question whether Protagoras was a pupil of Demokritos hangs together with the difficult question of age discussed in note 10. We prefer here also to leave it undecided. But even in case the predominant view, which makes Protagoras some twenty years older than Demokritos, should ever be sufficiently proved, the influence of Demokritos upon the Protagorean theory of knowledge remains extremely probable, and we must then assume that Protagoras, originally a mere rhetorician and teacher of politics, developed his own system later, indeed during his second stay at Athens, in intellectual intercourse with bis opponent Sokrates, at a time when the writings of Demokritos might already have had their influence. Zeller's attempt, following Frei (Quaestiones Protagoreae, Bonnae, 1845), to deduce the philosophy of Protagoras wholly from Herakleitos, disregarding Demokritos, splits on the want of a sufficient point of sun port for the subjective direction of Protagoras in the theory of knowledge. If it is proposed to regard as Herakleitic the origin of sensation from a mutual motion of sense and object (comp. Zeller, i. 585), the resolution of sense qualities into subjective impressions is wholly wanting in Herakleitos. On the other hand, the *'vdfiti) yvKd Kcli vifUf) iriKpbvJ* and so on (Fragm. Phys., 1), of Demokritos forms the natural transition from the purely objective view of the world of the older physicists to the subjective one of the Sophists. Protagoras must indeed reverse the standpoint of Demokritos in order to reach his own; but this is also his position towards Herakleitos, who finds all truth in the universal, while Protagoras seeks it in the particular. The circumstance that the Platonic Sokrates (comp. Frei, Quaest. Prot., p. 79) makes the principle of Protagoras, that all is motion, to be the original of all things, is historically not decisive. Generally it may be said that the influence of Herakleitos on the doctrine of Protagoras is unmistakable, and it is at the same timo probable that the elements due to this are the *original* elements to which Demokritos's reference of the sense qualities to subjective impressions was added later as a fermenting element.

The pride and love of display of the Sophists were no substitute for the respectable and reserved attitude of the old philosophers. Aristocratic dilletanteism in philosophy was thought more respectable than their professional business.

We are not yet far removed from the time when only the darker side of the Sophistic system was known to us. The ridicule of Aristophanes and the moral earnestness of Plato have joined with the innumerable anecdotes of later times to concentrate upon the name of the Sophists all that was to be found of frivolous pedantry, of venal dialectic, and systematic immorality. Sophist became the designation of all pseudo-philosophy; and long after the vindication of Epikuros and the Epikureans was, to the general profit of men of culture, an accomplished fact, that reproach, still clung to the name of the Sophists, and it remained an insoluble puzzle how Aristophanes could have represented Sokrates as the head of the Sophists.

Through Hegel and his school, in connection with the unprejudiced inquiries of modern philology, the way was deared in Germany for a more accurate view. A still more decided position was taken by Grote in his "History of Greece," and before him Lewes had entered the lists for the honour of the Sophists. He maintains Plato's *Euthydemus* to be just as much an exaggeration as the *Clouds* of Aristophanes. "The caricature of Sokrates by Aristophanes is quite as near the truth as the caricature of the Sophists by Plato; with this difference, that in the one case it was inspired by political, in the other by speculative, antipathy." 32 Grote shows us that this fanatical hatred was thoroughly Platonic. Xenophon's Sokrates occupies a much less hostile position towards the Sophists.

Protagoras marks a great and decisive turning-point in the history of Greek philosophy. He is the first who started, not from the object—from external nature, but from the subject—from the spiritual nature of man. He is in this respect an undoubted predecessor of Sokrates; he stands, indeed, in a certain sense, at the head of the whole antimaterialistic development, which is usually made to begin with Sokrates. At the same time, however, Protagoras has, in addition, the most intimate relations to Materialism, through his starting from sensation as Demokritos started from matter; whilst he was very decidedly opposed to Plato and Aristotle in this, that to him—and this trait also is related to Materialism—the *particular* and the *individual* is the essential, not the *universal,* as with them. With the Sensationalism of Protagoras is combined a relativity which may remind us of Eichner and Moleschott. The expression that something is, always needs a further determination *in relation to what* it is or is becoming; otherwise our predication has no meaning.4

In precisely the same way Buchner says, in order to combat the 'thing in itself,' that all things exist only for each other, and have no significance apart from mutual relations; 5 and still more decidedly Moleschott: "Ex cept in relation to the eye, into which it sends its rays, the tree *has no existence."* All such expressions are still in our own day regarded as Materialism. To Deniokritos, however, the atom was a 'thing in itself.' Protagoras dropped the Atomism. He regarded matter as something in itself completely undetermined, involved in eternal flow and change. It is what it appears to the individual.

Hist. of Phil., i. 106, 107. basis of the philosophy of Protagoras Comp. Frei, Quaest. Prot.,p. 110.—in its completion — and not the

"Mul to plus vero ad philosophiam Heraklitean *irdvra pet.* promovendam eo contulit Protagoras Frei, Quaest. Prot., p. 84 foil, quod hominem dixit omnium rerum Comp. Buchner, Die Stellung den' mensuram. Eo enim mentem sui Menschen inder Natur, Leipx., 1870, consciam reddidit, rebusque superi-p. cxvii. The expression of Mole orem praeposnit." But for this rea-schott will be more fully discussed in son this must be iegarded as the true the Second Book.

The most distinctive features of the philosophy of Protagoras are the following propositions underlying his Sensationalism:— i. Man is the measure of all things: of those that are that they are; of those that are not that they are not.

2. Contradictory assertions are equally true.

Of these propositions, the second is the most striking, and is also the one that most forcibly reminds us of the unscrupulous pedantry which is only too often considered as the essence of the

Sophistic system. It gains, however, a deeper sense so soon as it is explained from the first principle which contains the core of the Protagorean doctrines. Man is the measure of things, that is, it depends upon our sensations how things appear to us, and this appearance is all that is given us; and so it is not man in his universal and necessary qualities, but each individual in each single moment, that is the measure of things. If it is a question of the universal and necessary qualities, than Protagoras must be regarded wholly as a predecessor of the theoretical philosophy of Kant. Yet Protagoras as to the influence of the subject, as well as to the judgment of the object, kept close to the individual perception, and so far from viewing the 'man as such,' he cannot even, strictly speaking, make the individual the measure of things, for the individual is mutable; and il the same temperature appear to the same man at one time cool, at another warm, both impressions are in their own moment equally true, and there is no truth outside this.

We may now easily explain the second principle without contradiction, so soon as we proceed to the closer determination as demanded by the system of Protagoras— in the sense of two different individuals.

It was not the object of Protagoras to maintain the simultaneous truth and falsity of the same assertion in the mouth of the same individual; although, indeed, he teaches that, of every proposition maintained by any one, the opposite may be maintained with equal right, in so far as there may be any one to whom it so appears.-That in this way of regarding things there is contained a great element of truth cannot but be recognised; for the real fact, the immediately given, is in reality the phenomenon. But our mind demands something persistent in the flood of phenomena. Sokrates sought the path to this persistent element; Plato, in complete contrast to the Sophists, believed he had found it in the universal, in face of which the particular sank back into unreal seeming. In this controversy, if we view it quite theoretically, the Sophists are right, and Plato's theoretical philosophy can find its higher significance only in the deep-lying suspicion of a hidden truth, and in its relations to the ideal elements of life.

In Ethic the fatal consequences of the standpoint of Protagoras are most obvious. Protagoras, indeed, did not draw these consequences. He explained desire to be the principle of action, but he drew a sharp distinction between the good citizens and noble men who have desires only for what is good and noble, and the bad and vulgar who feel attracted towards evil. At the same time, the consequence must have followed from the theoretical conception of this unconditional relativity, that that is *right and good* for the man which in each case seems to him right and good.

As practical men, and, in fact, teachers of virtue, the Sophists helped themselves by simply adopting the traditional Hellenic morality as a whole for their own. There could be no question of deducing it from a principle: even the doctrine that those sentiments are to be favoured which further the prosperity of the state was not raised to an ethical principle, however nearly it may approach it Frai, Quaest. Prot., p. 99; Zeller, i. 916 foil.

So it is intelligible that the most important consequences from this principle of arbitrariness were drawn not only by fanatical opponents like Plato, but occasionally even by venturesome pupils of the Sophists. The famous art of making the worse appear the better cause is defended by Lewes as an art of disputation for practical people, as the art of being one's own advocate: the reverse of the picture is only too obvious. The defence is sufficient to show that, on the general ground of average Greek morality, the Sophists might boldly assert their blamelessness; it is not sufficient to refute the view that Sophistic was a dissolving element in Hellenic civilisation.

But if we look closely at the position that desire is the moving principle of action, we easily see that the ground was already prepared by the Sensationalism of Protagoras for the Cyrenaic doctrine of pleasure. The development of this germ was carried out by the 'Sokratic' Aristippos.

On the hot coasts of Northern Africa lay the Greek commercial colony of Cyrene; here Oriental luxury was combined with the refinement of Hellenic civilisation. Sprung from a wealthy mercantile family of this city, brought up with the sentiments and education of a man of the world, the young Aristippos went to Athens, attracted by the fame of Sokrates. Of handsome form, and gifted with the charm of the most refined demeanour and the most intellectual conversation, Aristippos found his way to every heart. He attached himself to Sokrates, and was regarded as a Sokratic, different as the direction taken by his doctrine was from the essence of the Sokratic theory. His personal inclination to a life of pleasure and display, and the powerful influence of the Sophists, brought about the development of his doctrine that pleasure is the object of existence. Aristotle calls him a Sophist; yet we may also recognise in him the influence of Sokratic views. Sokrates found the highest happiness in virtue, and taught that virtue is identical with true knowledge. Aristippos taught that self-control and temperance—that is, the genuine Sokratic virtues—alone render us capable of enjoyment, and keep us so; only the wise man can be really happy. Happiness, however, is with him, of course, only pleasure.

Lewes, Hist of Phil., i. 114.

He distinguished two forms of sensation: one which results from gentle motion, the other from violent rapid motion; the former is pleasure, the latter pain or absence of pleasure.

Now since sensual pleasure obviously produces a livelier sensation than intellectual pleasure, it was merely a consequence of the inexorable logic of Hellenic speculation when Aristippos inferred from this that physical pleasure is better than intellectual pleasure, physical pain worse than mental. Epikuros tried to escape this by a sophism.

Finally, Aristippos taught expressly that the true aim is not happiness, which is the permanent result of many single sensations of pleasure, but the individual sensual concrete pleasure itself. Happiness is of course good, but it must come spontaneously, and is therefore not the aim.

No Sensationalistic moralist of ancient or modern times has been more logically consistent than Aristippos, and his life constitutes the best commentary on his doctrine.

With Sokrates and his school, Athens had become the centre of philosophic tendencies. Though from this point, then, proceeded the great reaction against Materialism, which in Plato and Aristotle secured the most decided victory, yet even here the intellectual influences of Materialism were sufficiently powerful to challenge such a reaction.

Demokritos, it is true, felt no attraction towards Athens. ' I came to Athens," he is reported to have said, "and no man knew me." As a man of reputation then, he had hastened to the then newly flourishing centre of science to view closely the course of speculation there, and quietly again departed without revealing himself; and it may well be that the great and earnest system of Demokritos worked much less powerfully on the seething tendencies of the time than the less logical but more intelligible features of that Materialism, in the wider sense of the word, which dominates the whole pre-Sokratic period of philosophy. Above all things, however, had Sophistic, in the good and the bad sense of the word, found a favourable soil in Athens. Since the Persian war a change had taken place, under the influence of the new modes of thought, which extended through all grades of society. Under Perikles's powerful direction, the state had reached the consciousness of its destiny. Commerce and the sovereignty of the sea had favoured the development of material interests. A magnificent spirit of enterprise appeared amongst the Athenians. The time at which Protagoras taught almost coincided with the period which saw the elevation of the mighty buildings of the Acropolis.

The stiffness of antiquity disappeared, and art, in its passage to the beautiful, reached that elevation of style which we find in the works of Pheidias. In gold and ivory arose the wonderful statues of Pallas Parthenos, and of the Olympian Zeus; and while beliefs in all classes are beginning to totter, the festival processions of the gods reached the highest pitch of splendour and magnificence. More material and luxurious in every respect than Athens was Kotinth; but Korinth was not the city of philosophers. There intellectual apathy and degradation passed into sensuality, to which the traditional forms of worship not merely adapted themselves, but even gave encouragement.

Thus, even in antiquity, the interdependence of theoretical and practical Materialism, as well as the opposition of the two, is unmistakably obvious. If by practical Materialism we understand a dominant inclination to material acquisition and enjoyment, then theoretical Materialism is opposed to it, as is every effort of the spirit towards knowledge. Nay, we may say that the sober earnest which marks the great Materialistic systems of antiquity is perhaps more suited than an enthusiastic Idealism, which only too easUy results in its own bewilderment, to keep the soul clear of all that is low and vulgar, and to lend it a lasting effort after worthy objects.

Eeligious traditions, whose origin may be traced to high ideal elevation, are sometimes easily polluted in the course of centuries with the material and low sentiments of the masses, quite apart from the 'Materialism of dogma,' which may be found in every firmly-rooted orthodox system, so soon as the bare substance of religious doctrines is more highly valued than the spirit which has produced them. The mere decomposition, however, of tradition does not better this fault; since a religion will rarely have so petrified that no spark of ideal life will, from its higher forms, fall upon the soul; and, on the other hand, the progress of enlightenment does not make the masses into philosophers.

But the true notion of ethical Materialism is, of course, quite different: we must understand by it a moral doctrine which makes the moral action of man rise from the particular emotions of his spirit, and which determines the object of action, not by an unconditionally ruling idea, but by the effort after a desired condition. Such an ethical system may be named MateriaHstic, because, like theoretical Materialism, it starts from matter as opposed to form; only, that here is meant, not the matter of external bodies, not even the quality of sensation as matter of theoretical consciousness, but the elementary matter of practical conduct, the *impulses* and *the feelings oj pleasure and its opposite.* We may say that this is only an analogy, that there is no obvious unity of tendency, but history shows us almost universally that this analogy is powerful enough to determine the connection of the systems.

A fully-developed ethical Materialism of this sort is not only not ignoble, but it seems by a sort of internal neces sity to lead to noble and elevated forms of life, and to a love of those forms that rises far above the commonplace demand for happiness; just as, on the other hand, an idealistic ethical system in its full development cannot help being anxious for the happiness of individuals and the harmony of their impulses.

But we are concerned, in the historical development of nations, not with a purely ideal ethic, but with thoroughly fixed traditional forms of morality, the stability of which is disturbed and shaken by any new principle, because they do not rest upon the abstract reflection of the man himself, but on a taught and inherited product of the collective life of many generations. And thus our experience hitherto seems to teach us that all Materialistic morality, pure as it may otherwise be, operates especially in periods of transformation and transition, as a powerful solvent, while all great and decisive revolutions and reforms first break out in the shape of new ethical ideas.

Such new ideas were introduced in antiquity by Plato and Aristotle, but they could neither penetrate to the masses, nor gain over to their objects the old forms of the national religion. All the deeper on this account was the influence of these products of Hellenic philosophy upon the later development of mediaeval Christianity.

When Protagoras was driven from Athens for having begun his book on the gods with the words, "As to the gods, I do not know whether they exist or not," it was already too late for the salvation of the conservatism for which Aristophanes vainly set to work all the forces of the stage, and even the sacrifice of Sokrates could no longer stay the progress of the Spirit of the Times.

As early as the Peloponnesian war, soon after the death of Perikles, the great revolution in the whole life of the Athenians was decided; and of this revolution the especial promoters were the Sophists.

This rapid process of dissolution is unique in history: no people has ever lived so fast as the Athenians. And instructive as may be this turning-point of their history, the danger is proportionately great of our drawing false conclusions from it.

So long as a state, as in the case of Athens before Perikles, steadily develops, and holds fast to old traditions, all its citizens feel themselves held together by a common interest as against other states. On the other hand, the philosophy of the Sophists and that of the Cyrenaics had a cosmopolitan colouring.

The thinker embraces in a short series of conclusions results which history requires thousands of years to realise; and so the cosmopolitan idea may be in general quite right, and yet in the particular case prejudicial, because it destroys the interest of the citizens in their country, and in consequence cripples the country's vital force.

So long as men adhere to their traditions, there are certain ultimate limits set to the ambition and the talents of the individual. All these limits are removed by the principle that each individual man has in himself the measure of all things. The only security against this is the merely conventional; but the conventional is the unreasonable, because thought always impels us to new developments.

This was soon understood by the Athenians, and not the philosophers only, but even their most zealous opponents, learnt to argue, to criticise, to dispute, and to make projects. The Sophists created even an art of demagogy; for they taught rhetoric with the express object of understanding how one may turn the masses in the direction suitable to one's own interest.

Since contradictory assertions are equally true, many an imitator of Protagoras cared only to establish his own personal view, and so a kind of right of moral force was introduced. At all events, the Sophists must have possessed, in the art of influencing men's minds, great skill and deep psychological insight, or they could not have received an income which, compared with the fees of our

Vol. 1. D own days, stands at least in the relation of principal to interest. And, moreover, the underlying idea was not that of a reward for trouble, but that of the purchase of an art which was the making of its possessor.

Aristippos, who flourished in the fourth century, was a true cosmopolitan. The courts of the tyrants were his favourite resort, and at that of Dionysius of Syracuse he not unfrequently met with his intellectual opposite, Plato. Dionysius valued him beyond all other philosophers, because he knew how to make something out of every moment; also, of course, because he humoured all the tyrant's caprices. In the principle that nothing natural is blamable, Aristippos agreed with the 'dog' Diogenes; and hence he also was named by the popular wit the 'royal dog.' This is not a casual coincidence, but a similarity of principles, which exists in spite of the difference of the consequences drawn from them. Aristippos, too, had no necessities; for he had always what he needed, and felt just as secure and happy when wandering in rags as when living in regal splendour.

But the example of the philosophers, who were fond of foreign courts, and found it absurd to serve consistently the narrow interests of a single state, was soon followed by the political envoys of Athens and other republics, and no Demosthenes could avail to save the freedom of Greece.

As to religious beliefs, it deserves notice that simultaneously with the weakening of beliefs, which spread from the theatre through the influence of Euripides among the people, there appeared a number of new mysteries.

History has but too frequently shown that if the educated men begin to laugh at the gods, or to resolve their existence into philosophical abstractions, immediately the half-educated masses, becoming unsteady and unquiet, seize upon every folly in order to exalt it into a religion.

Asiatic cults, with fantastic, even immoral practices, found most favour. Kybele and Kotytto, Adonis-worship and Orphic prophecies, based upon impudently fabricated sacred books, became popular in Athens as well as in the rest of Greece. And so was prepared that great commingling of religions which connected the East and West after the campaign of Alexander, and which was so important in preparing the way for the later propagation of Christianity.

Upon art and science also the Sensationalistic doctrines exercised a great transforming influence. The materials of the empirical sciences were popularised by the Sophists. They were for the most part men of great learning, who were fully masters of their stores of solid knowledge, and had them always ready for practical use; but they were in the natural sciences not inquirers, but only popularisers. On the other hand, we owe to their efforts the foundation of grammar and the development of an admirable prose, such as was demanded by the progress of the times, instead of the narrow forms of poetry, and above all the great development of rhetoric. Poetry under their influence sank gradually from its ideal height, and in tone and contents approached the character of the modern. Plot, effort, wealth of wit and emotion, became more and more important.

No history shows more plainly than that of Hellas that, by a natural law of human development, there is no unbroken persistence of the good and the beautiful. It is the transitional points in the ordered movements from one principle to another that conceal within them the greatest sublimity and beauty. And therefore we have no right to complain of a worm-eaten blossom: the very law of blossoming it is that leads to decay; and in this respect Aristippos was at the highest point of his time when he taught that it is the present moment only that can alone bring happiness.

CHAPTER III. THE REACTION AGAINST MATERIALISM AND SENSATIONALISM: SOKRATES, PLATO, ARISTOTLE. -when we regard from the standpoint of a reaction against Materialism and Sensationalism those products of Hellenic speculation which are usually considered the highest and most perfect, we are in danger of undervaluing these products, and of criticising them with the bitterness ordinarily directed against Materialism. The temptation is indeed strong, for we have here, as soon as we disregard the other aspects of the great crisis, a reaction in the worst sense of the term. It is a reaction in which the lower standpoint is elevated above the higher, after the former had been surmounted consciously and by a genuine intellectual effort — a suppression of the beginnings of a better view by ideas in which the old errors of unphilosophical thought return in a new shape, with new prestige and power, but not without their old pernicious character. Materialism explained natural phenomena by immutable necessary laws: the reaction introduced a reason fashioned after human models haggling with necessity, and so demolished the basis of all natural science by the convenient instrument of arbitrary caprice.

Materialism conceived adaptations to be the highest products of nature, but without, therefore, sacrificing the unity of its principle: the reaction struggled fanatically to retain a teleology which even in its most brilliant forms conceals flat anthropomorphism, and whose radical extermination is the indispensable condition of all scientific progress. This doctrine is set forth repeat-cause: and no suggestion whatever is edly and at length in the *Timaeux* of made as to their coincidence. Reason

Plato; comp., *e.g.*, the passages p. 48 A, is higher than necessity, but does not 56 c. and 68 E. Everywhere here two rule unconditionally, but only to a kinds of cause are expressly spoken certain extent, and even so far only of—the Divine and rational, that is, by persuasion, the teleological; and the Natural

Materialism gave the preference to mathematical and physical investigations — that is, those departments in which the human mind is first able to secure results of permanent value: the reaction, to begin with, wholly threw over physical inquiries in favour of ethic, and when, under Aristotle, it again took up the neglected study, it thoroughly corrupted it by the reckless introduction of ethical ideas."

While we have in these points undoubted retrogression, the progress—at least that in which utterance was given to the determined opposition of the great philosophical school of Athens against Materialism and Sensationalism— is of a very doubtful nature. We have Sokrates to thank for the phantom of definitions which presuppose an alto s' The anthropomorphic character of this teleology, as well as the antimaterialistic zeal with which it was inculcated and defended, is seen most clearly from the passage of the *Phaedo* mentioned further on in the text (pp. 97 c- 99 D Steph.), in which Sokrates complains so bitterly of Anaxagoras, who had made no use whatever in his cosmology of the so promising 'reason,' but had explained everything by purely material causes.

Of ethical origin is teleology in particular. It is indeed true that even the Platonic teleology is less crudely anthropomorphic than the Sokratic, and in the teleology of Aristotle, again, we find a decided advance; but the ethical character, and the inconsistency with genuine physical inquiry, are common to all the three stages. In Sokrates everything just as it is has been created for human purposes. Plato recognises that things have an end of their own, and so their adaptation is more internal; while in Aristotle the end completely coincides with the notional essence of the thing. But even so we have imported a power of realising themselves into all natural things, which is absolutely inconceivable as a natural phenomenon, and has its only original in the practical consciousness of the forming and fashioning human being. There are, however, many other ethical ideas which Aristotle has carried into the study of nature, with the utmost injury to the progress of inquiry: thus, above all, the order of merit of all things in nature, and, in fact, the abstract relations of 'above' and 'below,' 'right' and 'left,' besides 'natural' and 'violent' motion, and pother imaginary agreement of name and thing, and Plato for the delusive method which rests one hypothesis upon another still more general, until at last the highest certainty is found in what is most abstract. Aristotle we have to thank for the juggle between the potential and the actual, and the fancy of a complete and all-comprehensive system of knowledge. That all these acquisitions of the Athenian school are, even to our own time, continually operative, especially in Germany, admits of no doubt; and therefore over the historical importance of this school we need waste no further word, but may rather ask, Was this historical importance a fortunate or an unfortunate thing?

So long as we regard these points in themselves and in their purely theoretical opposition to Materialism, our judgment must be necessarily an unfavourable one, and we may, indeed, go a long way further than this. It is usually said that with Protagoras the earlier Greek philosophy reached its dissolution, and that an entirely new foundation was required, which was afforded by Sokrates and his return to self-knowledge. We shall soon see how far the history of thought justifies this view. Such a view, moreover, can be supported only by the consideration of the. whole extent of Greek intellectual life. Philosophy, and especially theoretical philosophy in the strict sense, can scarcely be abolished through the attainment of truth, only to begin again from the beginning with the old errors. This might, indeed, appear to be possible if we consider, for example, the transition from Kant to Fichte; but all such phenomena must be explained from the whole history of thought, since philosophy never holds an isolated position in the intellectual life of any given people. Quite theoretically considered, the relativity of the Sophists was a thoroughly sound advance in the theory of knowledge, and not at all the end of philosophy, but much rather its true beginning. We see this most clearly in ethic; for it was just the Sophists, who apparently undermined every possible basis of morality, who made it their favourite occupation to teach virtue and statesmanship. They substituted in the place of what is good in itself that which is useful to the *state.* How very close this comes to Kant's ethical axiom: So act that the maxims of your conduct might be the principles of universal legislation.

It is, in fact, the step from the particular to the universal which should here in due course have followed, and, abstractly speaking, *might* have followed, without giving up the acquisitions of relativity and individualism made by the Sophists. In ethic this step has in effect been taken as soon as virtue, after the falling away of all externally-given objective rules, is not simply laid aside, but proceeds to identify itself with the principle of the conservation and progress of a community. This was the course the Sophists took, without, however, being conscious of its fundamental significance; but might not this consciousness in time have developed itself out of their doctrine? In that case, although, of course, the highest point would not have been at once attained, yet henceforward the ground would have been thoroughly firm and secure beneath their feet.

Sokrates resolved virtue into knowledge: is this principle, when quite theoretically tested, really higher than the standpoint of the Sophists? What, indeed, the objective notion of the good is, we can as little discover from the whole body of the Platonic dialogues as the nature of the philosopher's stone from the alchemistic writings. If we make the knowledge of virtue a consciousness of the right principles of conduct, then it is easily reconcilable with the foundation upon the common weal in the state. If we take the Sokratic illustration of the intemperate man, who only sins because he is not fully conscious of the painful consequences of his present desire, no Sophist would deny that the man who is so constituted that this consciousness is never lacking is the better constituted, but *for him* in consequence, quite subjectively and individually considered, the good is the better. He chooses the hotter not through a knowledge of the notion of the good, but through a psychological condition, differing at the moment of choice from that of the intemperate man. It is true, indeed, that from the consideration of such instances the necessity for the individual also of a general notion of the good embracing the different moments of time may be seen. Such a notion was possessed even by Demokritos. A pupil of Demokritos and Protagoras, who had continued, if I may use the expression, a tangential movement from their philosophy, instead of sweeping round again with Sokrates, might easily have reached the position that man is the measure of things: the individual man in his momentary condition of the individual phenomenon, the average man of a sum of phenomena.

Protagoras and Prodikos busied themselves also with the rudiments of grammatical and etymological studies, and we do not know how much is really due to them of what we are now accustomed to assign to Plato and Aristotle. It is sufficient, however, for our purpose, to know that the Sophists had already turned their attention to words and the meaning of words. Now the word, as a rule, stands as a sign for a group of sensations. Might they not in this way have very soon reached a theory of universals in the sense of the medieval Nominalism? In such a theory, of course, the universal would not have been more real and certain than the particular, but, on the contrary, would have been further removed from the object, and more uncertain—in fact, in direct opposition to Plato, the more uncertain as it became more universal.

If, finally, the Sophists, among human actions, which, if regarded from a strictly individual standpoint, are all equally good, discriminate between the praiseworthy and the blameworthy, and that according to a rule which is gathered from the universal life in a state, might they not also have reached the idea of discriminating amongst perceptions which in themselves are all equally true, the normal and the abnormal from the historical standpoint of universal thought? The position would then have remained quite unassailed, that 'true,' in the strictest sense, that is 'certain,' is merely the individual feeling of the particular person; but, besides, a fixed standard of values might have been attained for the different perceptions in accordance with their current acceptation in human intercourse.

If one would apply such a scale of current value to the just developed universals in the Nominalistic sense, the idea of probability would have almost irresistibly presented itself. So near, apparently, in this case, did the Sophistic standpoint lie to the ripest fruit of modern speculation. The path of progress was to all appearance open. Why must the great reaction intervene which was to lead the world for thousands of years in the mazes of Hatonic Idealism?

The answer to this question has been already indicated. The fact is, that we have to deal not with a philosophy that develops itself continuously, whether by antagonisms or in a direct line, but only with philosophising men, who, like their doctrines, are children of their time. The misleading appearance of an advance through antagonisms, as Hegel supposes, rests upon this very fact, that the thoughts which dominate an era, or which appear as philosophical ideas, form only one portion of the intellectual life of a nation, and that very different influences, often the more powerful because so little apparent, are at the same time in activity, until they suddenly become in turn the dominant ones, while the others retire into the background.

Ideas that hasten onwards too rapidly for their age live themselves out, and must invigorate themselves once more Dy a struggle with reaction before they painfully, and yet more surely, again struggle to the front. But how is it that this is brought about? The more rapidly the bearers of new ideas and new theories snatch at the control of public opinion, the more violent will be the opposition of traditional ideas in the minds of their contemporaries. After being long blinded and stunned, as it were, prejudice gathers itself together, either by external persecution and suppression, or by new intellectual creations to battle with and overcome the inconvenient opinions. If such new intellectual creations are in themselves poor and empty, and endured only from hatred of progress, they can, as in the case of Jesuitism against the Reformation, only prosecute their purpose in alliance with cunning and force and a policy of universal suppression. But if they have, in addition to their reactionary importance, a germ of life within themselves, a content which in other respects leads to progress, they may often produce more brilliant and satisfactory results than the activity of a faction which has become arrogant from the possession of new truths, and which, as happens only too frequently after a conspicuous success, becomes enfeebled and inadequate to the proper following up of what has been attained.

Of this latter kind was the situation in Athens when Sokrates faced the Sophists. We have shown above how, abstractly considered, the standpoint of the Sophists might have been further developed; but if we had to point out the forces which, but for the intervention of the Sokratic reaction, might have effected this development, we should have some difficulty. The great Sophists were content, of course, with their practical successes. The very boundlessness of their relativity, their vague acceptance of the middle-class morality without the establishment of any principle, the pliant individualism which everywhere assumes to itself the right to throw down or let stand as suits the purpose of the moment—these were, it is obvious, admirable foundations for the education of 'practical statesmen' of the well-known stamp, which, from the dim beginning of time until our own days, has everywhere secured the greatest external success. No wonder that the Sophists more and more went over from Philosophy to Politic, from Dialectic to Rhetoric! And we find, indeed, even in Gorgias, a clear consciousness that philosophy had been degraded to the level of a mere preparation for practical life.

Under such circumstances, it is no cause for surprise that the younger generation of Sophists betrayed not the least inclination to carry on the development of philosophy on the basis of the view reached by Protagoras, with the omission of the transcendental and mythical universal introduced by Plato, and so to press on to the standpoint of modern Nominalism and Empiricism. On the contrary, the later Sophists distinguished themselves merely by a confident insistance upon the principle of subjectivity or individual will, and by outbidding their masters in framing a convenient theory for the holders of power in the Greek states. There was, therefore, retrogression as regards the strictly philosophical germ in this philosophy—a sign that the more earnest and deeper natures no longer felt themselves drawn in this direction.

All this is, of course, not in the same degree applicable to the severe and earnest Materialism of Demokritos; yet we have seen that Demokritos founded no school. This was due, indeed, partly to his own tendency and inclination, but partly also to the character of the time. For once Materialism, with its belief in eternally existing atoms, was outbid by Sensationalism, which denied the existence of any thing-in-itself behind phenomena. It would have needed a great advance, however—a much greater than the just-mentioned continuations of the Sensationalist philosophy—to reintroduce the atom as a necessary mode of presentation of an unknown relation, and so to maintain the basis of physical science. Consequently, at this period, the interest in objective investigations generally disappeared. In this respect, Aristotle may almost be regarded as the true successor of Demokritos; of course, a successor who uses the results and the principles by which they have been attained for completely opposite purposes. In the summertide of the new Athenian philosophy, however, ethical and logical questions came so much to the front that they caused everything else to be forgotten.

Whence came this one-sided prominence of ethical and logical problems? The answer to this question must at once show us what was the inmost principle of life through which the new tendency arose, and whose force gives it a higher and more independent value than that of a mere reaction against Materialism and Sensationalism. Here, however, it is impossible to separate the men from the doctrines, the purely philosophical elements from the whole intellectual movement, if we wish to understand why certain philosophical innovations could attain such an important significance. It was Sokrates who called the new tendency into life. Plato gave it its idealistic stamp, and Aristotle, by connecting it with empirical elements, created out of it that ultimate system which thenceforth dominated the thought of so many centuries. Opposition to Materialism culminates in Plato; the Aristotelian system made the most obstinate stand against Materialistic theories; but the attack was begun by one of the most remarkable men of whom history tells, a character of rare greatness and resolution—the Athenian Sokrates.

All the portraitures of Sokrates show him to us as a man of great physical and intellectual force, a stout, stubborn nature, of stern self-command and few necessities, brave in fight, enduring not only of fatigues, but also, if need be, of the drinking-bout, moderately as he otherwise lived. His self-control was not the tranquillity of a nature which has nothing to control, but the preponderance of a great mind over strong sensual traits and a naturally passionate temperament.'! His thoughts and endeavours were concentrated upon a few important points, and the whole latent energy of his nature entered into the service of these thoughts and endeavours.

The earnestness that worked within him, the fire that glowed in him, lent to his address a marvellous influence. In his presence alone of all men could Alkibiades feel ashamed; the power of his unadorned address drew tears from impressionable souls. His was an apostle nature, burning with the desire to communicate to his fellow-citizens, and especially the young, the fire that lived within him. His work he him self felt was holy, and behind the playful irony that marked his dialectic lurked the eager energy of a spirit that knew and prized nothing but the ideas by which it was possessed.

We do not refer to the insuffi-ditionally rejected), but we hold to ciently authenticated stories of Zopy-his character as it is presented to us ros and the like, according to which in Xenophon and Plato, and espeSokrates, at all events in his youth, cially to the well-known description was choleric and licentious (com p. in the Symposion. We do not thereZeller, ii. 2 Aufl. 54, where, indeed, the fore assert that Sokrates at any peateries of Aristoxenos are too uncoilriod of his life did not control hig which was converted into the enthu- This is most clearly shown, ns siasm of the apostle of morality, must far as Sokrates is concerned, in his have assigned to it its due impor-discussion with Aristodemos (Xen. tnnce. Memor., i. 4), detailed at length in

Athens was a pious city, and Sokrates was a genuine Athenian. Enlightened as he was, his theory of the world still remained a distinctly religious theory. The teleological conception of nature, to which he adhered with zeal, not to say fanaticism, was to him only a proof of the existence and activity of the gods, as in truth the need of regarding the gods as creating and working in human fashion may be called the mainspring of all teleology.

That a man like this should be the very man to be arraigned for Atheism, need not, however, cause us overmuch surprise. At all times it has been the faithful reformers, and not the worldly freethinkers, who have been crucified and burnt; and the work of Sokrates, even in the sphere of religion, was that of a reformer. The whole tendency of the time set just then to the purification of religious ideas; not among the philosophers only, but even among the most influential Greek priestpassionate disposition, but merely in the Platonic Symposion, especially that this fierce natural foundation, 215 n, E.

Comp. the eulogy of Alkibiades Lewes, Hist. Phil., i. 168-173. hoods, there appears to have been a strong inclination, while retaining myth for the credulous masses, to frame a more spiritual idea of the gods, to arrange and unify the variety of local cults according to the inner relations of the theological idea, and to secure for the great national deities, such as the Olympian Zeus, and especially the Delphian Apollo, as wide a recognition as possible. To these endeavours Sokrates's manner of dealing with religion was to a certain point agreeable enough; and there is still some question whether we ought not to regard the remarkable answer of the oracle of Delphi, which declared Sokrates to be the wisest of the Hellenes, as a covert approval of his believing rationalism. Yet this very man could be more easily denounced to the people as a foe of religion, the more often he was accustomed openly, and with an avowed object of influencing his fellow-citizens, to discuss the most dangerous questions. This religious earnestness of the great man determined, then, his whole conduct in life and death, in a degree which lends to the man a still higher importance than to the doctrine, and which was quite calculated to make his pupils into disciples zealous to spread wider the flame of this lofty inspiration. The way in which Sokrates, following his sense of duty, opposed, as Prytanis, the passionate excitement of the populace, the way in which he refused to obey the Thirty Tyrants, and after his condemnation declined to flee, but, obedient to the law, with peaceful soul faced death, is a convincing proof that with him the doctrine and the life were completely fused. Mention has already been made late for a regeneration of Paganism, of the 'Theokrasy' (the mingling and it burst into full activity, we may fusion into one of different gods and learn, in particular, from the half worships) of the Delphic priesthood philosophical, half mystical cult of in Note *a* above. The place of 'King Helios,' which the Emperor Apollo in the Sokratic spiritual Julian would have opposed to Chrismovement has been recently pointed tianity. Comp. Baur, Gesch. d. out very curiously and markedly by Christl. Kirche, ii. (2 Ausg.) S. Nietzsche, Die Gcburt der Tragodie 23 ff.; Teuffel, Studien und Charakaus dem Geiste der Musik: Leipzig, teristiken: Leipzig, 1871, S. 190. 1872. How this tendency, in connec- Sokrates was Kpistates of the tion with the Platonic theories, for Prytanes, and had in that capacity centuries continued an exuberant to put the question to the vote, on growth, until, at last, although too the day when the excited populace wished to condemn the generals who put it to tho vote. The Thirty

It has been recently supposed that we must explain the philosophical significance of Sokrates by showing that he was anything but a mere teacher of morality, but that he has, on the contrary, left a very distinct mark upon the history of philosophy by certain definite innovations. To this there is no objection; only we wish to show how all these new views, with their bright and dark sides, have their roots directly in the theological and ethical principle by which Sokrates was guided in his whole conduct.

If we next ask how it was that Sokrates came to renounce speculation as to the essence of things, and instead to make the moral nature of man the supreme object of his philosophy, we have from himself and his pupils the explanation that he had in his younger days busied himself with physical science, but that everything in this province appeared to him so uncertain that he had abandoned this kind of inquiry as unprofitable. Much more important was it for him, according to the Delphic oracle, to know himself: the object, however, of this effort after self-knowledge is to become as good as possible.

We need not now concern ourselves with the question whether Sokrates had really at one time zealously pursued physical investigation, as would seem to follow from the satirical picture drawn by Aristophanes. In the period of his life which we know from Plato and Xenophon it was no longer so; on the contrary, we know from Plato that Sokrates had read many of the writings of the earlier philosophers without finding any satisfaction in them. He read, for instance, Anaxagoras, and when he found that Anaxagoras explained the creation by referring it to reason, he was uncommonly delighted, for he supposed that Anaxagoras would find in reason some explanation of all the arrangements of the universe, and show, for example, if the earth is flat, why it is best thus; or, if it is in the centre of the universe, why this must be so, and so on. Instead of this, he was rudely disenchanted when Anaxagoras spoke of physical causes only. That is as if some one should propose to explain *why* Sokrates is sitting in this particular place, and then when he began should explain the 'sitting' according to the principles of anatomy and physiology, instead of mentioning that the Athenians had thought good to condemn him, and how he had thought good in disdain of flight to sit here and await his fate. 6 had neglected to pick up the derid Tyrants ordered him and four others after the battle of Arginusae. The to bring Leon back to Athens from proposal was not only unjust in Salamis; the other four obeyed, but itself, but it had a defect of form, Sokrates quietly went back home, and therefore Sokrates, at the risk although he knew that it was at the of his own life, steadily refused to peril of his life.

We see from this illustration how Sokrates came to the study of such treatises with a ready-made view. His entire conviction is that the reason which has created the world-structure proceeds after the manner of human reason; that we can follow its thoughts everywhere, although we must at the same time admit its infinite superiority. The world is explained from man, not man from the universal laws of nature. In the order of natural events, then, there is presupposed throughout that antithesis of thoughts and acts, of plan and material execution, which we find in our own consciousness. Everywhere we have an anthropomorphic activity. A plan, a purpose must first be provided, and then the matter and the force to set it going. We see here how much of a Sokratic Aristotle still was at bottom with his antithesis of form and matter, and the government of efficient causes by the final purpose. Without having dealt himself with physical science, Sokrates had yet already marked out for it the path in which it was afterwards to travel with such steady persistence. But the peculiar principle of this theory of the universe is the theological. The architect of the worlds must be a Person who can be conceived and imagined by man, though he may not be understood in all his actions. Even the apparently impersonal expression that 'reason' has done all this receives a religious stamp through the unconditional anthropomorphism with which the work of this 'reason' is regarded. And therefore we find, even in the Platonic Sokrates—and this trait must be genuine—the expressions 'Reason' and 'God' often employed as quite convertible terms.

Lewes, Hist. of Phil., i. 81 foil., thinks it to be genuinely Sokratic, gives this passage of the *Phaedo* and shows how Anaxagoras was mis(comp. Note 39) at length. He rightly understood by Sokrates.

That Sokrates in his conception of these things rests upon essentially monotheistic views need not surprise us, for it lay entirely in the time. It is true this monotheism was nowhere dogmatic; on the contrary, the plurality of the gods is expressly maintained, but the preponderance of the God who is regarded as creator and preserver of the world makes the others beings of a lower rank, who may, for many speculative purposes, be left entirely out of sight.

So that we may perhaps assume that the uncertainty of physical speculations, of which Sokrates complains, was nothing but the too obvious impossibility of constructing a complete and rational explanation of the whole structure of the universe, such as he had vainly sought from Anaxagoras. For efficient causes are regarded by Sokrates, wherever he deals with them, as something entirely indifferent and unimportant; which is quite intelligible if they are conceived not as universal laws of nature, but merely as the implements of a reason which personally thinks or creates. The more exalted or majestic this is conceived to be, so much the more indifferent and insignificant will the implement be considered; and so Sokrates can scarcely speak with sufficient contempt of 'the search after external causes.' VOL. L B

One sees from this how at bottom the doctrine of the identity of thought and existence has a theological root, since it supposes that the reason of a world-soul, or a God, and a reason, moreover, differing from the human reason only in degree, has so contrived and disposed everything that we can think it again, and, if we use our reason quite rightly, *must* think it again.

The religious tendency inaugurated by Sokrates may be compared with the Eationalism of modern times. Sokrates is perfectly ready to retain the ordinary forms of religious cultus, only he imparts to them everywhere a deeper meaning; thus, for example, when he demands that we shall not pray for particular blessings, but much rather require 'good' from the gods, since they know best what is good for us. This doctrine seems as harmless as it is reasonable, until we reflect how deeply in Hellenic faith prayer for particular blessings was bound up with the very existence of particular deities. The gods of the popular belief were thus made by Sokrates only the representatives of a purer creed. Unity of worship between the people and the educated was preserved, but by the aid of an interpretation of traditional creeds which we may well call rationalistic. That Sokrates praises the oracles is quite in harmony with this tendency, for why should not the deity, who has taken thought in the smallest details for the good of man, also hold intercourse with him and afford him counsel? And even in our modern civilisation, and in England also, although more especially in Germany, a very powerful tendency has arisen, which thought it its duty to spread purer forms of faith, exactly out of zeal for the restoration of religion and its influence, and the main impulse of which, with all its rationalism, was a *positive* one. Zeal against Materialism, and the anxious assertion of the ideal benefits of faith in God, freedom, and immortality, was nowhere greater than amongst men of this tendency. So Sokrates also, who is under the double sway of destructive culture and love for the ideal content of faith, will, above all things, preserve the latter. The conservative element,-which pervades his whole being, by no means prevents him from putting his hands to very radical changes, even in the sphere of politics, in order that the most essential and noble element of political existence, the living sense of community, may be permanently secured against the torrent of the predominant individualism.

Lewes, who gives us what is in many respects an admirable picture of Sokrates, would like to prore from his doctrine that virtue is knowledge, that philosophy, and not morality, was the special occupation of his life. This distinction leads to misconceptions. A mere 'moralist' Sokrates certainly was not, if by that we mean a man who, without regard to the deeper establishing of his doctrines, only attempts to make himself and others more moral. But yet his philosophy in its inmost essence was moral philosophy, and moral philosophy based upon a religious foundation. In this is the mainspring of all his activities, and the presupposition of the intelligibility and teachableness of morality is from the beginning implied in his peculiar religious standpoint. That he went further, and not only asserted the intelligibility of morality, but identified practical virtue with the theoretical comprehension of morality, is his personal conception of the relationship; and here also we may venture to trace religious influences.

The Delphic god, who was especially a god of moral elevation, called upon man, by the inscription on his temple, to 'Know himself.' This utterance became to Sokrates in a twofold respect the guide of his philosophical career: first, in the establishment of moral science instead of the apparently fruitless natural science; but, secondly, in the principle of striving after moral elevation by means of knowledge.

The relativity of the Sophists must to a man of this intellectual tendency have been thorougldy hateful. The religious sense calls for its sure points, especially in all that concerns God, the soul, and the rule of life. For Sokrates, therefore, it is an axiomatic principle that there must be an ethical knowledge. Eelativity, which scouts it, rests upon the right of individual impressions. A3 against this, then, the universal and the universally true must be established.

We have seen above how the step to the universal might have been taken from the standpoint of relativity without any change of principle. But in that case the universal would have been conceived in a strict Nominalistic sense. Knowledge might have extended itself to infinity on this field without ever getting beyond empiricism and probability. It is interesting to observe how the Platonic Sokrates, in arguing against the relativity of Protagoras, often begins exactly as a genuine disciple of the Sophists must have begun, if he would venture on the step to the consideration of the universal. But the controversy never stops there; it always aims beyond the immediate goal, in order to embrace the universal in that transcendental sense in which Plato had introduced it into science. And the ground had, without doubt, been already prepared for this by Sokrates. If the Platonic Sokrates proves, for example (in the Kratylus), that names are not arbitrarily assigned to things, but that they correspond to the innermost nature of the object, there is already contained in this nature of things, in a germinal shape, that essence which Plato later exalted so high above the individual things, that they were reduced and degraded to mere appearances.

Aristotle attributes to Sokrates two essential innovations in method—the use of *definitions* and *induction.* Both, as methods of dialectic, turn upon universals; and the art of discussion, in which Sokrates was a master, consisted chiefly in the sure and skilful reference of the single case to a universal, and employment of the universal to conclude back to the particular. And it is just here, of course, that we find in the Platonic dialogues quantities of logical tricks, ambuscades, and sophisms of all kinds on the side of the always victorious Sokrates. He plays often with his opponents, as a cat with a mouse, entraps them into far-reaching admissions, only to show them himself immediately that the reasoning contained an error; but scarcely is this repaired, than the opponent is again caught in a snare, which is, in fact, no more real than the first.

There is no doubt that here the general treatment is genuinely Sokratic, although the particular arguments are for the most part Plato's. It will also be admitted that this sophistical manner of opposing the Sophists is much more profitable in speech, in the direct conflict of argument, where one man tries his intellectual strength against another, than in the calm literary discussion which, at least according to our ideas, must be measured by a far severer standard of soundness in its proofs.

Sokrates scarcely ever consciously confused his opponents, and merely overmatched them instead of thoroughly refuting them. It is his firm belief in his own principles that blinds him to the errors of his own reasoning, while he instantly discovers those of his opponents, and employs them with all the force of a practised athlete. Although, however, we cannot charge Sokrates with any dishonesty in debate, yet the confusion of the defeat of an opponent with the refutation of his opinion belongs to him also, as it had already belonged to his predecessors and to Greek dialectic from its first beginnings. The picture of the intellectual wrestling-match, or, as we find in Aristotle in particular, of the contest of two parties before a tribunal, is everywhere present, the thought appears linked with the person, and the vivid picturesqueness of debate replaces a calm and complete analysis.

The Sokratic 'irony,' moreover, with which he professes ignorance and asks instruction from his opponent, is often only the thin veil of a dogmatism which is ever ready, in the least embarrassment, innocently, and to all appearance only tentatively, to foist in a ready-made opinion, and, unobserved, to gain it acceptance. Yet this is a dogmatism which consisted in the constant repetition of few and simple dogmas: virtue is knowledge; the just man alone is really happy; self-knowledge is the first duty of man; to improve himself is of more consequence than any care for external things, and so on.

With regard to the special meaning of self-knowledge ana the doctrine of virtue, Sokrates remains always a seeker only. He seeks with all the energy of a believing nature, but he does not venture to assert definite contusions. His method of definitions leads much more frequently to the mere postulation of a definition, to the statement of the idea of the thing that is to be known, than to the actual establishing of a definition. When we reach the point where something more should be given us, we find either a mere attempt or the everlasting Sokratic ignorance. He is apparently content with the negation of negation, and reminds us of the oracle which declared him to be the wisest of the Greeks because he knew his own ignorance, whilst other men do not so much as know that they know nothing. This result, however, purely negative as it appears, is far as the heavens removed from scepticism; for whilst the sceptic denies the very possibility of certain knowledge, to Sokrates the idea that such a knowledge there must be is the very guiding star of all his activity. He contents himself, however, with making room for genuine knowledge by destroying mere sham knowledge, and by the constitution and employment of a method which shall be capable of discerning true from seeming knowledge. Criticism therefore, as opposed to scepticism, is the function of this method; and in the vindication of criticism as the instrument of science we have at least one achievement of his activity that possesses a permanent value. And yet his chief significance in the history of philosophy does not lie here, but in his belief in knowledge and its object; the universal essence of things, the stationary pole in the flight of phenomena. Although this belief may have overshot the mark, yet thus was taken the indispensable step that the flagging energies of Kelativism and Materialism were incapable of taking—the treatment of the universal in its relation to the individual, of conceptions in contrast to mere perception. The tares of Platonic Idealism grew up together with the wheat; but the ground was yet again prepared: when a strong hand took the plough, the field of philosophy again bore fruit a hundredfold, just when it seemed destined to be unproductive.

Of all the disciples of Sokrates, Plato was the one most deeply affected by that religious glow which proceeded from him, and it was Plato also who carried out most purely, though also most one-sidedly, the thoughts of the master. And it is especially the errors which lie at the foundation of the Sokratic philosophy which, in the hands of Plato, attain a mighty development, to endure for thousands of years. These Platonic errors, however, because of their deep opposition to the philosophy which springs from experience, are for us of especial importance. They are also errors of universal significance, like those of Materialism; for although they may not be connected with the nature of our thinking faculties by such immediate points of connection as is Materialism, yet they rest only the more surely on the broad basis of our whole psychical organisation. Both theories are necessary stages of human thought, and although Materialism may, as compared with Platonism, upon special points always maintain its position; yet it may be that the whole picture of the world which this latter affords stands nearer to the unknown truth: in any case it has deeper relations to the life of the emotions, to art, to the moral functions of mankind. Noble, however, as these relations may be, and beneficently" as Platonism at various epochs may have acted through them on the whole development of humanity, the indispensable duty nevertheless remains of laying thoroughly bare the errors of Platonism without regard to their nobler aspects.

But first a word as to Plato's general tendency. We called him the purest of the Sokratics, and we found in Sokrates a Eationalist. This is far from agreeing with the widely current view which regards Plato as a mystic and a poetical enthusiast; but this view is thoroughly false. Lewes, who has opposed this notion with special energy, thus characterises him: "He wrote poetry in his youth; in mature age he wrote vehemently against it. In his dialogues he appears anything but 'dreamy;' anything but' an Idealist, ' as that phrase is popularly understood. He is a dialectician, a severe and abstract thinker, and a great Sophist. His metaphysics are of a nature so abstract and so subtle that they frighten away all but the most determined students. His views on morals and politics, so far from having any romantic tinge, are the *neplus ultra* of logical severity; hard, uncompromising, and above humanity. He had learned to look upon human passion as a disease, and human pleasure as a frivolity. The only thing worth living for was truth. Dialectics was the noblest exercise of humanity." Lewes, Hist. of Phil., i. 197. scriptions are just, and not irreconcil

Compare, on the other hand, the apable; for the plastic beauty, clear as proving words of Zeller, ii. (2te Aufl.), the god of light, of the form in Plato, p-355) to 'l poetical character of is indeed ' poetical,' in the wider sense the Platonic philosophy: "Asanar-of the word, but is not mystical or tistic nature was necessary to the pro-romantic. At the same time, how duction of such a philosophy, so in ever, the stubborn and pretentious turn this philosophy would necessarily dialectic, to which Lewes holds, is require to be embodied in artistic carried to an extent which is in fact shape. The phenomenon brought into not only extravagant, but is even dis such near contact with the idea as we turbing to the artistic form; but it find with Plato becomes a beautiful stands, moreover, with its dogmat phenomenon, the intuition of the idea ism and its special pretentions to a in the phenomenon an aesthetic intui-'knowledge' which is only gained by tion. Where science and life so inter-a systematic struggle, also in contra penetrate each other as with him, diction with the genuine poetical there science will only be communi-principle of true speculation, which cated in lively description; and since relies more upon intellectual vision what is to be communicated is an ideal, than upon mediate knowledge, this description will necessarily be a Plato's philosophy might indeed, if poetical description." No doubt Lewes this artistic element had been carried has undcr-estimnted the artistic ele-out, have become the best model for ment in Plato's dialogues. Both de-the speculation of all time; but the combination of this element with the tifio form. It is wrong, however, to

For all this, it cannot be denied that, historically, Platonism frequently appears in connection with enthusiasm, and that even the-widely-digressing Neoplatonic systems find some support in Plato's doctrine; nay, amongst the immediate followers of the great master there were those who may be described as mystics; and the Pythagorean elements which they combined with the teachings of Plato find in these very teachings support and authority. We have besides these, of course, the extremely sober ' middle academy,' which also connected itself with Plato, and the beginnings of whose theory of probability may in fact be traced in Plato.

The truth is, that in Plato the Sokratic Eationalism outruns itself, and in the effort to elevate the sphere of reason high above the sensations, went so far that a relapse into mythical forms became inevitable. Plato ascended into a sphere for which man has been granted neither language nor powers of conception. He saw himself thus compelled to fall back upon figurative expression; but his system is a speaking proof that figurative expression for what is entirely supersensual is a chimera, and that the attempt to climb by this ladder to impossible heights of abstraction revenges itself in the predominance exercised by the figure over the thought, and by rushing to consequences in which all logical consistency perishes beneath the glamour of associations of sensuous ideas. abstract dialectic, and logical severity, regard this as a weakness in the phi so sharply emphasised by Lewes, pro-losopher, who is here merely too much duces a heterogeneous whole, and of a poet still, and too little of a philo especially by its total confusion of sopher. It lies rather in the nature of science and poetry created great con-the problems on which Plato has here fusion in later philosophy. ventured that they cannot be treated Zeller, ii. 2 Aufl., p. 361 ff. in any but a figurative method. An fE. T. 160 foil., recognises, quite adequate scientific knowledge of the rightly, that the Platonic myths are not absolutely transcendental is impos the mere garments of thoughts which sible, and modern systems which the philosopher possessed in another calls up the phantom of an intellectual shape, but that they are employed knowledge of transcendental things.

In those cases where Plato wishes to are in truth no whit higher in this express something which he has no respect than the Platonic, means of conveying in rigorous scien

Plato, before attaching himself to Sokrates, had been introduced to the philosophy of Herakleitos, and had so learnt that there is no quiet persistent being, that everything is in constant flux. When, then, he thought he had discovered something permanent in the Sokratic definitions, and in the universal essence of things which is expressed in these definitions, he combined this doctrine with a Herakleitean element, in such fashion that he attributed true being, and the undisturbed permanence inseparable from it, to the universal alone; the individual things, on the other hand, *are* strictly not at all, but merely *become.* The phenomena flow away without reality: being is eternal.

We now know that the only ideas capable of definition are abstract, self-constituted ideas, such as those employed by the mathematician in order to approach infinitesimally near to the quantitative constitution of things, without, however, exhausting it by his formulas. Every attempt to define *things* breaks down: the conventional employment of a word may be arbitrarily fixed, but when this word is used to indicate a class of objects according to their common nature, it becomes evident, sooner or later, that the things have other relations and other distinguishing qualities than was originally supposed. The old definition becomes useless, and must be replaced by a new, which has in its turn no more pretensions to eternal validity than the first. No definition of a fixed star can prevent it from moving; no definition can draw a permanent boundary between meteors and other heavenly bodies. As often as research makes a great step forward, the definitions must give way, and individual things do not regulate themselves in accordance with our general notions, but these must, on the contrary, be determined by the particular objects which we perceive.

Plato carried further the elements of logic he had received from Sokrates. In him we find, for the first time, a clear idea of *genera* and *species,* of the co-ordination and subordination of concepts; and he is fond of using the new achievement that he may, by the aid of division, bring light and order into the objects of discussion. This was, indeed, a great and important step forward, and yet even this immediately enlisted itself in the service of as great an error. There arose that hierarchy of ideas in which that which is most void of content was placed highest. Abstraction was the Jacob's ladder by which the philosopher ascended to certainty. The further he was from facts, the nearer he thought himself to truth.

Whilst Plato, however, exhibited universal ideas as the permanent in the fleeting phenomenal world, he saw himself further compelled to the pregnant step of separating the universal from the particular, and attributing to it a separate existence. Beauty is not only in beautiful objects, goodness not only in good men, but the beautiful, the good, quite abstractly regarded, are self-existent realities. It would lead us too far to discuss fully here the Platonic ideal theory: it is enough for our purpose to examine its foundations, and to see how from these foundations sprang that intellectual tendency which raised itself so high, as it supposed, above the vulgar empiricism, and which must, nevertheless, at all points, yield again to empiricism wherever it is a question of the positive progress of science.

So much is clear, that we need the universal and the process of abstraction in order to attain to knowledge. Even the particular fact, in order to become an object of knowledge, must be exalted above the Individualism of Protagoras by the supposition and demonstration of a perception of something implying regular recurrence; that is, of the universal as against the individual—of the average as against fluctuations. But knowledge thus begins at once to rise above mere opinion before it has directed itself to any special class of similar objects. We require, however, in addition, even before we can accurately know whole classes, general terms in order to fix our knowledge, and to be able to communicate it; for the simple reason that no language could suffice to express all particulars, and because, with a language that did this, no understanding, no general knowledge would be possible, and the retention of such an infinity of meanings would be impossible. On this point Locke was the first to throw a clear light; but we must never forget that Locke, long as he lived after Plato, nevertheless stands in the midst of the great process by which the modern world freed itself from the Platonic and Aristotelian theory of things. Sokrates, Plato, and Aristotle, like their whole age, allowed themselves to be deceived by words. We have seen how Sokrates believed that every word must originally express the essence of the thing; the general name, therefore, would express the nature of the class of objects in question. Where there was a name, there a real existence was presupposed. Justice, Truth, Beauty, must mean 'something;' and there must accordingly be realities corresponding to these expressions.

Aristotle points out that Plato first distinguished the universal essence of things from the individuals, which Sokrates had not yet done. But Sokrates had, moreover, not held that peculiar doctrine of Aristotle as to the relation of the universal to the particular which we shall soon have to consider. Yet Sokrates had got as far as the theory that our knowledge has reference to the universal, and that is something quite different from the indispensableness of general notions for knowledge explained above. The virtuous man is, according to Sokrates, the man who knows what is pious or impious, what is noblo or disgraceful, what is just or unjust; but in saying this, he had always in his eye the definition which he was ceaselessly in search of. The universal nature of the just, of the noble, not what is in the particular case just and noble, is sought. From the universal we must obtain the particular, but not conversely; for induction serves him in reaching the universal, only to make it clear to the mind, *not* to found the universal upon the sum of particular instances. From this standpoint it was only consistent to allow the universal to exist by itself, because only thereby did it seem to attain to complete independence. Only later could the attempt be made to establish for the universal an immanent and yet fundamentally independent relation to the particular objects. It must not be left out of sight, however, that the Herakleitean foundation of Plato's education very materially contributed to bring about this separation between the universal and the particular.

But we must not fail to understand that from this paradoxical method of working of course only paradoxical results could follow. The name is made a thing, but a thing having no similarity with any other thing, and to which, in the nature of human thought, only negative predicates can be attached. But since there is an absolute necessity for some positive assertion, we find ourselves from the outset in the region of myth and symbol.

The very word elfios or *IBea,* from which our word idea has come, bears this stamp of the symbolical. There is a similar notion of the species as distinguished from the individual. We may very easily represent to ourselves in imagination a pattern of any species which is free from all the accidents of the individual, and will therefore stand for the type or pattern of all individuals, and be moreover an absolutely perfect individual. We cannot imagine a lion as such, a rose as such; but we may represent in imagination a definitely-outlined picture of a lion or a rose, wholly free from all those accidents of individual formation which may collectively be regarded as deviations from this norm, as imperfections. This is, however, not the Platonic idea of the lion or the rose, but an ideal that is a creation of the senses, intended to express the abstract idea as perfectly as possible. The idea itself is invisible, for everything that is visible belongs to the fleeting world of mere phenomena: it has no forms in space, for the supersensuous cannot be linked with space. Similarly nothing whatever positive can be expressed of the ideas without conceiving them in some sensuous fashion. They cannot be called pure, sovereign, perfect, eternal, without our connecting with them by these very words ideas of sense. So Plato, in his ideal theory, is obliged to have recourse to mythus. and so, at a single step we pass from the highest abstraction to the true life-element of all mysticism—the sensuous supersensuous. The mythus is, however, to have only a figurative or metaphorical force. By its means, what is in itself only an object of the pure reason is to be represented in the forms of the phenomenal world; but what kind of *figure* can that be of which the original cannot be supplied?

The idea itself is said to be perceived by the reason, though but imperfectly in this earthly life, and the reason stands related to this supersensuous existence as the senses are related to sensible objects. And this is the origin of that sharp separation of reason and sensation which has ever since dominated all philosophy, and has excited endless misunderstandings. The senses are said to have no share in knowledge; they can only feel or perceive, and reach only to phenomena. The reason, on the other hand, is capable of comprehending the supersensuaL It is completely separated from the rest of the human organisation, especially by Aristotle, who has developed this doctrine further. Certain special objects are supposed to be known by the pure reason—the 'Noumena' which, in opposition to 'Phenomena' or appearances, form the object of the highest kind of knowledge. But, in fact, not only are these noumena cobwebs of the brain, but even the 'pure reason,' which is to apprehend them, is equally fabulous. Man has no such reason, and no idea of such a reason, wldch can perceive the universal, the abstract, the supersensuous, the ideas without the mediation of sensation and perception. Even where our thought carries us beyond the limits of our sensible experience, where we are led to the conjecture that our space, with its three dimensions, our time, with its present springing out of nothing and vanishing into nothing, are only human forms of the conception of an infinitely more comprehensive reality,—even here we must avail ourselves of the ordinary understanding, whose categories, one and all, are indissolubly connected with sensation. We cannot imagine either the one and the many, or substance as opposed to its qualities, or even a predicate of any kind, without an infusion of the sensible.

We are here, therefore, everywhere in the presence of mythus, and of mythus whose inner core and significance consists of the utterly unknown, not to say an absolute nonentity. All these Platonic conceptions, therefore, have been, down to our own days, only hindrances and *ignesfatui* for thought and inquiry, for the mastery of phenomena by the understanding and by sure methodical science. But just as the human spirit will never be content with the world of understanding, which an exact empiricism might afford us, so the Platonic philosophy will ever remain the first and most elevated type of a poetical exaltation of the spirit above the unsatisfying patchwork of knowledge, and we are as much justified in this exaltation on the wings of imaginative speculation as in the exercise of any function of our mental and physical faculties. Nay, we shall attach to it a high importance when we see how the free play of spirit which is involved in the search after the One and the Eternal in the change of earthly things, reacts with a vitalising and freshening influence upon whole generations, and often indirectly affords a new impulse even to scientific research Only the world must, once for all, clearly comprehend that we have here not knowledge, but poesy, even though this poesy may perhaps symbolically represent to us a real and true aspect of the true nature of all things, of which the immediate apprehension is denied to our reason. Sokrates wished to make an end of the rampant individualism, and to pave the way to objective knowledge. The result was a method which completely confused subjective and objective, rendered impossible the direct advance of positive knowledge, and appeared to open to individual thought and speculation a sphere of the most unlimited license. But this license was, nevertheless, not really so unlimited. The religious and moral principle from which Plato and Sokrates started guided the great speculative movement to a determined goal, and made it capable of affording a deep content and a noble character of completeness to the moral efforts and struggle of thousands of years, while it became completely fused with foreign and anything but Hellenic conceptions and doctrines. And even to-day the ideal theory, which we are obliged to banish from the realm of science, may by its ethical and aesthetic content become a source of plentiful blessings. The 'form' *(Gestalt),* as Schiller has so beautifully and vigorously rendered the faded expression 'idea,' still lives and moves divinely amongst gods in the abodes of light, and still to-day, as in old Hellas, has the power of lifting us upon its wings above the anxieties of earth that we may flee into the realm of the ideal

As to Aristotle, we shall here speak very briefly, since we must discuss the influence of his system when we come to medieval times. Then we will enter more fully into the most important notions which the middle ages and modern times have, with various modifications, borrowed from his system. Here we are rather concerned with its general nature and its relation to Idealism and Materialism.

Aristotle and Plato being by far the most influential and important of the Greek philosophers whose works we possess, we are easily led to suppose a sharp antithesis between them, as though they represented two main philosophical tendencies — *a priori* speculation and rational empiricism. The truth is, however, that Aristotle devised a system in close dependence upon Plato, which, though not without internal inconsistencies, combines an apparent empiricism with all those errors which in the SokraticoPlatonic theories radically corrupt empirical inquiry.

It is still a very widely prevalent opinion that Aristotle was a great physical inquirer. But since we have known how much had been previously accomplished in this sphere, and how unhesitatingly Aristotle appropriated the observations of others, and all kinds of information, without mentioning his authority; moreover, how many of his statements bear an impression of being his own observations which cannot have been observed, because they are wholly false; criticism of this opinion has been excited, although it has scarcely as yet thoroughly gone to work. But what must in any case remain to Aristotle is the praise, bestowed on him by Hegel, of having subordinated the wealth and the detail of the actual universe to the Notion. However great or however small may have been his independent work in the special sciences, the most important element of his whole activity will still be the collection of the matter of all existing sciences around speculative points of view, and therefore an activity which in principle coincides with that of the modern systematisers, and above all of Hegel.

The proofs of this we will take from a book recently published, although not written with this object: Eucken, Die Methode der aristotelischen Forschung in ihrem Zuaammenhang mit den philosophischen Grundprincipien des Aristoteles: Berlin, 1872. In this very careful and learned little book is a striking support of the view, which we have long held, that the neo-Aristotelian school, which was founded by Trendelenburg, must in the end chiefly contribute to our definitive emancipation from Aristotle. In Eucken philosophy resolves itself into the Aristotelian philology; but then this philology is thorough and objective. We nowhere find the deficiencies of the Aristotelian method so clearly and comprehensively stated as here; and although the author, nevertheless, holds that there is a balance of advantages, yet no careful reader can help seeing how weak the proofs of this are. The small success of Aristotle in scientific discoveries is attributed by the writer almost exclusively to the want of instruments necessary to perfect the powers of observation, although it is historically established that modern progress in all the departments of natural inquiry began with almost the same means which were at the service of the ancients, and that it has for the most part VOL. I. created for itself the magnificent tools which are to-day at its disposal. Copernicus had no telescope, but he dared to shake off the authority of Aristotle. That was the decisive step, and it was the same in all other departments. This point has, of course, escaped Eucken, who (Meth. d. arist. Forschung, S. 153), on the contrary, makes it appear how little had been done before him. Yes, if the *extant* literature were all! Comp. on the other side the Note 1 1 above on the use made of Demokritos, and the manner in which Aristotle, as described by Eucken, S. 7 foil, made use of his predecessors without quoting them—unless they were to be introduced for the purpose of being refuted. Examples in Eucken, S. 154 ff.: that men only have palpitation of the heart; that male creatures have more teeth than females; that the skull in woman has, nnlike that of man, a circular suture; that there is an empty space in the back part of the human skull; and that men have eight ribs. Again, S. 164 foil., what are said to be experiments: that eggs float in strong brine; that it is possible to collect in a close vessel or wax drinkable water from the sea; that the yolk of several eggs shaken together collects into the middle.

F

Demokritos also mastered the whole extent of the science of his time, and that probably with greater independence and thoroughness than was the case with Aristotle; but we have no trace whatever of his having brought all these sciences under the yoke of his system. With Aristotle the carrying out of the speculative basis is the chief aim. The one and the permanent, which Plato sought outside things, Aristotle wants to find in the manifoldness of the things themselves. As he makes the external universe an enclosed sphere, with the earth resting in the centre, so the world of science is pervaded by the same method, the same manner of conception and representation, and everything gathers round the knowing subject, whose ideas, with a naive forgetfulness of all the limitations of knowledge, are viewed as the true and ultimate objects of apprehension.

Bacon advanced the assertion that the co-ordination of knowledge into a system was a hindrance to further progress. This view Aristotle could scarcely have opposed, for he held the task of science as a whole to be exhausted, and never for a moment doubted that he was in a position to supply a satisfactory answer to all really essential questions. As in the sphere of ethic and politic he confined himself to the types exhibited in the Hellenic world, and had little sense of the great changes which were going on beneath his eyes, so he troubled himself little with the crowd of new facts and observations which were made accessible to the man of science by the campaigns of Alexander. That he accompanied Alexander in order to satisfy his desire of knowledge, or that plants and animals were sent to him for examination from distant climates, is mere fable. Aristotle confined himself in his system to the knowledge of his own day, and was convinced that this was all that was of real importance, and sufficed to solve all the principal problems. It was this very limitation of his views, and the certainty with which he moved in the narrow circle of his universe, that recommended Aristotle so eminently to the philosophical teachers of the Middle Ages, while modern times, with their inclination to progress and revolution, had no task more important than to burst asunder the fetters of this system.

More conservative than Plato and Sokrates, Aristotle everywhere attaches himself to tradition, to popular opinion, to the conceptions contained in language; and his ethical demands keep as near as possible to the ordinary customs and laws of Hellenic communities. He has therefore always been the favourite philosopher of conservative schools and tendencies.

The unity of his theory of things Aristotle secures by the most reckless anthropomorphism. The corrupt teleology which argues from man and his aims is one of the most essential elements of his system. As in human production and activity, for example in the building of a house or ship, the idea of the whole is always the first thing present as the end of activity, and as this idea then, by the carrying out of the parts, realises itself in matter, nature must be supposed to proceed in the same way, because in his view this sequence of end and thing, of form and matter, is typical of all that exists. After man with his aims, the world of organisms is established. These serve him not only to show the real potentiality of the tree in the seed-corn, not only as types for the classification by species and genus, as model examples of the teleological principle, and so on, but especially, by the comparison of lower and higher organisms, to establish the view that everything in the universe is capable of being arranged in degrees of rank, and according to notions of value—a principle which Aristotle does not fail to go on to apply to the most abstract relations, such as above and below, right and left, and so on. And he obviously believes that all these relations of rank do not merely exist in the human method of comprehension, but are grounded upon the nature of things. So everywhere the universal is explained by means of the special, the easy by means of the difficult, the simple by the compound, the low by the higher. And this it is which in great measure has secured the popularity of the Aristotelian system; for man, to whom nothing is of course more familiar than the subjective circumstances of his thought and action, is always inclined to regard as clear and simple their causal relations to the world of objects, since he confounds the obvious succession in time of the internal and external with the mysterious motive power of efficient causes. Thus, for example, Sokrates could regard as a very simple matter the ' thinking and electing' by which human actions come about according to the notion of the end; the result of a determination seemed no less simple, and the precedent circumstances in muscles and nerves become merely indifferent accidents. Things in nature seem to betray a certain designedness, and therefore they also must arise by this so natural process of thought and election. A Creator constituted like man is therefore assumed; and as he is infinitely wise, the whole way of looking at things is rested upon a firm basis of optimism.

Cuvier observed that Aristotle cal writings of Aristotle exhibit no describes the Egyptian fauna not from trace of any addition to knowledge his personal observation, but from made by the campaigns of Alexander. the details furnished by Herodotus, (Eucken, *loc. cit.* p. 16 and p. 160; as although the description reads as if to his view of the completion of scien he had himself seen the animals, tific knowledge, p. 5 foil.) Humboldt remarks that the zoologi

Aristotle had, of course, made a great advance in the method in which he conceives the end as operative in things. (Comp. note 40.) When man came to reflect more closely on the way and manner in which the end was realised, that most naive anthropomorphism which made the Creator work with human hands was no longer to be entertained. A rationalistic view of things, which regarded the popular religious ideas as the figurative presentation of supernatural facts, could, of course, make no exception in the case of teleology; and as here also, as everywhere, Aristotle endeavoured, after his manner, to attain to complete clearness, he was necessarily led by teleology itself, and by the consideration of the organic world, to a pantheistic theory, which makes the divine thought everywhere permeate matter, and realise itself and become immanent in the growth and becoming of all things. By the side of this view, which was capable, with very slight modification, of being developed into a complete Naturalism, there is in Aristotle a transcendental idea of God, which theoretically rests upon the truly Aristotelian thought that all motion must ultimately proceed from a something itself unmoved.53

The traces of empiricism in Aristotle are to be found partly in isolated expressions, of which the most important are those which require us to respect facts, but partly also in his doctrine of substance *ovala),* which, of course, offends us by an irreconcilable contradiction. Aristotle, in this point differing essentially from Plato, calls, in the strict and proper sense, the individual existences and things substances. In them the form, the essential part, is united with matter; the whole is a concrete and thoroughly real existence. Nay, Aristotle sometimes speaks as though complete reality belonged properly to the concrete thing alone. This is the standpoint of the medieval Nominalists, who, however, have not, as a matter of fact, the opinion of Aristotle thoroughly on their side; for Aristotle spoils everything again by admitting a second kind of substance, especially in the notions of species, but also in universals generally. Not only is this apple-tree here before my window a reality, but the notion of kind also indicates a similar reality; only that the universal essence of the apple-tree does not dwell in the vague cloud-land of ideas, from which it radiates an influence into the things of the phenomenal world, but the universal essence of the apple-tree has its existence in the individual apple-trees.

The principle of the Aristotelian foundation; but the ontological suptheology is very-well and very sue-port of the transcendentality of God cinctlyexpressedinUeberweg,Grund-lies in the proposition that all morisa, i. 4 Auil. p. 175 foil., 1 E. T. tion, including the development from 162, 163: "The world has its prin-potentiality to reality, has a moving ciple in God, and this principle exists cause which is itself unmoved, not merely as a form immanent in "Every particular object which is the world, like the order in an army, the result of development implies an but also as an absolute self-existent actual moving cause; so the world, substance, like the general in an as a whole, demands an absolutely army." The conclusion of the theo-first mover to give form to the natulogy with the words of Homer, *oiiK* rally passive matter which constitutes *dyaBtit* iroXwcoipaWij, els *xoiparot larto,* it" *loc. cit. 162).* betrays the ethical tendency at its

There is here, in fact, so long as we confine ourselves to organisms, and compare only species and individual, a deceptive appearance which has already dazzled many moderns. Let us endeavour to indicate precisely the point where truth and error separate.

Let us begin by placing ourselves at the Nominalistic standpoint, which is perfectly clear. There are only individual apple-trees, individual lions, individual maybugs, and so on; and besides these names, by which we colligate the sum of existing objects, where similarity or likeness connects them together. The 'universal' is nothing but the name. It is not difficult, however, to give this way of looking at things an appearance of superficiality, by pointing out that we are here treating not of casual similarities, depending on the casual perception of the subject, but that objective nature offers certain obviously distinctive groups which, by their real similitude, compel us to this common conception of them. The most unlike individuals amongst lions or maybugs are yet much nearer to each other than the lion is to the tiger, or the maybugs to the stag-beetle. This observation is doubtless true. Yet a very brief examination of its force will show us that the real connecting link, which we will for brevity's sake admit without discussion, is in any case something quite different from the universal type of the genus which we in our fancy associate with the name apple-tree.

We might, then, from this point carry much further the metaphysical discussion of the relation of the individual to the universal, of the one to the many. Supposing that we knew a formula of the combination of matter, or of the state of things in a germ-cell, by which it could be determined whether the germ *will* develop itself into the form of an apple or of a pear tree; then it may be conjectured that every individual germ-cell, besides the conditions of this formula, has also its individual variations and peculiarities, and really is at bottom in all cases, at first, the result of the universal and particular, or rather the concrete fact, in which there is no distinction whatever of the universal and the particular. The formula lies purely in our mind.

We easily see that here again realistic objections might be made; but it is not necessary to follow this chain further in order to understand the error of the Aristotelian doctrine of the universal. This error lies much further back; for Aristotle keeps close by the word. He seeks nothing unknown behind the universal essence of the apple-tree. This is much rather fully known. The word directly indicates a reality, and this goes so far that Aristotle, in the transference of that which was found in the organism to other objects, in the case of a hatchet distinguishes the individuality of this particular hatchet from its hatchetness.' The 'hatchetness' and the material, the metal, taken together, compose the hatchet, and no bit of metal can become a hatchet until it is seized and possessed by the form corresponding to the universal. This tendency to infer the existence immediately from the name is the fundamental error of the Aristotelian theory of notions, and leads, in its logical consequences, little as Aristotle cares to trouble himself with these, to the same exaltation of the universal over the particular which we find in Plato. For if it is once conceded that the essence of the individual lies in the species, the most essential part of the species must again lie on a still higher plane, or, in other words, the ground of the species must lie in the genus, and so on.

As a matter of fact, then, this thoroughgoing influence of the Platonic modes of thought is clearly shown in the method of inquiry usually employed by Aristotle. For we speedily discover that his proceeding from facts, and his inductive mounting from facts to principles, has remained a mere theory, scarcely anywhere put in practice by Aristotle himself. At the most, what he does is to adduce a few isolated facts, and immediately spring from these to the most universal principles, to which he thenceforward dogmatically adheres in purely deductive treatment. So Aristotle demonstrates from universal principles that outside our enclosed world-sphere nothing can exist; and in the same manner he reaches his destructive doctrine of the 'natural' motion of bodies in opposition to the ' enforced' motion, to the assertion that the left side of the body is colder than the right, to the doctrine of the transformation of one kind of matter into another, of the impossibility of motion in empty space, to the absolute distinction of cold and warm, light and heavy, and so on. So again he proves *a priori* how many species of animals there can be, demonstrates from universal principles why animals must be endowed with this member or that, and numerous other propositions, which are then employed in their turn, with the most logical consistency, and which in their totality render successful inquiry completely impossible. The science to which the Platonic and Aristotelian philosophy best adapts itself is naturally mathematics, in which the deductive principle has attained such brilliant results. Aristotle, therefore, views mathematics as the type of all sciences, only he prevents its employment in natural researches by everywhere referring the quantitative back to the qualitative; and so adopts a precisely opposite course to that taken by modern physical science.

Eucken, *loc. cit.,* S. 167 sqq., in den verschiedenen Gebieten der shows that even the strict notion Naturwissenachaft im Allgemeinen of induction in Aristotle is not easy vie im Eesondern manchmal mit to fix, because he often uses the grosser Zuversicht von einigen weniexpression for mere analogy, which gen Erscheinungen aus auf das Allgemust, however, differ from indue-meine geschlossen und daher oft Betion; and even for the mere ex-hauptungen aufgestellt, die weit iiber planation of abstract ideas by in-den Umfang des von ihm thatsachlicb. stances. Where the term is used Beobachteten hinausgehen." Exammore strictly (for the reaching of the pies of this, S. 171 ff., as to a priori universal out of the particular), Aris-conclusions, where induction should totle was still inclined *(loc. cit.* , S. rather have been employed, com p. 171) to pass hastily from the particu- Eucken, SS. 54 ff., 91 ff., 113 ff., 117 lar to the universal. "So hat er denn ff., *kc.*

Closely connected with deduction is the dialectical treatment of controverted points. Aristotle is fond of a historico-critical exposition of the views of his predecessors. They are to him the representatives of all possible opinions, to which he finally opposes his own particular view. Universal agreement is a complete proof; the refutation of all other views gives an appearance of necessity to what appears to be the one remaining view. Plato had already distinguished knowledge from correct opinion by the capacity of him who has a ready answer to all possible objections, and can maintain his own view successfully in the struggle of opinions. Aristotle himself introduces the opponents, makes them expound their opinions—often inaccurately enough—disputes with them on paper, and then sits as judge in his own cause. So victory in discussion takes the place of proof, the contest of opinions the place of analysis, and the whole remains a purely subjective treatment, out of which no true science can be developed.

If we now ask how it was possible that such a system could prove a barrier for hundreds of years, not only to Materialism, but to every empirical tendency, and how it is possible that the 'organic-world theory of Aristotle' is still to-day maintained by an influential school of philosophy to be the axiomatic impregnable basis of all true philosophy, we must, in the first place, not forget that speculation is in general fond of starting from the naive notions of the child and the charcoal-burner, and so of connecting together in the sphere of human thought the highest and the lowest, as opposed to the relativistic mean. We have already seen how consistent Materialism is able, as no other system can, to bring order and relation into the sensible world, and how it is entitled, from this starting-point, to regard even man, with all his various activities, as a special case of the universal laws of nature; and yet, how between man as an object of empirical research, and man as he is in the immediate self-knowledge of the subject, there is fixed an eternal gulf. And hence the attempt is ever repeated to see whether, by starting from self-consciousness, we may attain a more satisfying philosophy; and so strong is the secret tendency of man in this direction, that this attempt will a hundred times be regarded as successful, in spite of the recognised failure of all previous efforts.

It will indeed be a most important step in philosophical progress if these efforts are finally abandoned; but that will never be the case unless the longing of the human reason for unity receive satisfaction in some other way. We are constituted not merely to know, but also to imagine and construct; and though with more or less mistrust of the definite validity of what the understanding and the senses have to offer us, yet mankind will ever hail with joy the man who understands how, by the force of genius, and by employing all the constructive impulses of his era, to create that unity in the world and in our intellectual life which is denied to our knowledge. This creation will, indeed, be only the expression of the yearning of the age after unity and perfection; yet even this is no small thing, for the maintenance and nourishment of our intellectual life is as important as science itself, although not so lasting as this is: since the investigation of the details of positive knowledge, and of the relations which are the exclusive objects of our knowledge, is absolute, owing to its method, while the speculative apprehension of the absolute can only claim a relative importance as the expression of the views of an epoch.

Although, then, we must ever regard the Aristotelian system as an opposing hostile force in relation to the clear distinction of these spheres—although it is the standing type of a perverted method, the great example of all that is to be avoided, in its mingling and confusion of speculation and inquiry, and in its pretensions not merely to comprehend but to dominate positive knowledge—yet we must, on the other hand, recognise that this system is the most perfect example as yet afforded in history of the actual establishment of a theory of the universe which forms a united and self-included whole. If, therefore, it is my duty to lessen the reputation of Aristotle as an investigator, yet, nevertheless, the manner in which he united in himself, and collected into a harmonious system, the whole sum of the learning of his time, still remains a gigantic intellectual achievement, and, by the side of the perverseness which we have been obliged to point out, we find in every department abundant marks of penetrating acuteness. In addition to this, as the founder of logic, Aristotle deserves a place of high honour in philosophy, and if the complete fusion of his logic with his metaphysic, taken abstractly, lessens the value of this science, yet this very combination lends force and charm to the system. In an edifice so firmly built, the spirit could take rest and find its support in the seething and impetuous time when the ruins of the ancient culture, with the enthralling ideas of a new religion, excited in the Western mind so great and troubled an excitement, and a stormy endeavour after new forms. How content were our forefathers on their earth, resting in the hounded sphere of the eternally-revolving vault of heaven, and what agitation was excited by the keen current of air that burst in from infinity when Copernicus rent this curtain asunder!

But we are forgetting that we have not yet to set forth the importance of the Aristotelian system in medieval times. In Greece it was only very gradually that it acquired the predominance over all other systems, when, after the close of the classical period which precedes Aristotle, the rich blossoming of scientific activity which began after him, also declined, and the vacillating spirit grasped here also at the strongest prop that seemed to be offered. For a time the star of the Peripatetic School blazed brightly enough beside other stars, but the influence of Aristotle and his doctrine could not prevent the invasion of Materialistic views with exalted force soon after him, nor indeed prevent these from seeking to find points of connection even in his own peculiar system

CHAPTER IV.

MATERIALISM IN GREECE AND ROME AFTER ARISTOTLE: EPIKUROS.

We have seen in the previous chapter how that progress by antitheses, which Hegel has made so important for the philosophical treatment of history, must always be based upon a general view of all the facts in the history of culture. A tendency, after spreading vigorously and completely permeating its whole epoch, begins to die out, and loses its hold upon new generations. Meanwhile fresh forces arise from other and hitherto in visibly-working currents of thought, and adapting themselves to the changed character of the nations and states, issue a new watchword. A generation exhausts itself in the production of ideas, like the soil which produces the same crop too long; and the richest harvest always springs from the fallow field.

Such an alternation of vigour and exhaustion meets us in the history of Greek Materialism. Materialistic modes of thought dominated the philosophy of the fifth century B.C., the age of Demokritos and Hippokrates. It was toward the end of this century that a spiritual movement was inaugurated by Sokrates, which, after undergoing various modifications in the systems of Plato and Aristotle, dominates the succeeding century.

But again from the school of Aristotle himself there proceeded men like Dikaearchos and Aristoxenos, who denied the substantiality of the soul. And finally there appeared the famous physicist Strato of Lampsakos, whose doctrine, so far as it can be made out from the scanty traditions, is scarcely distinguishable from purely Materialistic views.

The *vow* of Aristotle Strato regarded as consciousness based upon sensation. He supposed the activity of the soul to consist in actual motion. All existence and life he referred to the natural forces inherent in matter.

But although we find that the whole of the third century is marked by a revival of Materialistic modes of thought, yet Strato's reform of the Peripatetic School does not on this head make good more than a position of compromise. The decisive impulse is given by the system and school of Epikuros; and even his great opponents, the Stoics, in the sphere of physics incline distinctly to Materialistic conceptions.

The historical circumstances which prepared the way for the new influence were the destruction of Greek freedom and the collapse of Hellenic life—that brief but unique flowering-time, at the conclusion of which arises the Athenian philosophy. Sokrates and Plato were Athenians, and men of that genuine Hellenic spirit which was beginning to disappear before their eyes. Aristotle, in point of time and character, stands on the threshold of the transition, but by his resting upon Plato and Sokrates he was closely connected with the preceding period. How intimate are the relations in Plato and Aristotle of ethic to the idea of the state! For the radical reforms of the Platonic state are, like the conservative discussions of the Aristotelian politic, devoted to an ideal which was to offer strong opposition to the rising flood of Individualism. But Individualism was of the essence of the time, and an entirely different stamp of men arises to take control of the thought of the age. Again, it is the outlying districts of the Greek world which produce most of the principal philosophers of the next epoch; but this time, it is true, not the old Hellenic colonies in Ionia and Magna Graecia, but chiefly districts where the Greek element had come in contact with the influences of foreign, and especially Oriental culture. The love of positive scientific research became more pronounced again in this era, but the various departments of inquiry began to diverge. Although we never find in antiquity that keen enmity between natural science and philosophy which is so common at present, yet the great names in the two spheres cease to be the same. The connection of men of science with a school of philosophers became much freer; while the chiefs of the schools were no longer inquirers, but were above all things advocates and teachers of their system.

As, generally speaking, the most familiar form of Materialism among the Greeks was the *anthropological,* so wo observe that Aristotle's doetrine of the separable, divine, and yet individual, soul in man met with the strongest opposition amongst his successors in antiquity. Aristoxenos, the musician, compared the relation of the soul to the body to that of harmony to the strings by which it is produced. Dikaearchos. in place of the individual soul-substance, put a universal principle of life and sensation, which becomes only temporarily individualised in corporeal objects. (Ueberweg, Grund., i. 4Aufl. S. 198, E. T., Hist. of Phil., i. p. 183). One of Aristotle's most important interpreters under the empire, Alexander of Aphrodisias, conceived the separable soul (the Koos Irohttktos) to be no portion of the man, but only as the divine essence which inBuences and develops the natural and inseparable human soul, and by which, in consequence, the process of thinking takes place. (Comp. Zeller, fix. 1, 2 Aufl. S. 712). Amongst the Arabian interpreters, Averroes in particular conceived the doctrine of the penetration of the divine soul into man quite pantheistically; while contrariwise the Christian philosophers of the Middle Ages carried further than Aristotle the individuality and separability of the reason, from which they got their immortal *anima rationalit* (apart, that is, from the strictly orthodox doctrine of the Church, which requires that the immortal soul should include not tho reason alone, but the lower faculties), so that in this particular too the exact view of Aristotle was scarcely anywhere accepted.

The practical standpoint which Sokrates had asserted in philosophy allied itself now with Individualism, only to become the more one-sided in consequence. For the supports which retigion and public life had previously offered to the consciousness of the individual now completely gave way, and the isolated soul sought its only support in philosophy. So it came about that even the Materialism of this epoch, closely as it also, in the contemplation of nature, leaned upon Demokritos, issued chiefly in an ethical Comp. Zeller, iii. 1, 2 Au.t., p. 26, E. T. (Beichel, Stoics, &c), p. 36. aim—in the liberation of the spirit from doubt and anxiety, and the attaining of a calm and cheerful peacefulness of soul. Yet before we speak of Materialism in the narrower sense of the term (see Note i), let us here interpose some observations on the 'Materialism of the Stoics.'

At the first glance we might suppose that there is no more consistent Materialism than that of the Stoics, who explain all reality to consist in bodies. God and the human soul, virtues and emotions, are *bodies.* There can be no flatter contradiction than that between Plato and the Stoics. He teaches that that man is just who participates in the idea of justice; while, according to the Stoics, he must have the substance of *justice* in his body.

This sounds Materialistic enough; and yet, at the same time, the distinctive feature of Materialism is here wanting —the purely material nature of matter; the origination of all phenomena, including those of adaptation and spirit, through movements of matter according to universal laws of motion.

The matter of the Stoics possesses the most various forces, and it is at bottom force that makes it what it is in each particular case. The force of all forces, however, is the deity which permeates and moves the whole universe with its influence. Thus deity and undetermined matter stand opposed to each other, as in the Aristotelian system the highest form, the highest energy, and the mere potentiality of becoming everything that form produces from it —that is, God and matter. The Stoics, indeed, have no transcendental God, and no soul absolutely independent of body; yet their matter is thoroughly pervaded, and not merely influenced by soul; their God is identical with the world, and yet he is more than mere self-moving matter; he is the ' fiery reason of the world,' and this reason works that which is reasonable and purposeful, like the 'reasonstuff" of Diogenes of Apollonia, according to laws which man gathers from his consciousness, and not from his observation of sensible objects. Anthropomorphism, therefore, teleology, and optimism profoundly dominate the Stoic system, and its true character must be described as 'Pantheistic.'

The Stoics had a strikingly pure and correct doctrine of the freedom of the will. Moral accountability is involved in the fact that conduct flows from the will, and so from the innermost and most essential nature of man; but the manner in which each man's will shapes itself is only a result of the mighty necessity and divine predestination which govern all the machinery of the universe down to the smallest detail. For his thought also man is responsible, because even our judgments are shaped by the influence of our moral character.

The soul, which is bodily in its nature, subsists for a certain time after death: wicked and foolish souls, whose matter is less pure and durable, perish quicker; the good mount to an abode of the blessed, where they remain till they are resolved in the great conflagration of the universe, with everything that exists, into the unity of the divine being.

But how was it that the Stoics, from their lofty theory of morals, proceeded to a theory of the universe standing in many points so near to Materialism? Zeller thinks that, in consequence of their practical tendency, they had conceived their metaphysic in the simplest form in which it is supplied by the immediate experience of practical life. There is a good deal to be said for this view of the question; but there is in the system of Epikuros a still deeper link between ethical and physical science. And is such a link wanting in the case of the Stoics? May it not be, perhaps, that Zeno found a support for his theory of virtue just in this thought of the absolute unity of the universe? Aristotle leaves us stranded in the dualism of a transcendental God and the world he governs, of the body with an animal soul and the separable immortal spirit: an excellent foundation for the consciousness of medieval Christianity, broken and yearning from the dust towards eternity, but not for the haughty self-sufficiency of the Stoic.

Zeller, iii. 1, S. 113 ff., E. T. jects. The objects then presented to (Reichel, Stoics, &c.), p. 129: "Ori-the senses are regarded by them as ginally devoting themselves with all real things, nor is an opportunity their energies to practical inquiries, afforded for doubting their real being. in their theory of nature the Stoics Their reality is practically taken for occupied the ground of ordinary com-granted, because of the influence they mon sense, which knows of no real exercise on man, and because they object except what is grossly sensible serve as objects for the exercise of and corporeal. In all their specula-man's powers. In every such exertions their primary aim was to dis-cise of power both subject and object cover a firm basis for human actions, are material. Even when an impresIn actions, however, men are brought sion is conveyed to the soul of man? into direct contact with external ob-the direct instrument is something VOL. I. G ,

The step from absolute Monism to the physic of the Stoics is now easy, for either all bodies must be reduced to pure idea, or all spirits, including that which moves in them, must become bodies; and even if, with the Stoics, we simply define body as that which is *extended in space,* the difference between these two views, utterly opposed as they seem to one another, is not really great.—Yet here we must break off, since whatever may have been the connection between the ethic and the physic of the Stoics, the speculations as to space, in its relation to the world of ideas and of bodies, belong to modern times.—We turn now to the revival by Epikuros of a consequent Materialistic theory, resting upon a purely mechanical theory of the world.

The father of Epikuros is said to have been a poor schoolmaster of Athens, who became a *kleruchos,* or colonist, at Samos. There Epikuros was born towards the end of the year 342, or at the beginning of 341. In his fourteenth year, it is said, he studied Hesiod's *Cosmogony* at school, and finding that everything was explained to arise from chaos, he cried out and asked, Whence, then, came chaos? To this his teacher had no reply that would content him, and from that hour the young Epikuros began to philosophise for himself.

material—the voice or the gesture. merely from the predominance of

In the region of experience there are practical interests. But, in fact, no such things as non-material im-Materialism, in the wider sense pressions." Comp. *ibid.,* S. 325 If., E. (pantheistic or mechanical), was for

T. 362, where an admirable parallel the ancients an almost inevitable is drawn between the Stoical ethic consequence of rigorous Monism and their theoretical views of the and Determinism; for they were absolute sway of the divine will in still far removed from the

modern the world, while, on the other hand, Idealism of a Descartes, Leibniz, or

'Jlaterialism there too is deduced Kant.

Epikuros must, in fact, be regarded as self-taught, although the most important ideas which he incorporated in his system were individually already commonly known. His general education is said to have been deficient. He joined himself to none of the then prevailing schools, but studied the more industriously the writings of Demokritos, which supplied him with the corner-stone of his cosmology, the doctrine of atoms. Nausiphanes, a somewhat sceptical follower of Demokritos, is said to have first introduced this doctrine to him at Samos.

Nevertheless, we cannot assume that it was through ignorance of other systems "that Epikuros took his own course; for already as a youth of eighteen he had been to Athens, and heard probably Xenokrates, the pupil of Plato, whilst Aristotle, accused of atheism, was at Chalcis, looking towards his end.

How different then the state of Greece from what it had been a hundred years before, whilst Protagoras was still teaching! Then Athens, the home of free culture, had reached its highest point of external power. Art and literature were in their fullest bloom. Philosophy was animated by all the vigour and arrogance of youth. Epikuros studied at Athens at the time of the downfall of liberty.

Thebes had perished, and Demosthenes lived in exile. From Asia were heard the news of Alexander's victories. The East disclosed its marvels-and as the circle of vision was widened, the Hellenic fatherland, with its glorious past, appeared more and more as a step that had been taken on the way to new developments, whose whence and whither no man yet knew.

Alexander died suddenly at Babylon; the last convulsive struggle of freedom followed, only to be cruelly repressed by Antipater. Amidst this confusion Epikuros again left Athens, in order to return to his parents' Ionian home. Afterwards he is supposed to have taught at Kolophon, Mitylene, and Lampsakos; and at the last-named place he gained his first disciples. He only returned to Athens in the maturity of years, and there bought a garden, where he dwelt with his disciples. It is said to have borne as an inscription, "Stranger, here will it be well with thee: here pleasure is the highest good." Here lived Epikuros with his followers, temperately and simply, in harmonious effort, in heartfelt friendship, as in a united family. By his will he bequeathed the garden to his school, which for a long time still had its centre there. The whole of antiquity furnishes no brighter and purer example of fellowship than that of Epikuros and his school.

Epikuros never filled any public office; and yet he is said to have loved his country. He never came into conflict with religion, for he sedulously honoured the gods with all conventional observance, without pretending to a belief concerning them which he did not really feeL

The existence of the gods he based upon the pure subjective knowledge which we have of them: and yet that man is not an atheist, he taught, who denies the gods of the multitude, but much rather he who subscribes to the opinions of the multitude concerning the gods. We are to regard them as eternal and immortal beings, whose holiness excludes every thought of care or occupation; and therefore all the events of nature proceed according to eternal laws, and without any interference from the gods, whose majesty is insulted if we suppose that they trouble themselves about us: we must worship them, nevertheless, for the sake of their perfection.

If, now, we put together these partly contradictory Expressions, there can be no doubt that Epikuros did really respect the *idea of the gods* as an element of noble human nature, and not the gods themselves as actual objective existences. Only from this point of view, of a subjective and soul-harmonising reverence for the gods, can we explain the contradictions in which otherwise the Epikurean system would necessarily leave us involved.

For if the gods *exist* indeed, but *do nothing,* that would be reason enough for the credulous frivolity of the masses to *believe* in them but not to *worship* them, while Epikuros did in fact just the reverse of this. He reverences the gods for their perfection: this he might equally do whether this perfection is exhibited in their outward actions, or whether it is only developed as an ideal in our thoughts; and this latter seems to have been his view.

In this sense, however, we must not suppose that his reverence for the gods was mere hypocrisy in order to keep on good terms with the mass of the people and the dangerous priesthood: it came really from his heart; for these careless and painless gods did in fact represent, as it were, an incarnated ideal of bis philosophy.

It was at the utmost a concession to existing circumstances, and certainly, at the same time, a habit endeared by the associations of youth, when he attached himself to the forms which must of course, from his standpoint, seem at least arbitrary and indifferent.

Thus Epikuros could at once impart a flavour of piety to his life, and still make the central point of his philosophy the effort to win that calmness of the soul which finds its only immovable foundation in deliverance from foolish superstitions.

Epikuros, then, taught expressly that even the motion of the heavenly bodies is not dependent upon the wish or impulse of a divine being; nor are the heavenly bodies themselves divine beings, but everything is governed by an eternal order which regulates the interchange of origination and destruction.

To investigate the reason of this eternal order is the business of the physical inquirer, and in this knowledge perishable beings find their happiness.

The mere historical knowledge of natural events, with out a knowledge of causes, is valueless; for it does not free us from fear nor lift us above superstition. The more causes of change we have discovered, the more we shall attain the calmness of contemplation; and it cannot be supposed that this inquiry can be without result upon our happiness. For the deepest anxieties of the human heart arise from this, that we regard these earthly things as abiding and satisfying, and so we must tremble at all the changes which nevertheless occur. But he who regards change in things as necessarily inherent in their very existence is obviously free from this terror.

Others, believing the old myths, are in fear of eternal torments to come; or, if they are too sensible to believe in these, yet apprehend at least the loss of all feeling which death brings with it as an evil, just as if the soul could still feel this deprivation.

But death is really quite indifferent to us, just because it deprives us of feeling. So long as we are, there is as yet no death; but as soon as death comes, then we exist no more. And yet we cannot but dread even the approach of a thing which in itself has nothing terrible about it. Still more foolish is it, of course, to sing the praises of an early death, which we can always secure for ourselves at a moment's notice. There is no more misfortune in life to the man who has really convinced himself that not to live is no misfortune.

Every pleasure is a good, every pain is an evil; but we are not on that account to pursue after every pleasure and to flee from every pain. Peace of soul and freedom from pain are the only lasting pleasures, and these are therefore the true aim of existence.

On this point Epikuros diverges sharply from Aristippos, who placed pleasure in motion, and declared the individual pleasure to be the true object. The tempestuous life of Aristippos, as compared with the quiet garden-life of Epikuros, shows how their opposite theories were carried out in practice. Unquiet youth and retired age, as well of the nation as of philosophy, seem at once reflected in these contrasts.

None the less was Epikuros opposed to Aristippos, from whom he had learnt so much, in teaching that intellectual pleasure was higher, and to be preferred to physical pleasure; for the mind is stimulated not only by the present, but also by the past and the future.

Yet Epikuros also was so far consistent that he explained that the virtues must be chosen for pleasure's sake alone, just as we resort to medicine for the sake of health; but he added, that virtue is the only permanent element of pleasure; all besides may be separated from it as being perishable. So near, logically, stood Epikuros to his opponents Zeno and Chrysippus, who declared that virtue is the only good; and yet, in consequence of the difference in the points of departure, we find the utmost difference in the systems.

All the virtues are derived by Epikuros from wisdom, which teaches us that man cannot be happy unless he is wise, noble, and just; and, conversely, that man cannot be wise, noble, and just, without being really happy. Physics, in the Epikurean system, were in the service of ethic, and this subordinate position could not but react upon his explanation of nature. For as the whole object of the explanation of nature is to free us from fear and anxiety, the stimulus to inquiry ceases when once the object is attained; and it is attained so soon as it is shown how events can be explained from universal laws. The possibility is enough here; for if an effect *can* be ascribed to natural causes, I need not any longer seek after supernatural ones. Here we recognise a principle which the German Eationalism of the last century frequently applied to the explanation of miracles.

But we are forgetting to ask whether and how we can prove what is the *real* cause of the events, and this want of a certain distinction has its revenge; for only those explanations will give us lasting satisfaction in which we find a coherence and a principle of unity. Epikuros, as we shall see further on, possessed such a principle in the bold thought that, given the infinity of worlds, then everything that is at all possible is somewhere at some time realised in the universe; but this general idea has very little to do with the ethical aim of physics, which must have reference to *our* world.

Thus, with regard to the moon, Epikuros supposed that it might have its own light, but its light might also come from the sun. If it is suddenly eclipsed, it may be that there is a temporary extinction of the light; it may also be that the earth has interposed between the sun and moon, and so by its shadow causes the eclipse.

The latter opinion seems indeed to have been specially held by the Epikureans; only it is so combined with the other that we see how unimportant it was considered to decide between them. You may choose which view you prefer—only let your explanation remain a natural one. This natural explanation must rest upon analogy with other known cases; for Epikuros declares that the right study of nature must not arbitrarily propose new laws, but must everywhere base itself upon actually observed facts. So soon as we abandon the way of observation, we have lost the traces of nature, and are straying into the region of idle fantasies.

In other respects Epikuros's theory of nature is almost entirely that of Demokritos, only fuller accounts of it have been preserved to us. The following propositions contain what is most important in it:—

Out of nothing nothing comes, for otherwise anything could come out of anything. Everything that is is body; the only thing that is not body is empty space.

Amongst bodies some are formed by combination; the others are those out of which all combinations are formed. These are indivisible and absolutely immutable.

The universe is unbounded, and therefore the number of bodies must also be endless.

The atoms are in constant motion, in part widely removed from each other, while in part they approach each other and combine. But of this there was never a beginning. The atoms have no qualities except size, figure, and weight.

This proposition, which formally denies the existence of intrinsic qualities as opposed to external motions and combinations, forms one of the characteristic features of all Materialism. With the assumption of intrinsic qualities the atom has already become a monad, and we pass on into Idealism or into pantheistic Naturalism.

The atoms are smaller than any measurable size. They have a size, but not this or that particular size, for none that can be mentioned will apply to them.

Similarly the time in which the atoms move in the void is quite inexpressibly short; their movement is absolutely without hindrance. The figures of the atoms are of inexpressible variety, and yet the number of actually occurring forms is not absolutely infinite, because in that case the formations possible in the universe could not be confined within definite, even though extremely wide, limits.

In a finite body the number as well as the variety of the atoms is limited, and therefore there is no such thing as infinite divisibility.

In void space there is no above or below; and yet even here one direction of motion must be opposed to another. Such directions are innumerable, and with regard to them we can in thought imagine above and below.

For the divergences of Epiknros Lucretius's *De Watura,* which will be from Demokritos we must refer partly found further on, and the special dis to the section on Demokritos (p. 25 cussions in connection with it. full.), partly to the extracts from

The soul is a fine substance distributed through the whole mass of body, and most resembles the air with an infusion of warmth.—Here we must again interrupt the ideas of Epikuros to make a brief remark.

To our present Materialists, this very theory of a soul like this, consisting of fine matter, would, of all others, be most repugnant. But whilst we now find such theories, for the most part, only amongst fanciful Dualists, the case was quite different when nothing was known as to the nature of nerve-force or the functions of the brain. The material soul of Epikuros is a genuine constituent of the bodily life, an *organ,* and not a heterogeneous substance existing independently, and continuing to exist after the dissolution of the body. This is quite clear from the following developments:—

The body encloses the soul, and conducts sensations to it: it shares in sensation by means of the soul, and yet imperfectly, and it loses this power of sensation at the dissolution of the soul. If the body is destroyed the soul must also be dissolved.

The origin of mental images is due to a constant streaming of fine particles from the surface of bodies. In this manner actual material copies of things enter into us.

Hearing, too, takes place through a current proceeding from sounding bodies. As soon as the sound arises, the report is formed by certain billows, which produce, as it were, a current of air.

More interesting than these hypotheses, which, in the absence of all true scientific inquiry, could only be childishly inadequate, are those explanations which are more independent of clear, positive knowledge. Thus Epikuros attempted to explain by natural laws the development of speech and of knowledge. The names of things did not originate as a formal system, but through men's uttering peculiar sounds varying according to the nature of things. The use of those sounds was confirmed by convention, and so the various languages were developed. New objects occasioned new sounds, which, then spread through employment, and became generally intelligible.

Nature has taught man many things, and so placed him that he must act. When he is brought into contact with objects, reflection and inquiry arise, in some cases quicker, in others more slowly; and so the development of ideas progresses ceaselessly through certain stages.

Epikuros did least for the extension of logic, and that deliberately, and from reasons which do all honour to his intelligence as well as his character. If one reflects how the great mass of the Greek philosophers sought to shine by paradoxical assertions and dialectic tricks, and for the most part confounded things instead of explaining them, we can only praise the sound sense of Epikuros, which led him to reject dialectic, as not only useless but pernicious. For the same reasons he employed no strange-sounding technical terminology, but explained everything in mere household words. From the orator he desired nothing but clearness; nevertheless he sought to establish a canon of truth.

And here again we come upon a point on which Epikuros is almost universally misunderstood and undervalued. That his logic is very simple is generally admitted, but with a contemptuous sneer that is not justified by the true state of the case. The logic of Epikuros is distinctly sensationalistic and empirical; from this standpoint, then, it is to be judged, and it can be shown that its essential principles, so far as we can gather them from the mutilated and in many ways obscure accounts which have come to us, are not only clear and consistent, but are also irresistible up to the point where the one-sidedness of all empiricism finds its limits.

The ultimate basis of all knowledge is sensible perception. And this is in itself always true: only through its relation to an object does error arise. If a madman sees a dragon, this perception, as such, is not deceptive; he does perceive the picture of a dragon, and no reason and no law of thought can alter the fact. But if he believes that this dragon will devour him, there he is wrong. The error lies in the referring of the perception to an objective fact. It is an error of the same kind as wheu a scientific man, after the most sober inquiry, incorrectly explains some celestial phenomenon. The perception is true, the reference to an assumed cause is false.

Aristotle of course teaches that true and false are shown only in the synthesis of subject and predicate in the judgment. A chimera is neither false nor true, but if any one asserts that the chimera exists or does not exist, then these propositions are either true or false.

Ueberweg maintains that Epikuros has confounded truth and psychical reality. But in order to maintain this he must define truth as the "agreement of the psychical image with a really existing object," and this definition agrees indeed with Ueberweg's logic, only it is neither commonly accepted nor necessary.

Let us dismiss the logomachy. If Epikuros's madman forms to himself the judgment, 'This phenomenon is the image of a dragon,' Aristotle can no longer object to the truth of this judgment. That the judgment of the madman in reality (though not always) is quite a different one is here irrelevant.

This remark should also be a sufficient reply to Ueberweg; for there is certainly nothing which has, in the strongest sense of the term, so 'independent' an existence as our ideas, from which everything else is first derived. But Ueberweg understands the matter differently, and therefore here too a different reply shall be made to the mere verbal misapprehension. In his phraseology Epikuros's perception can no longer be called 'true,' but yet it may be called 'certain,' because it is simple, incontrovertible, immediately given.

And now it may be asked, Is this immediate certainty 1 Hist. PbiL, i. 4th ed. p. 220, E. T. 204.— Tn.
of the particular individual concrete perceptions the foundation of all 'truth,' even if we understand it in Ueberweg's sense, or not? The Empiricist will say Yes; the Idealist (that is, the Platonic, not perhaps the Berkeleian) will say No. Further on we will go more deeply into this contradiction. Here it is sufficient to make Epikuros's train of thought perfectly clear, and so to secure his justification.

So far the standpoint of Epikuros is that of Protagoras, and it is therefore a complete misapprehension to suppose that he can be refuted by drawing the inference: So then contradictory propositions according to Epikuros, as according to Protagoras, may be equally true. Epikuros answers: Yes, they are true—each for its object. The contradictory assertions as to the same object have, however, only nominally the same object. The objects are different: for they are not the 'things in themselves,' but the mental images of them. These are the only real starting-point. The 'things in themselves' do not even form the second, but only the third step in the process of knowledge. Zellcr iii. I, 2 Aun, p. 365 foil., tive thing, is broken, and will theretreats this point as a "difficulty," as fore appear so out of the water also, to the solution of which Epikuros is indeed false; but it can be easily appears to have troubled himself but corrected by a second perception, little. But the expression is remark-If now the perceptions taken in able that, on the view of Pythagoras, themselves were not collectively *errors of the tenses become impossible;* quite trustworthy, and the basis of while shortly afterwards follows the all further knowledge, one might procorrect remark that the error lies not pose to annul one of them entirely, in the *perception* but in the *judgment.* as we simply and absolutely abandon The eye, for example, looking upon an incorrect judgment. But it is a stick plunged into the water, sees it obvious that that is quite impossible, broken. This perception, however, Even such errors of the senses (errors of a broken stick, is not only thor-unknown to the ancients), in which oughly true and trustworthy (com-an incorrect judgment (false induopare what is said in the text against tion) immediately and unconsciously TJeberweg), but it is, moreover, a interferes with and affects the function very important basis of the theory of perception, as, for instance, the pheof the refraction of light, which, nomena of dark spots on the retina, without such perceptions, could never are as *perceptions* trustworthy. When have been attained. The judgment Zellcr believes that the difficulty that the stick, conceived as an objec-would be only carried a step further

Epikuros goes beyond Protagoras in the safe path of Empiricism, since he recognises the formation of memorypictures, which arise from *repeated* perception, and which,' therefore, as compared with the individual perception, have already the character of a universal. This universal, or what is equivalent to a universal, idea (for example, the idea of a horse after one has seen different animals of this kind), is less certain than the original individual idea, but can at the same time, just because of its universal nature, play a much greater part in thought.

It forms the middle term in the passage to the causes, that is, in the inquiry after the 'thing in itself.' This inquiry it is that first results in science, for what is all Atomism but a theory as to the ' thing in itself,' which lies at the bottom of phenomena? Similarly the criterion of the truth of all universals is always their ratification by perception, the basis of all knowledge. The universals are not, therefore, by any means especially certain or true. They are, primarily, only ' opinions' which are spontaneously developed out of the contact of man with things.

These opinions are true if they are ratified by percep back by the distinction between the stance, the way in which Rousseau perception of a *picture* and perception makes his Emile develop the notion of an *object,* that seems to rest upon f the refraction of light out of the a misunderstanding. The question, picture of the broken stick. And "How may the true be distinguished although Epikuros may not have from the untrue pictures?" is thus treated the question with this keento he answered, that every picture is ss, yet obviously bis remark (if "true;" that is, the object is given Cicero reports correctly), that it i with complete certainty in that modi-the task of the wise man to disth.fication which necessarily follows ii opinion *(opinio)* from cerfrom the constitution of the media tainty (pei-/,i'cut'«Mi), is not the whole and of our organs. Our proper task answer that Epikuros's system affords is never, therefore, to reject a picon the matter. Nay, it is perfectly ture absolutely as "untrue," and to clear that this very distinction must substitute another for it, but to re-be produced in the same way as all cognise as such a *modification* of the other knowledge; by tho formation original picture. This takes place quite of a notion, and, in connection with simply, like all other recognition, it, a belief naturally developed frsm through the formation of a irpoXijts the perception itself as to the causes and then of a Sofa out of repeated of the modified phenomenon, perceptions. Let us compare, for in tions. The Empiricists of our own day demand that they shall be ratified by 'facts.' But as to the existence of a fact, we can again only appeal to perception. If the logician objects that it is not perception but methodical proof that determines the existence of a fact, we must remind him in turn that this methodical proof, in the last result, can only be referred to perceptions and their interpretation. The elementary fact, therefore, is always the perception, and the difference of the standpoints shows itself only in this—whether the method of verification is purely empirical, or whether it rests eventually upon propositions which are viewed as necessarily prior to all experience. This controversy we need not here decide. It is enough that we have shown that, even in the matter of logic, we have been led by hostile traditions into unfairly reproaching Epikuros with superficiality and inconsistency, whilst from his own standpoint he goes to work at least as rationally as Descartes, for example, who also rejects the whole traditional logic, and substitutes a few simpler rules of investigation.

Epikuros was the most fertile writer amongst the ancients, with the exception of the Stoic Chrysippos, who wished to surpass him in this respect, and succeeded; but whilst the books of Chrysippos abounded in borrowed passages and quotations, Epikuros never made a quotation, but carved everything out of his own materials.

In this disdain of all quotations, we cannot but recognise that radicalism which is not unfrequently united with Materialistic views—a disdain of the historical, as compared with the scientific, element. Let us take these three points together: that Epikuros was self-taught, and attached himself to none of the dominant schools; that he hated dialectic, and employed a universally intelligible mode of speech; finally, that he never quoted, and, as a rule, simply ignored those who thought differently from himself; and we have here an adequate explanation of the hatred that so many narrow philosophers have poured upon him. The charge of want of thoroughness flow9 from the same source, for still in our own days nothing is so common as the tendency to seek the thoroughness of a system in an elaborate scheme of unintelligible phrases. If our contemporary Materialists in their opposition to philosophical terminology go too far, and often condemn for want of clearness terms which have a quite fixed meaning, although one not to be guessed at once by a beginner, this is chiefly to be ascribed to a neglect of the historical and exact meaning of the expressions. Without having grounds for making definitely a similar reproach against Epikuros, we must-''-I overlook this common feature of the neglect of history. In this, as in so many other respects, the keenest contrast to Materialism is to be found in Aristotle.

It is worth noticing that Greek philosophy, so far as it is expressed in sound systems, having a character of unity, and based upon purely ethical and intellectual ideas, terminates with Epikuros and his school, as it begins with the Ionian natural philosophers. The further developments belong to the positive sciences, while speculative philosophy, in Neo-Platonism, becomes thoroughly degenerate.

As the aged Epikuros cheerfully closed his life in the midst of his circle of disciples at Athens, a new theatre of Greek intellectual life was already opened at Alexandria. "''

Within very recent times it was the fashion to use the 'Alexandrian spirit' as the synonyme for superficial sciolism and peddling pedantry; and even yet, while we recognise the claims of Alexandrian research, we usually couple with this recognition the thought that only the complete shipwreck of a vigorous national life had been able to supply such room for the purely theoretical need of knowledge.

In the face of these notions, it is important for our object to point out the creative energy, the living spark of noble effort—an effort as bold and comprehensive in its aims as it was bold and honest in its means—which the learned world of Alexandria presents to us on a nearer view.

For if the Greek philosophy, springing from a Materialistic origin, after a short and brilliant passage through all conceivable standpoints, found its termination in Materialistic systems and Materialistic modifications of other systems, we are entitled to ask what was the final result of all these transformations?

But the 'final result' may be variously understood. Philosophers have somtt' 3 approved of a construction which compares the career of philosophy to the course of a day from night through morning, noon, and evening again to night. The natural philosophers of Ionia on the one hand, and Epikureanism on the other, fall on this theory in the region of night.

We must not forget, however, that the conclusion of Greek philosophy in the return of Epikuros to the simplest principles did not lead the nation back to the condition of poetical childhood, but much rather formed the natural transition to a period of the most fruitful inquiries in the sphere of the positive sciences.

Historians are very fond of maintaining that in Greece the rapid developments philosophy produced a hopeless separation between 'the thought of the intellectual aristocracy and the imaginat' ns and aspirations of the people, and that this separation brought about the national catastrophe. "We may, indeed, grant all this, and yet hold that the fall of individual nations does not hinder the progress of humanity; nay, that in the very fall of the nation the result of its efforts, like the seeds of the dying plant, reaches its utmost ripeness and perfection. If we see, then, how such residts became really in later times the life-germs of new and unlooked-for progress, we shall regard the career of philosophy and of scientific inquiry from a higher and freer standpoint. And it may be VOL. I. H actually proved that the brilliant scientific outburst of our own times, at the era of its development, at every point connects itself with

Alexandrian traditions.

All the world has heard of the libraries and schools of Alexandria, of the munificence of her kings, the zeal of her teachers and scholars. But it is not all this that constitutes the historical importance of Alexandria: it is much more the very marrow of all science, the method which here appeared first after a sort that determined the course of all after-time; and this progress in methodology is not confined to this or that science, nor to Alexandria itself, but is much rather the common note of Hellenic research after the decadence of speculative philosophy.

Grammar, the first foundations of which had been laid by the Sophists, found in this period an Aristarchos of Samothrace, the pattern of critics, a man from whom the philology of our own day has still found something to learn.

In history, Polybios began to set causes and effects in organic connection. In Manetho's chronological inquiries the great Scaliger sought in modern times a point of departure.

Euklid created the method of geometry, and provided the elements which yet constitute the basis of this science.

Archimedes found in the theory of the lever the foundation of all statics: from him until Galilei the mechanical sciences made no more progress.

But amongst the sciences of this epoch, astronomy shines with special brilliancy, after having rested from the time of Thales and Anaximander. With great emphasis speaks Whewell of the 'inductive age of Hipparchos,' for it was in fact the inductive method in all its thoroughness and fertility that was for the first time handled by Hipparchos. The cogency of the inductive method rests, however, upon the presupposition of that uniformity and necessity in the course of nature which Demokritos had firat brought distinctly into view. Henco is to be explained, moreover, the far-reaching influence of astronomy in the days of Copernicus and Keppler, the true restorers of that method which Bacon formulated.

The necessary complement of the inductive method, the second cornerstone of our modern science, is, of course, experiment. This, too, had its birth in Alexandria, and in its schools of medicine.

Anatomy was made the basis of medical knowledge by Herophilos and Erasistratos, and even vivisection appears to have been employed. A school of great influence grew up, which made experience, in the best sense of the word, its grand principle, and great progress was the reward of their efforts. If we include all these brilliant phenomena in one view, the intellectual activity of Alexandria must inspire in us a high regard. It was not the want of internal vitality, but the course of history, which speedily put an end to this activity; and we may say that the renascence of the sciences was chiefly a revival of Alexandrian principles.

Nor must we undervalue the results of positive research in antiquity. We here leave out of sight grammar and logic, history and philology, whose great and permanent achievements none will controvert. We will rather point out that in those very sciences, in which the last few centuries have attained such an unequalled development, the preparatory achievements of Greek inquiry were of high importance.

Whoever contemplates the Homeric world, with its ceaseless miracles, the narrow space of its earth-surface, and its naive conceptions of the heavens and the stars, must confess that the capable among the Greeks had entirely to remodel their notions of the world. Of the wisdom of the Indians and the Egyptians only fragments reached them, which, without answering efforts of their own, could never have attained to any serious development. The distorted representation of the few countries around the Mediterranean, which it was already clear to Plato must form only a very small portion of the whole earth, the fables of the Hyperboreans and the peoples inhabiting the farthest west beyond the setting of the sun, the myths of Scylla and Charybdis: all these are traits from which we learn at once that the conceptions of science and poetry are as yet scarcely distinguished. The events correspond with the scene. Every natural occurrence appears muffled by some divine apparition. Those beings out of which the popular sense of beauty created such splendid types of human strength and grace, are everywhere and nowhere, and subvert every thought of a rigid connection between cause and effect. The gods are not wholly omnipotent, and yet there are no fixed limits to their power. Everything is possible, and nothing can be depended upon. The *reductio ad absurdum* of the Greek Materialists—"since in that case anything might arise from anything"—has in this world no application: anything may actually arise from anything, and since no leaf can fall, no streak of mist rise up, no ray of light shine—not to speak of lightning and thunder—without the intervention of some deity, no starting-point lor science is here to be discerned.

With the Romans, apart from the fact that they received their first scientific impulses from the Greeks, it was, if possible, still worse; except that the augury by birds, and especially the observation of storms, so studiously pursued by the Etruscans, made known a series of positive facts in the sphere of natural occurrences. But the nascent Graeco-Eoman culture found scarcely the barest rudiments of astronomy and meteorology, no trace of physics and physiology, not a suspicion of chemistry. Whatever happened was commonplace, accidental, or miraculous, but not an object of scientific cognisance. In a word, there was still lacking the very beginning of natural science— Hypothesis.

At the termination of the short and brilliant career of ancient civilisation, we find a complete change. The axiom of the uniformity and knowableness of natural events stands removed above all doubt; the effort after this knowledge has found its destined path. Positive natural science, directed to the precise investigation of particular facts, and the clear co-ordination of the results of these inquiries, has already completely separated itself from the speculative philosophy of nature, which seeks to reach beyond the bounds of experience, and rise to the ultimate causes of things.

Physical research has attained a definite method. Deliberate has supplanted merely casual observation: instruments lend precision to observation and secure its results; experiments even are being made.

The exact sciences, by a brilliant elaboration and perfecting of mathematics, had secured that instrument which, in the hands of the Greeks, the Arabs, and the Teutono-Eomanic peoples of modern times, step by step brought about the most magnificent practical and theoretical results. Plato and Pythagoras inspired their pupils to the cultivation of a mathematical sense.

The books of Euklid constitute still in the country of Newton, after more than two thousand years, the foundation of mathematical instruction, and the primitive synthetic method celebrated in the Mathematical Elements of Natural Philosophy—*(Naturalis philosophiae principia mathtmaticd)*—its last and greatest triumph.

Astronomy, under the guidance of subtle and complicated hypotheses as to the motion of the heavenly bodies, accomplished incomparably more than those primitive diviners of the stars, the peoples of India, Babylon, and Egypt, had ever succeeded in attaining. A very nearly exact calculation of the positions of the planets, of eclipses of the sun and moon, an accurate representation and grouping of the fixed stars, does not exhaust the list of what was achieved; and even the root-idea of the Copernican system, the placing of the sun in the centre of the universe, ia to be found in Aristarchos of Samos, with whose views Copernicus was very probably acquainted.

If we inspect the map of Ptolemy, we find still, it is true, the fabulous southern land uniting Africa to Further India, and converting the Indian Ocean into a second and greater Mediterranean; but Ptolemy represents this country as purely hypothetical; and how charming it looks already in Europe and the inner portions of Asia and Africa! Long before the spherical shape of the earth had been generally recognised. A methodical indication of place by means of degrees of longitude and latitude forms a strong support for the maintenance of what has been reached, and the incorporation of all fresh discoveries. Even the circumference of the earth had been already estimated by means of an ingenious astronomical method. Though this estimate contained an error, yet this very error led to the discovery of America, when Columbus, relying upon Ptolemy, sought the western passage to the East Indies.

Long before Ptolemy the researches of Aristotle and his predecessors had diffused a mass of information on the fauna and flora of more or less distant countries. Accurate description, anatomical examination of the internal structure of organic bodies, paved the way for a comprehensive survey of the forms which, from the lowest upward to the highest, were conceived as a progressive realisation of formative forces, which end by producing in man the most perfect of earthly things. Although in this view again numerous errors were involved, yet so long as the spirit of inquiry remained active, the foundation was of infinite value. The victorious campaigns of Alexander in the East enriched the sciences, and by the help of comparison still further enlarged and opened the field of observation. The industry of Alexandria accumulated and sifted materials. And so, when the elder Pliny attempted in his encyclopedic work to represent the whole field,of nature and art, a nearer insight into the relations between human life and the universe was already possible. To this restless spirit, who closed his great work with an invocation to Nature, the universal mother, and ended his life whilst engaged in observing a volcano, the influence of nature upon the intellectual life of mankind constituted a fruitful point of view, and an inspiring stimulus to inquiry.

The physics of the ancients embrace a notion, built upon experiment, of the main principles of acoustics, of optics, of statics, and the theory of gases and vapours. From the researches of the Pythagoreans into the pitch and depth of musical tones, as conditioned by the relative masses of the sounding bodies, to the experiments of Ptolemy on the refraction of light, the spirit of Hellenic research accomplished a long career of fruitful productiveness. The mighty buildings, war-engines, and earthworks of the Romans were based upon a scientific theory, by the exact application of which they were carried out with the utmost possible care and expedition, while the much more colossal works of the Oriental nations were produced rather by the prodigal expenditure of time and labour under the coercion of despotic dynasties.

Scientific medicine, culminating in Galen of Pergamos, had already explained the bodily life in its most difficult element—the nervous activity. The brain, previously regarded as an inert mass, whose use was still less understood than that of the spleen in modern times, had been elevated to the seat of the soul and the functions of sensation. Sommering, in the last century, found the theory of the brain almost where Galen had left it. The ancients were acquainted with the importance of the spinal marrow, and thousands of years before Sir Charles Bell they had distinguished the nerves of sensibility and movement; and Galen cured paralysis of the fingers, to the astonishment of his contemporaries, by acting upon those parts of the spine from which the implicated nerves took their rise. No yjonder, then, that Galen already regarded ideas as results of bodily conditions.

When we behold knowledge thus accumulating from all sides—knowledge which strikes deep into the heart of nature, and already presupposes the axiom of the uniformity of events—we must ask the question, How far did ancient Materialism contribute to the attainment of this knowledge and these views?

And the answer to this question will at first sight appear very curious. For not only does scarcely a single one of the great discoverers—with the solitary exception of Demokritos—distinctly belong to the Materialistic school, but we find amongst the most honourable names a long series of men belonging to an utterly opposite, idealistic, formalistic, and even enthusiastic tendency.

And special notice must here be paid to mathematics. Plato, the first father of an enthusiasm which became in the course of history at one time beautiful and profound, at another fanatical and delirious, is at the same time the intellectual progenitor of a line of inquirers who carried the clearest and most consequent of all sciences, mathematics, to the highest point it was to reach in antiquity. The Alexandrian mathematicians belonged almost wholly to the Platonic school, and even when the development of Neo-Platonism began, and the troubled fermentations of the great religious crisis made their way into philosophy, this school still produced great mathematicians. Theon and his noble daughter Hypatia, martyred by the Christian rabble, may serve to indicate this stage. A similar tendency proceeded from Pythagoras, whose school produced in Archytas a mathematician of the first order. By the side of these the Epikurean Polyaenos is scarcely to be mentioned. Even Aristarchos of Samos, the forerunner of Copernicus, clung to Pythagorean traditions. The great Hipparchos, the discoverer of the precession of the equinoxes, believed in the divine origin of the human souL Eratosthenes belongs to the middle academy, which corrupted Platonism by a sceptical element. Pliny, Ptolemy, Galen, without any exact system, leaned to pantheistic views, and would perhaps, two hundred years earlier, have been confounded with the proper followers of Materialism under the common name of Atheism and Naturalism. But Pliny favoured no philosophical system, although he stands in open opposition to popular beliefs, and leans in his views to Stoicism. Ptolemy was entangled in astrology, and in the general principles of his philosophy, at all events, follows Aristotle rather than Epikuros. Galen, who was more of a philosopher than any of them, is an Eclectic, and is acquainted with the most various systems, yet he shows himself least inclined to the Epikurean: only in the theory of knowledge he held the immediate certainty of sense-perceptions; but he supplemented it by assuming immediate truths of the reason, which are certain previous to all experience.

We see easily enough, however, that this slender participation of Materialism in the achievements of positive inquiry is not casual; that it is especially not to be attributed merely to the quietistic and contemplative character of Epikureanism, but that, in fact, the ideal element *(Moment)* with the conquerors of the sciences stands in the closest connection with their inventions and discoveries.

Here we must not allow an appreciation to escape us of the great truth that it is not what is objectively right and reasonable that most furthers us, not even that which The passage contained at p. 65 of morphologischen Ansichten des Statue first edition, in which the Index of giriten lagen gleichsam die Keime Humboldt's "Kosmos " was employaller spaterer Fortschritte der Natured to prove the scientific importance wissenschaft." We must not, indeed, of Aristotle, has been retracted on overlook the importance of teleologiconsidering that the preservation of cal hypotheses in the sphere of orgathe Aristotelian writings in the gene-nic discovery, but the great developral destruction of the Greek literature ment of modern science rests upon the was sufficiently decisive on this point, liberation from the tyranny of this It is therefore perhaps to be doubted 'organic view of things.' The knowwhether the influence of Aristotle has ledge of inorganio nature, and therenot been too favourably estimated with of the most universal laws of in the passage of Humboldt: "In nature, connects itself, in fact, much Plato's hoher Achtung fur mathema-more closely with the principle of Detisclle Gedankenentwicklung, wie in mokritos, through which physics and den alle Organismen umfassenden chemistry first became possible.

leads us to the greatest fulness of objective truth. As the falling body reaches the goal more quickly upon the brachystochrone than upon an inclined plane, so it is a result of the complex organisation of man that in many cases the roundabout course through the play of imagination leads more quickly to the apprehension of pure truth than the sober effort to penetrate the closest and most various disguises.

There is no room to doubt that the Atomism of the ancients, though far from possessing absolute truth, yet comes incomparably nearer to the essential reality of things, so far as science can understand it, than the Numerical theory of the Pythagoreans or the Ideal theory of Plato; at least it is a much straighter and directer step to the existing phenomena of nature than those vague and hesitating philosophemes which spring almost wholly out of the speculative poesy of individual souls. But the ideal theory of Plato is not to be separated from the man's immeasurable love for the pure forms in which all that is fortuitous and abnormal falls away, and the mathematical idea of all figures is regarded. And so it is with the number-theory of the Pythagoreans. The inner love for all that is harmonious, the tendency of the spirit to bury itself in the pure numerical relations of music and mathematics, produced inventive thought in the individual soul. So from the first erection of the MijSei? tryew/ teVpTo? *eurirea* until the termination of the ancient civilisation, there ran this common characteristic through the history of invention and discovery—that the tendency of the spirit to the supersensuous helped to open the laws of the sense-world of phenomena on the path of abstraction.

Where, then, are the services of Materialism? Or, in addition to all its other services to art, poetry, and sensibility, must the preference also be given to fanciful speculation in relation even to the exact sciences? Obviously not: the thing has its reverse side, and this appears if we regard the indirect effects of Materialism and its relation to scientific method.

Although we may assign great importance to the subjective impulse, to the individual conjecture of certain final causes for the tendency and force of the movement towards truth, yet we must not for a moment lose from view how it is just this fantastic and arbitrary mythological standpoint which has so long and so seriously hampered the progress of knowledge, and to the widest extent still continues to do so. As soon as man attains to the sober, clear, and definite observation of individual events, so soon as he connects the product of this observation with a definite, though, it may be, an erroneous theory, if it be at least a firm and simple one, further progress is secured. This, when it occurs, is easily to be distinguished from the processes of the devising and imagining certain final causes. Though this, as we have just shown, may have, under favourable circumstances, a high subjective value, depending on the interchange of intellectual forces, yet the beginning of this clear, methodical observation of things is in a sense the first true beginning of contact with things themselves. The value of this tendency is objective. Things, at the same time, demand that we shall so approach them, and only when we put a carefully considered question, does nature afford us an answer. And here we must refer to that starting-point of Greek scientific activity which is to be sought in Demokritos and the rationalising influence of his system. This rationalising influence benefited the whole nation; it was completed in the simplest and soberest observation of things which can be imagined—in the resolution of the varying and changeful universe into unalterable but mobile particles. Although this principle, most closely connected as it was with the Epikurean Materialism, has only attained its full significance in modern ages, yet it obviously exercised, as the first instance of a complete and vivid representation of all changes, a very deep influence upon the ancients also. So even Plato himself resolved into mobile elementary bodies his 'non-existent,' yet nevertheless indispensable, matter; and Aristotle, who opposes with all his might the assumption of a void, who maintains the dogma of the continuity of matter—seeks, so far as may be done from this difficult standpoint, to compete with Demokritos in the vividness of his doctrine of change and motion.

It is indeed true that the Atomism of to-day, since chemistry has been worked out, since the theory of vibration, and the mathematical treatment of the forces at work in the smallest particles, stands in very much more direct connection with the positive sciences. But the connecting of all these otherwise inexplicable events of nature, of becoming and perishing, of apparent disappearance, and of the unexplained origin of matter with a single pervading principle, and, as one might say, a palpable foundation, was, for the science of antiquity, the veritable Columbus's egg. The constant interference of gods and demons was set aside by one mighty blow, and whatever speculative natures might choose to fancy of the things that lay behind the phenomenal world, that world itself lay free from mist and exposed to view, and even the genuine disciples of a Plato and a Pythagoras experimented or theorised over natural occurrences without confusing the world of ideas and of mystic numbers with what was immediately given. This confusion, so strongly manifested in some of the modern native philosophers of Germany, first appeared in classical antiquity with the decay of all culture at the era of the Neo-Platonic and Neo-Pythagorean extravagances. It was the healthy morality of thought which, sustained by the counterbalance of sober Materialism, kept the Greek Idealists so long away from such errors. In a certain sense, the whole thought of Greek antiquity, from its beginning till the period of its complete destruction, wa3 under the influence of a Materialistic element. The phenomena of the sensible world were, for the most part, explained out of what was perceived by the senses or repreeented as so perceived.

Whatever judgment, then, we may in other respects pass upon the whole of the Epikurean system, so much, at all events, is certain, that the scientific research of antiquity drew profit not out of this system, but much more from the general Materialistic principles which underlay it. The school of the Epikureans remained, amongst all the ancient schools, the most fixed and unalterable. Not only are the instances extremely rare in which an Epikurean went over to other systems, but we find scarcely a single attempt to extend or modify the doctrines once accepted until the very last developments of the school. This sectarian narrowness bears witness to the strong predominance of the ethical over the physical side of the system. When Gassendi, in the seventeenth century, revived the system of Epikuros, and opposed it to that of Aristotle, he sought, of course, to maintain the ethics of Epikuros so far as was compatible with Christianity, and it cannot be denied that this too had a strong leavening influence in the development of the modern spirit; but the most important fact was the immediate release of the old Demokritean principle out of the chains of the system. Variously modified by men like Descartes, Newton, and Boyle, the doctrine of elementary corpuscles, and the origin of all phenomena from their movements, became the corner-stone of modern science. Yet the work which had secured for the Epikurean system ever since the revival of learning a powerful influence on modern modes of thought, was the poem of the Eoman Lucretius Carus, to whom, on the special ground of his historical importance, we will dedicate a special chapter, which will at the same time afford us a deeper view of the most important portions of the Epikurean doctrine.

CHAPTER V. THE DIDACTIC POEM OF LUCRETIUS UPON NATURE.

Among all the peoples of antiquity, none perhaps was by nature further removed than were the Romans from Materialistic views. Their religion had its roots deep in superstition; their whole political life was circumscribed by superstitious forms. They clung with peculiar tenacity to the sentiments they inherited; art and science had little charm for them, and they were still less inclined to bury themselves in the contemplation of nature. A practical tendency, more than any other, governed their life, and yet this was by no means materialistic, but was thoroughly spiritual. They valued dominion more than wealth, glory rather than comfort, and triumph more than all. Their virtues were not those of peace, of industrial enterprise, of righteousness, but those of courage, of fortitude, of temperance. The Roman vices were, at' least in the beginning, not luxury and wantonness, but hardness, cTuelty, and faithlessness. Their power of organisation, in conjunction with their warlike character, had made the nation great, and of this they were proudly conscious. For centuries after their first contact with Greeks there continued that antipathy which sprang from the difference in their characters. It was only after the defeat of Hannibal that Greek art and literature gradually forced their way into Rome. At the same time came luxury and wantonness, with the fanaticism and immorality of the Asiatic and African peoples. The conquered nations crowded to their new capital, and brought about a confusion of all the elements of the old Roman life, while the great more and more acquired a taste for culture and refined sensuality; generals and governors made spoil of the works of Greek art; schools of Greek philosophy and rhetoric were opened, and frequently again forbidden: men were afraid of the dissolving element in Greek culture, but were less and less able to resist its charms. Even old Cato himself learnt Greek; and when once the language and literature were known, the influence of philosophy could not remain inactive.

In the last days of the Eepublic this process had been so far completed that every educated Eoman understood Greek, the young nobles pursued their studies in Greece, and the best minds endeavoured to form the national literature on Greek models.

At that time, among all the schools of Greek philosophy, there were two which especially captivated the Eomans— the Stoic and the Epikurean: the first, with its blunt pride in virtue, naturally related to the Eoman character; the second, more in accord with the spirit of the times and their state of progress, but both—and this marks the Eoman character—of practical tendency and dogmatic form.

These schools, which, despite their sharp contrasts, had nevertheless so much in common, came into more friendly contact in Eome than in their native land. It is true that the unmeasured calumnies of the Epikureans, which since Chrysippos had been industriously disseminated by the Stoics, were speedily transplanted to Eome. There, too, the mass of men regarded an Epikurean as a slave of his lusts, and, with a double measure of superficiality, ventured to deny his philosophy of nature, because it was protected by no barrier of unintelligible phrases.

Cicero, too, unfortunately, popularised the Epikurean doctrine in the bad sense of the word, and so threw a ludicrous colour over many things which disappears when they are more seriously regarded. But for all that, the Eomans were for the most part admirable dilettanti, who were not so deeply concerned for their own school but that they were able to value opposing views. The security of their position in the world, the universality of their intercourse, kept them free from prejudice; and therefore. we find expressions, even in Seneca, which gave Gassendi some authority for making him an Epikurean. Brutus the Stoic and Cassius the Epikurean together imbrue their hands in Caesar's blood. But this same popular and superficial conception of the Epikurean doctrine, which in Cicero seems so detrimental to it, not only makes it possible for friendship to exist between Epikureanism and the most divergent schools, but it weakens the character of the greater number of the Roman Epikureans, and so gives a certain foundation in fact for the general reprobation. Even at a time when Greek culture was still quite foreign to them, the Eomans had begun to exchange the rude austerity of primitive manners for an inclination to indulgence and wantonness, which, as we see so often in the case of individuals, was the more unrestrained in proportion to the novelty of the freer state of things. The change had become distinctly marked so early as the time of Marius and Sulla. The Eomans had become practical Materialists, often in the very worst sense of the term, before they had yet learnt the theory.

The theory of Epikuros was, however, in every way purer and nobler than the practice of these Eomans; and so now two courses were open to them—they either allowed themselves to be purified, and became modest and temperate, or they corrupted the theory, and so combined the conceptions of its friends and foes that they ended by having a theory of Epikureanism which corresponded to their habits. Even nobler natures and more thorough philosophers tended to hold by this more convenient form. So it was with Horace when he spoke of himself as a "hog of Epikuros's herd," obviously with sportive irony, but not in the serious and sober sense of the old Epikureanism. And, in fact, Horace not unfrequently points to the Cyrenaic Aristippos as his model.

A more serious attitude was that of Virgil, who also had an Epikurean teacher, but appropriated manifold elements of other systems. Amongst all these semi-philosophers stands a thorough and genuine Epikurean in Titus Lucretius, whose didactic poem, "De Eerum Natura," contributed more than anything else, when learning revived, to resuscitate the doctrines of gikuros, and to set them in a more favourable light. The Materialists of the last century studied and loved Lucretius, and it is only in our own days that, for the first time, Materialism seems to have broken completely away from the old traditions.

T. Lucretius Cams was born in the year 99, and died in the year 55 B.C. Of his life scarcely anything is known. It appears that amidst the confusion of the civil war, he sought some stay for his inner life, and found it in the philosophy of Epikuros. His great poem was undertaken to make a convert to this school of his friend the poet Memmius. The enthusiasm with which he opposes the salvation to be found in his philosophy to the troubles and nihilism of the times, gives to his work an elevated tone, a fervour of belief and imagination which rises far above the innocent serenity of Epikurean life, and often assumes a Stoic impetus. And yet it is a mistake when Bernhardy maintains in his 'Eoman Literature,' that " from Epikuros and his followers he took nothing but the skeleton of a philosophy of nature." This contains a misapprehension of Epikuros, which is still more conspicuous in the following expression of the eminent philologist:

"Lucretius builds indeed upon this foundation of mechanical Nature, but as he was concerned to save the right of personal freedom and of independence of all religious tradition, he seeks to introduce knowledge into practice, to free man, and to place him upon his own feet, by insight into the origin and the nature of things."

We have already seen that this striving after emancipation is the very marrow of the Epikurean system. In Cicero's superficial statement, this was indeed left in the

Vol. 1. I background; but not in vain has Diogenes Laertius preserved for us in his best biography the very words of Epikuros, which are the basis of the view we have already given.

But if there was anything that attracted Lucretius to Epikuros, and inspired him with this eager enthusiasm, it was just this boldness and moral vigour with which Epikuros robbed the theistic beliefs of their sting, in order to base morality upon an impregnable foundation. This is shown clearly enough by Lucretius, for immediately after the splendid poetical introduction to Memmius, he goes on:

"When human life to view lay foully prostrate upon earth, crushed down under the weight of religion, who showed her head from the quarters of heaven with hideous aspect lowering upon mortals, a man of Greece ventured first to lift up his mortal eyes to her face, and first to withstand her to her face. Him neither story of gods, nor thunderbolts, nor heaven with threatening roar, could quell, but only stirred up the more—the eager courage of his soul filling him with desire to be the first to burst the fast bars of Nature's portals."

That Lucretius had recourse to many additional sources, that he industriously studied Empedokles, and perhaps in the scientific parts of his theory has added much from his own observation, we will not deny; yet we must here again remind ourselves that we do not know what treasures were contained in the lost books of Epikuros. Almost all judges assign to the poem of Lucretius a very high place among the productions of pre-Augustan times, in respect of its genius and vigour; and yet the didactic portions are often dry and careless, or connected by sudden transitions with the poetical pictures.

A refutation of the attempts of sued with dispassionate calmness. Bitter to distinguish between the We may, of course, at the same time, theories of Lucretius and Epikuros attribute some part of this differmay be found in Zeller, iii. 1, 2 A u (1. ence to the special hatefuluess and p. 499. Everything is to be said on harmfulness of Roman as compared the other hand for the emphasis laid with Greek religious systems; but upon his enthusiasm for ' deliverance yet there remains a kernel still, from the darkness of superstition,' which may be regarded as a bitter in Teuffel, Gesch. d. riim. Liter., p. condemnation of religion absolutely; 326 (2 Aufl. p. 371). We might say and undoubtedly the importance still more confidently, that the really which Lucretius has acquired in mooriginal element in Lucretius is the dern ages rests no less upon this burniug hatred of a pure and noble special feature than upon his strict character against the degrading and Epikureanism. demoralising influence of religion, Lib. i. 61 sqq. In this and other whilst in Epikuros deliverance from passages from Lucretius, I hava religion is indeed an essential aim of availed myself of Mr. Munro's tran philosophy, but an aim which is pur-slation.—Ta.

In point of language, Lucretius has an extreme degree of antique roughness and simplicity. The poets of the Augustan age, who felt themselves to be far above the rude art of their predecessors, had great reverence for Lucretius. Virgil has devoted to him the lines—

"Felix qui potuit rerum cognoscere causas,
Atque nietus omnes et inexorabile fatum
Subjecit pedibas strepitumque Acheroitis avari."

Lucretius, then, without doubt had a powerful influence in the propagation of the Epikurean philosophy among the Romans. This reached its highest point under Augustus; for though it had then no such representative as Lucretius, yet all the gayer spirits of the band of poets who gathered around Maecenas and Augustus were inspired and guided by the spirit of this system.

"When, however, under Tiberius and Nero, abominations of all kinds made their appearance, and nearly all enjoyment was poisoned by danger or by shame, the Epikureans retired, and in this last period of heathen philosophy it was the Stoics especially who undertook the struggle against vice and cowardice, and with untroubled courage, as in the case of a Seneca or a Paetus Thrasea, fell a sacrifice to tyranny.

Doubtless the Epikurean philosophy also in its purity, and especially in the extension which had been given ta it by the strong moral character of Lucretius, was quite fitted to afford such sublimity of sentiments, only that the purity, and vigour, and force of comprehension which were displayed by Lucretius were rare in this school, and perhaps from the days of Lucretius to our own are net again to be met with. It is well worth the trouble, then, to look more closely into the work of this remarkable man.

The Introduction to this poem consists of an invocation to the goddess Venus, the giver of hfe, of prosperity, and of peace, which is marked by a picturesque mythological imaginativeness, a clear and yet profound reach of thought.

Here we are at once face to face with the peculiar Epikurean attitude towards religion. Not only the ideas of religion, but its poetical personifications are employed with an unmistakable fervour and devotion by the same man who, immediately afterwards, in the place quoted above, represents it as the strongest point of his system that it conquers the humiliating terror of the gods.

The early Eoman conception of religion, which, in spite of the uncertainty of the etymology, yet certainly expresses the element of the dependence and obligation of man to the divine beings, must, of course, convey to Lucretius exactly what he most deprecates. He challenges the gods, therefore, and attacks religion, without, on this point, our being able to discover any shade of doubt or contradiction in his system.

After he has shown how, by the bold unfettered investigations of the Greeks—where he refers to Epikuros, for though he also celebrates Demokritos, he stands further away from him—religion, which once cruelly oppressed mankind, had been thrown down and trodden underfoot, he raises the question whether this philosophy does not lead us into the paths of immorality and sin.

He shows how, on the contrary, religion is the source of the grossest abominations, and how it is this unreasonable terror of eternal punishments which leads mankind to sacrifice their happiness and peace of mind to the horrors of the prophets. 62 / Then the first principle is developed that nothing can fever come from nothing. This proposition, which to-day would rather be regarded as a generalisation from experience, is, quite in accordance with the then scientific standpoint, to be posited as a directive principle at the foundation of all scientific experience.

Any one who imagines that anything can arise out of nothing, can find his prej udice confirmed every instant. He who is convinced of the contrary has the true spirit of inquiry, and will discover also the true causes of phenomena. The proposition is, however, established by the consideration that, if things could arise from nothing, this mode of development could, of course, have no limits, and anything might then arise from anything. In that case men might emerge out of the sea, and fishes spring from the soil; no animal, no plant, would continue to propagate itself only after its kind.

This view has so much truth in it, that if things could spring from nothing, we could no longer conceive of any absolute reason why anything should not arise; and such an order of things must become an ever-varying and senseless play of the birth and death of grotesque creations. On the other hand, the regularity of nature, which offers us in spring roses, in summer corn, in autumn grapes, will lead us to conclude that creation accomplishes itself through a concourse of the seeds of things taking place at a fixed time, and thence we may assume that there exist certain bodies which are common constituents of many things, as letters are of words. / Similarly it is shown that nothing, again, is really destroyed, but that the particles of perishing things are dispersed, just as they come together in order to constitute the thing.

Here occurs, i. 101 (we cite "Tantnm religio potuit suadere mafrom the edition of Lachmanu), the lorum." of con-quoted and pregnant vers —

The ohvious objection that we cannot perceive the particles which are gathered together or dispersed, Lucretius meets by the description of a violent storm. To make his meaning more clear, he introduces also the picture of a rushing torrent, and shows how the invisible particles of the wind produce effects as obvious as the visible particles of the water. Heat, cold, sound are in the same way adduced to prove the existence of an invisible matter. Still finer observation is to be seen in the following examples: Garments which are spread on a surfy shore become damp, and then, if they are placed in the sun, become dry, without our seeing the particles of water either come or go. They must, therefore, be so small as to be invisible. A ring worn on the finger for many years becomes thinner; the falling of water wears away stone; the ploughshare gets used away in the field; the pavement is worn away by the treading of feet; but nature has not made it possible for us to see the particles that disappear every instant. Just so no power of sight can discover the particles which come and go in all the processes of generation and decay. Nature, therefore, jworks by means of invisible bodies or atoms.

Then follows the proof that the universe is not filled iwith matter, that it is rather a void space in which the,,atoms move.

Here, again, the weightiest argument is supposed to be the *a priori* one—that if space were absolutely filled with matter, motion would be impossible, and yet this we perceive constantly. Then come the arguments from experience. Drops of water force their way through the thickest stone. The nourishment of living beings permeates the whole body. Cold and sound force their way through walls. Finally, differences of specific gravity can only be referred to the greater or smaller proportion of void space. The objection that, in the case of fishes, the water they displace goes into the space they leave behind them, Lucretius meets by maintaining that in this case it would be quite inconceivable that the motion should commence; for where is the water before the fish to go, while the void it is to occupy does not yet exist? So, again, when two bodies start asunder, there must, for an instant, be a void between them. The facts cannot be explained by saying that the air is condensed and then again rarefied, for supposing this were so, it could only happen in case the particles could cohere more closely by filling up the void that previously held them apart.

There is nothing, however, besides the atoms and void. All existing things are either combinations of these two or an ' event of these.' Even time has no separate existence, but is the feeling of a succession of occurrences earlier and later: it has not even so much reality as void space; but the events of history are to be regarded only as accidents of bodies and of space.

These bodies are all either simple—atoms, or 'beginnings,' as Lucretius usually calls them, principia or primordia rerum—or are compound; and if simple, cannot be destroyed by any violence. Infinite divisibility is impossible, for in that case, as things are so much more easily destroyed than they are reconstituted, the process of dissolution in the course of endless time would have proceeded so far, that the restoration of things would have become impossible. It is only because there are limits to the divisibility of matter that things are preserved. Infinite divisibility, moreover, would be incompatible with the laws regulating the production of things, for if they were not composed of minute indestructible particles, then all things might arise without fixed law and order. ƒThis rejection of endless divisibility is the keystone of the doctrine of atoms and void space. After its assertion, then, the poet makes a pause, which is devoted to a polemic against different conceptions of nature, especially against Herakleitos, Empedoklea and Anaxagoras. But we must note his praise of Empedokles, whose close relations to Materialism we have already dwelt upon. After a very lofty poetical eulogy of the island of Sicily, the poet proceeds: "Now though this great country is seen to deserve, in many ways, the wonder of mankind, and is held to be well worth visiting, rich in all good things, guarded by large force of men, yet seems it to have held within it nothing more glorious than this man, and nothing more holy, marvellous, and dear. The verses, too, of his godlike genius cry with a loud voice, and set forth in such wise his glorious discoveries, that he hardly seems born of a mortal stock." 3

Passing over the polemic, we come to the conclusion of the First Book, a discussion of the constitution of the universe. Here, true as ever to the example of Epikuros, he I declines, above all things, to admit definite limits to the j world. Let us suppose an extreme limit, and imagine a spear hurled with a strong arm from this limit: will it be stopped by something, or will it continue its course into the infinite? In either case it is clear that we cannot conceive an actual limit to the world.

There is here a singular argument, that if-there were fixed limits to the world, all matter must long ago have been collected on the floor of the limited space. Here we find a weak point in Epikuros's whole scheme of nature. He j expressly combats the notion of gravitation towards the centre, which had already been accepted by many ancient thinkers. Unfortunately this passage of the Lucretian poem is very much mutilated; yet we may still see the essential features of the argument, and recognise the fallacy I. *v.* 726-738:—

"Quae cum magna modis multis miranda videtur
Gentibus humanis regio visendaque fcrtur,
Rebus opima bonis, multa munita virum vi,
Nil tamen hoc habuiase viro praeclarius in se
Nee sanctum magis et minim, carumque videtuiv
Carmina quinetiam divini pectoris eius
Vociferantur et eiponunt praeclara reperta,
TJt viz humana videatur stirpc creatus."

-which underlies it. Epikuros there assumes that weight I or gravity, as well as resistance, is an essential property of, the atoms. On this point the profound thinkers who created the Materialism of antiquity did not succeed altogether in freeing themselves from ordinary notions; for although Epikuros expressly teaches that, strictly speaking, there is in space no above and no below, yet he clings to a determinate direction in the falling of the atoms that make up the universe. To escape from the ordinary notions of weight was, in fact, no easy achievement for the human intellect. The doctrine of the Antipodes, which had developed from the shock inflicted upon the belief in Tartarus, together with the study of astronomy, struggled in vain in antiquity against the ordinary conception of an absolute *above* and *below.* With what reluctance these notions, which are constantly impressed upon us by our senses, yield to scientific abstraction, we may see from another example in modern times,—namely, the doctrine of the revolution of the earth. Even so late as a century after Copernicus, there were scientifically trained and freethinking astronomers, who advanced their natural feeling of the solidity and fixity of the earth as a proof of the incorrectness of the Copernican system.

Starting, then, from the basis of the gravity of the atoms, the Epikurean system cannot suppose that these have a twofold direction, ceasing in the centre. For since, as everywhere else, so in this centre also, there remains void space between the particles, they cannot support each other. But if we wished to suppose that they had already become compressed in the centre to a certain absolute density by immediate contact, then, according to the theory of Epikuros, already in the infinite duration of time all atoms must have been collected here, and therefore nothing more could happen in the world

We need not critically demonstrate the weaknesses of this whole manner of thinking.61 It i much more interesting to the thoughtful observer of human development to see how difficult it was to attain to a correct theory of nature. We wonder at Newton's discovery of the law of gravitation, and scarcely reflect how much progress had to be made in order so far to pave the way for this doctrine that it must inevitably be discovered by some great thinker. When the discovery of Columbus instantaneously placed the old theory of the Antipodes in an entirely new light, and finally disposed of the Epikurean theories on this point, there was involved the necessity of a reform in the whole conception of gravity. Then came Copernicus, then Keppler, then the inquiry into the laws of falling bodies made by Galilei, and so at last everything was ready for the exposition of an entirely new theory.

4 It deserves, however, to be re-viewed from the standpoint of the marked, that the theory of Epikuros, knowledge and ideas of that time, adduces much better reasons in many tion once begun could not be stopped, important points than the Aristotelian while Aristotle, starting from his theory, and that the latter, more by Ideological idea of motion, finds in chance than by force of its proofs, the centre its natural goal. But the happens to be nearer to our present superiority is most evident in the views. Thus, for example, the whole argumentation of the Epikurean systheory of Aristotle rests upon the con-tem to overthrow the nat-

ural upward ception of a *centre of the universe,* (centrifugal) motion of Aristotle, which Lucretius (i. 1070) rightly con-which is very well refuted by Lutroverts from the standpoint of the cretius (ii. 185 foil.; probably also infinity of the universe. In the same in the last passage of the first book, way Lucretius has the better concep-according to v. 1094), and referred tion of motion when he maintains (i. to upward motion necessitated by 1074 foil.) that in a void, even though the laws of equilibrium and of colliit were the centre of the universe, mo-sion. Compare above pp. 32-33. The verses (i. 21-34) run thus:—"Nam certe neque consilio primordia rerum Ordine se sua quaeque sagaci mente locarunt Nee quos quaeque darent motus pepigere profecto, Sed quia multa modis multis mutata per omne Ex infinite vexantur percita plagis, Omne genus motus et coetus experiundo Tandem deveniunt in talis dispositions, Qualibus haec rerum consist it summa creata, Et multos etiam magnos servata per annos

Towards the end of the First Book Lucretius briefly announces the magnificent doctrine, first proposed by Empedokles, that all the adaptation to be found in the universe, and especially in organic life, is merely a special case of the infinite possibilities of mechanical events.5

If we find any magnificence in the Aristotelian teleology, yet we must none the more refuse this character to the uncompromising denial of the idea of design. We are here dealing with the peculiar keystone of the whole edifice of Materialistic philosophy, a part of the system which has by no means always received its proper share of attention from recent Materialists. If the doctrine of design is one for which we have naturally more sympathy, yet it also contains a larger infusion of human one-sidedness of view. The entire dismissal of what has been imported into our view of things from human narrowness may be repugnant to us, but feeling is not argument; it is at the best but a divining principle, and in face of keen logical consequences is, it may be, an intimation of further possible explanations, which, however, lie beyond, and never before, these consequences.

"For verily not by design did the first beginnings of things station themselves each in its right place, guided by keen-sighted intelligence, nor did they bargain, sooth to say what motions each should assume, but because many in number, and shifting about in many ways throughout the universe, they are driven and tormented by blows during infinite time past; after trying motions and unions of every kind, at length they fall into arrangements such as those out of which this our sum of things has been formed, and by which too it is preserved through many great years, when once it has been thrown into the appropriate motions, and causes the streams to replenish the greedy sea with copious river-waters, and the earth, fostered by the heat of the sun, to renew its produce, and the race of liv TJt semel in motus conjectast convcnientis.

Efficit ut largis avidum mare fluminis nndis

Integrant omnes et solis terra vapore

Fota novet fetus smmmissaque gens animantum

Floreat et vivant labentes aetheris ignes. "

A more special treatment of the Empedoklean principles, follows in rise of organic existence, according to Book v. 836 foil.

ing things to come up and nourish, and the gliding fires of ether to live."

To conceive adaptations as only a special case of all conceivable possibilities is as magnificent an idea, as it is an ingenious one to refer the adaptations in this world to the persistence of adaptations. Thus this world, which maintains itself, is merely the one case which, among the innumerable combinations of atoms, must in the course of eternity spontaneously result; and it is only the fact that the very nature of these movements leads to their upon the whole maintaining and constantly renewing themselves that lends to the actual facts of this world the persistency which they enjoy.

In the Second Book Lucretius explains more fully the motion and the properties of the atoms. They are, he declares, in everlasting movement, and this movement is originally a perpetual, equable falling through the boundless infinity of void space.

But here arises a formidable difficulty for the Epikurean system: How is this everlasting and equable descent of the atoms to result in the formation of the world? According to Demokritos the atoms fall with varying degrees of rapidity; the heavy strike against the light, and thus becoming is first occasioned. Epikuros rightly enough refers the various speed with which bodies fall in the air or in water to the resistance of the medium. In this he follows Aristotle, only to take up later a more decided opposition to him. Aristotle not only denies a void, but even the possibility of motion in a void. Epikuros, with a more accurate conception of motion, finds, on the contrary, that motion in a vacuum must be only the more rapid because there is no resistance. But how rapid will it be? Here lies another sunken rock in the system.

As a comparison, it is suggested that the atoms must move in space with incomparably greater speed than the sun rays which in an instant traverse the space from the Lucret., i. 1021-1034, Munro.

sun to the earths But is this a standard? Have we here any standard whatever of speed? Obviously not; for, in fact, any given space must be traversed in infinitely little time, and as space is absolutely endless, this motion, so long as there are no objects by which it may measure itself, will be quite undeterminate; but the atoms, which move in parallel lines and with equal rapidity, are relatively in complete rest. This consequence of his departure from the view of Demokritos, Epikuros does not seem to have realised to himself with sufficient clearness. Very singular, however, is the expedient he adopts in order to begin the formation of the world.

How came the atoms, which naturally move in a simple course of straight parallel lines, like drops of rain, to attain oblique movements, rapid eddying and innumerable combinations, now inextricably fixed, now releasing themselves, and engaging in new groups with eternal regularity? It must be impossible to fix the time at which they began to deviate from their straight course.? The slightest aberration from the parallel lines must, in the course of time, bring about a meeting, a collision of atoms. When this has once occurred, the various forms of the atoms will soon result in the most complicated eddying movements, combinations, and separations. But how did it begin? Here is a fatal gap in the system of Epikuros. Lucretius solves the riddle, or rather cuts the knot, by having recourse to the voluntary movements of men and animals. Because the sun rays, subtle as means through empty space (ii. 150they may be, do not consist of single 156). On the other hand, we may atoms, but of combinations of atoms, say of the atoms that they must fall and their course lies through a very many times quicker than light (ii. rare medium it is true, but by no 162-164).

"Et multo citius ferri quam lumina solis,
Multiplexque loci.spatium transcurrere eodem
Tempore quo solis pervolgant fulgura coelum."

II. 216 foil. of his stronger moral character; for, II. 251-293. It is hard to underleaving out of view that the point stand how it can have been supposed occurs also, of course, in Epikuros, that this doctrine of the 'freedom of we here find a serious inconsistency the will' constitutes a superiority of with the physical theory, which lends Lucretius over Epikuros, and a result no support whatever to a theory of moral responsibility. On the con-the *equilibrium arbitrii,* since no

Whilst, therefore, it is one of the most important efforts of recent Materialism to deduce the whole mass of voluntary movements from mechanical causes, we find Epikuros adopting a quite incalculable element into his system. True, according to him, most human actions are a consequence of the given movements of the material parts, since one motion regularly occasions another. But here we have not only an obvious and violent break in the causal chain, but there lurks behind a further indistinctness as to the nature of the movement. In the case of a living creature, free will—as we see also in the examples mentioned by Lucretius—quickly works very important results, as with the horse that bursts into the course when the barriers are removed. And yet the origin of this is only an infinitely slight collision of individual atoms of the soul. Here we have at bottom a notion apparently very like that of the doctrine that the earth stands still in the midst of the universe, of which more will be said below.

In these errors Demokritos had probably no share; and yet we shall judge them more leniently if we reflect that, even to our own day, the essence of the doctrine of the freedom of the will, with whatever metaphysical subtlety it is elaborated, consists simply of the uncertainty and perplexity of phenomenal appearances.

In order to account for the apparent stillness of objects whose constituent parts are, nevertheless, in the most constant violent motion, the poet employs the illustration of a grazing flock with merpily skipping lambs, of which we see nothing more from a distance than a white spot on the green hillside.

The atoms are represented by Lucretius as extremely various in form. Now smooth and round, now rough and pointed, branched or hook-shaped, they exercise, according to their configuration, a particular influence upon our senses, or upon the properties of the bodies into whose composition they enter. The number of different forms is limited, but there are an unlimited number of each form, and in every body the most various atoms form special relationships with each other; and thus, by means of this combination, as in the combination of letters in words, an incomparably greater variety of bodies is possible than could otherwise result from the different shapes of the atoms.

irary, we might almost regard the image could make it clearer how, by unconscious arbitrariness with which the assumption of such a decision in the soul-atoms decide this way or equilibrium, any intimate connection that, to determine the direction and between the actions of a person and operation of the will, as a satire upon his character is destroyed.

We cannot forbear from taking an extract from a poetical passage proceeding right from the poet's heart, and which is bound up with a criticism of the mythological conception of nature:—" And if any one thinks proper to call the sea Neptune, and corn Ceres, and chooses rather to misuse the name of Bacchus than to utter the term that belongs to that liquor, let us allow him to declare that the earth is mother of the gods, if he only forbear in earnest to stain his mind with foul religion." 69

After Lucretius has further explained that colour and the other sensible qualities do not proceed from the atoms themselves, but are only consequences of their operation in particular relations and combinations, he proceeds to t he important question of the relation between sensation and matter. The fundamental position is that the sentient is developed out of the non-sentient. This view is limited by the poet to this, that it is not possible for sensation to proceed from *anything* under any circumstances,

» H, 655-660 (680):—

"Hie signis maje Neptunum Ceremque vocare Constituit fruges et Bacchi nomine abnti Movolt quam laticis propriam proferre vocamen, Conceilamus ut hie terrarum dictitet orbem Esse deum matrem, dum vera re tamen ipse Beligione animum turpi contingere parent." yor the reading, compare Lach-MSS., but the correction (which Bermann'a "Commentary," p. 112 or nays also adopts) is obvious, since the Munro, in *loc* The last verse has words "dum venire tamen ipse" would fallen out of its right place in the otherwise only weaken the thought.

but that much depends upon the fineness, shape, motion, and arrangement of matter whether it shall produce the sentient or capable of feeling. Sensation is found only in the organic animal body, and here belongs, not to the parts in themselves, but to the whole.

We have thus reached the point where Materialism, however consistently it may be developed in other respects, always, either more or less avowedly, leaves its own sphere. Obviously with the union into a whole a new metaphysical principle has been introduced, that, by the side of the atoms and void space, appears as a sufficiently original supplement.

The proof that sensation belongs not to the individual atoms but to the whole is adduced by Lucretius with some humour. It would not be a bad thing, he thinks, if human atoms could laugh and weep, and speak sagely of the composition of things, and ask in their turn what were their original constituent parts. In any case, they must have such in order to be capable of sensation; and then, again, they would no longer be atoms. It is here, of course, overlooked that developed human sensation may also be a whole composed of various lesser sensations through a peculiar combination of influences, but the essential difficulty, nevertheless, remains unsolved. This sensation of the whole can in no case be a mere consequence of any possible functions of the individual, unless the wbole also has a certain substantial reality, since out of an otherwise impossible summation of the non-sentiency of the atoms no sensation in the whole can arise.

II. 904 foil.: " Nam sensus jungi-special structure, and that the atom tor omuis Visceribus nervis venis." of a sentient body has no separate

The whole passage (a little uncertain existence, and is therefore incapable in its readings) indicates chiefly the in itself of sensation. The poet here *softness* of these particles, which are too comes tolerably near to the Aris therefore specially perishable, and are totelian notion of organisms, and we by no means eternal, or capable, as have no reason to doubt that this waa sentient elements, of propagation the doctrine of Epikuros. (Comp.

from one sentient being to another. 912 sqq.: "Necmanus a nobis potis

Lucretius, however, shows often in estsecreta neque ulla Corporis omnino tho whole passage that they have a sensum pars sola tenere.")

The organic whole is, then, a wholly new principle by the side of the atoms and the void, though it may not be so recognised.

The conclusion of the Second Book consists of a bold and magnificent corollary from the views thus far propounded: the theory of the ancient Materialists of the infinite number of worlds which, at enormous periods and distances, arise near, above, and below each other, last for aeons and then are again dissolved.

Far beyond the limits of our visible universe there exist on all sides innumerable atoms not yet formed into bodies, or that have been for endless ages dispersed again, whicb pursue their quiet fall through spaces and times which no man can measure. But as in every direction through the vast whole the same conditions exist, the phenomena also must repeat themselves. So that above us, below us, beside us, exist worlds in an innumerable host; and if we consider these, all idea of a divine government of the whole must disappear. All these are subject to the processes of becoming and passing away; since they at one time are constantly attracting new atoms from the infinite space, and at another, through the separation of the parts, undergo ever-growing losses. Our earth is already old. The aged peasant shakes his head with a sigh, and ascribes to the piety of our ancestors the bitter fruits of earlier times, which have been more and more corrupted for us by the decay of our world.

In the Third Book of his poem, Lucretius summons all the forces of his philosophy and of his poetry to elucidate the nature of the soul, and to refute the doctrine of immortality, and he starts by trying to get rid of the fear of death. To this terror, which poisons every pure pleasure, the poet ascribes a large share of those passions which drive a man to sin. Poverty seems to those whose hearts are not lightened by the truth to be the gate of death. That he may fly from death man heaps up for himself riches by the vilest sins; nay, the fear VOL. 1. K.

of death can so far blind us that we seek that from which we fly; it may even drive us to suicide, since it makes life intolerable.

Lucretius distinguishes soul *(anima)* and spirit *(animus):* both he explains to be closely united parts of man. As hand, foot, eye, are organs of the living being, so also is the spirit. He rejects the view that makes the soul consist only in the harmony of the whole physical life. The warmth and the breath which leave the body at death are formed by the soul; and the finest inmost portion of it, which is situated in the breast, and alone possesses sensation, is the spirit; both are corporeal, and are composed of the smallest, roundest, and most mobile atoms.

If the bouquet of wine disappears, or the perfume of an unguent is dissipated into the air, we observe no loss of weight; just so is it with the body when the soul has disappeared.

The difficulty which here again suggests itself of fixing the exact seat of sensation is in the most important point completely evaded by the Epikurean system, and in spite of the immense progress of. physiology, the Materialism of the last century found itself at precisely the same point. The individual atoms do not feel, or their feelings could not be fused together, since void space which has no substratum cannot conduct sensation, and still less partake of it. We must therefore constantly fall back on the solution—the motion of the atoms is sensation.

Epikuros, and with him Lucretius, in vain seek to veil this point by saying that, besides the subtle atoms of air, vapour, and heat, of which the soul is supposed to consist, there is still a fourth constituent associated with them, wholly without name, and of the utmost fineness and mobility, which forms the soul of the soul. But with regard to these subtlest soul-atoms, the difficulty still remains the same, as it also does for the vibrating brainfilaments of De la Mettrie.

In another aspect, of course, the defi-

ciency of the theory of motion, supposition of this unnamed ex-Epikuros appears to have supposed— trcmely subtle matter appears to in sharp contrast with our theory of have a carefully considered value; the conservation of force—that a subtle that is, in connection with a great body may pass on its own movement to a heavier, independently of the first the sentient (and will-endowed:
How can the motion of a body, in itself non-sentient, be sensation? Who is it, then, that feels? How does the sensation come about? Where? To these questions Lucretius gives us no answer. Later we shall perhaps meet them again.

An extended refutation of any possible form of the theory of immortality constitutes an important section of the book. We see what stress the poet laid upon this point, since the conclusion is already fully contained in what has preceded. The sum of the whole argument is to show that death is indifferent to us, because when it appears upon the scene there is no longer a subject capable of feeling any evil.

In his fear of death, says the poet, man has, in looking upon the body which decays in the grave, or is destroyed by the flames, or is torn by beasts of prey, ever a secret relic of the idea that he himself must suffer this. Even where he denies this idea he yet nurses it, nor does he "separate himself from that self, nor withdraw himself from the body so thrown out." And so he overlooks the fact that when he really dies he cannot have a duplicate existence, only to torture himself with such a fate. "Now no more shall thy house admit thee with glad welcome, nor a most virtuous wife and sweet children run to be the first to snatch kisses, and touch thy heart with a silent joy. No more mayst thou be prosperous in thy doings, a safeguard to thine own" — so they complain—" one disastrous day has taken from thee, luckless man, in luckless wise, all the many prizes of life." But they forget to add—" And now no longer does any craving for these things beset thee withal." If they would but rightly apprehend this, they would deliver themselves from great distress and fear. "Thou, even as now thou art, sunk in the sleep of death, shalt continue so to be all time to come, and freed from all distressful pains; but we, with a sorrow that would not be sated, wept for thee when close by thou didst turn to ashes on thy appalling funeral pile, and no length of days shall pluck from our hearts our ever-during grief." When any one so speaks, we must ask him what is there in it so passing bitter, if it come in the end to sleep and rest, that any one should pine in never-ending sorrow?
bulk, and this in turn to a still comp. ii. 251-93) element moves the heavier; so that the sum of mechani-caloric, this then in turn the breath cal work done, instead of remaining of life, this the air mingled with the stationary, goes on multiplying from soul, this the blood, and the blood at step to step. Lucretius describes length the solid parts of the body, this gradual rise iii. 246 foil; that

The whole conclusion of the Third Book, from the passage here quoted, contains much that is admirable and remarkable. Nature itself is made to speak, and proves to the man the vanity of his fear of death. Very beautifully also the poet employs the terrible myths of the lower world, which are all transferred to human life and its pains and passions. One might often fancy one's self listening to a Bationalist of the last century, except that we are in the sphere of classical ideas.

It is not that Tantalus in the lower world feels a vain terror of the rock that threatens his head, but that mortal men are so tormented in life by fear of God and death. Our Tityos is not the giant of the under world, who covers nine acres as he lies stretched, and is eternally torn by vultures, but every one who is eaten up by the torments of love or of any other desire. The ambitious man, striving after high office in the state, rolls, like Sisyphos, the huge stone up the mountain, which will straightway roll down again to earth. The grim Cerberus and all the terrors of Tartarus typify the punishments that the transgressor has to fear; since though he escape prison and the ignominy of execution, his conscience must yet punish him with all the terrors of justice.

Heroes and kings, great poets and sages, have died, and men whose life has far less value think it a grievance that they must die. And yet their whole life is spent in tormenting dreams and useless anxieties; they find the cause of their unhappiness now in this thing and again in that, and do not know what they really lack. If they knew this, they would neglect all else, and devote themselves to the study of nature, since it is a question of the state in which man will continue to be for ever after the termination of this life.

The Fourth Book contains the special anthropology. It would lead us too far were we to introduce the numerous and often surprising observations upon which the poet builds his doctrines. These doctrines are those of Epikuros; and as we are concerned not so much with the first beginnings of physiological hypotheses as with the development of important principles, the little we have already recounted of the Epikurean theory of the sensations will suffice.

The conclusion of the book consists of an extended discussion of love and the relations of the sexes. Neither the ordinary notions of the Epikurean system which possess one's mind, nor the brilliant poetical invocation of Venus at the beginning of the poem, lead one to expect the seriousness and impressiveness which the poet here displays. He deals with his theme from a purely physical point of view, and in seeking to explain the development of the sexual impulse, he treats it from the beginning as an evil.

The Fifth Book is devoted to the more special exposition of the development of all that is—of earth and sea, of the stars, and of living beings. Very peculiar is the passage about the stationariness of the earth in the middle of the universe.

The cause assigned for this is the inseparable connection of the earth with atmospheric atoms, which are spread under it, and which are not compressed by it, just because they are from the begimiing in firm union with it. That a certain want of clearness lies at the bottom of this notion we will admit; moreover, the comparison with the human body, which is not burdened by its own members, and is borne about and moved by the fine gaseous particles of the soul, does not help to bring the conception home to us. Yet we must observe that the idea of an absolute rest of the earth lies as far from the poet as it would be obviously inconsistent with the whole system. The universe must, like all the atoms, be conceived as falling, and it is only surprising that the free deviation downwards of the gaseous atoms beneath the earth is not employed as a solution.72

Of course, if Epikuros or his school had fully explained the relations of rest and motion, they would have been many centuries ahead of their time.

The tendency to explain the universe by the possible instead of the actual we have already learnt to know in the case of Epikuros. Lucretius expresses it with such precision, that, taking it in connection with the traditions of Diogenes Laertius, we must come to the conclusion that on this point we have before us not indifference or superficiality, as many suppose, but a determinate, and, as far as is possible with such a foundation, an exact method of the Epikurean school.73 The matter is differently con-sion is expressly admitted by Lucreceived by Zeller (iii. 1, p. 382, E. T. = this (v. 366-372) to be possible, whilst lieichel, Stoics, &c., 425), who main-destruction by many smaller collitains, indeed, that the consistency of sions from the outside is at the same the system would require a falling of time enumerated as one of the natural the worlds (and therefore a *relative* causes for the death of the ageing inotionlcssness of the earth as com-world. As to the manner in which pared with our universe), but without the earth is kept suspended by consupposing that Epikuros drew this stant collisions of subtle atmospheric conclusion. It is not correct, how-atoms, here again the above-menever, to say that in this falling protioned (note 71) peculiarity of the Epicess the world must very soon come kurean theory of motion seems to into collision. Such an accident is underly it, according to which the much more likely to happen only after mechanical influence of impact (as exu long time, considering the immense pressed in our language) multiplies distances which must be supposed to itself in the transition from subtler exist between the individual worlds, to heavier particles. A catastrophe of the worlds by a colli

On the occasion of the question as to the causes of the motions of the stars the poet says:

"For which of these causes is in operation in this world, it is not easy to affirm for certain; but what can be and is done throughout the universe in various worlds formed on various plans, that I teach; and I go on to set forth several causes which may exist throughout the universe for the motions of stars; one of which, however, must in this world also be the cause that imparts lively motion to the signs; but to dictate which of them it is, is by no means the duty of the man who advances step by step." 7

The idea that the entire series of possibilities is in the infinity of worlds somewhere in actual existence, is in complete accordance with the system; to make the sum of the conceivable correspond to that of the actually possible, and therefore the actually existing in some of the infinitely numerous worlds, is a thought which even today may throw a useful cross-light upon the favourite doctrine of the identity of Existence and Thought. Whilst the Epikurean nature-study directs itself to the sum of the conceivable, and not to certain detached possibilities, it passes on also to the sum of the actually existing; only that in the decision as to what is in our particular case, the sceptical *hreyeiv* seizes upon a place and covers an expression which goes further than our real knowledge. With this profound and cautious method, however, the theory of the greater probability of a particular explanation admirably harmonises; and we have, as a matter of fact, many traces of such a preference of the most plausible explanation.

Obviously, of course, there is somewhere and at some time realised here no question of an exact scientific, in the universe, and, in fact, has often but only of an exact philosophical, been realised, and that as an inevitmethod. Further details on this able consequence, on the one hand, of point will be found in the, Neue Beitr. the absolute infinity of the universe, s. Gesch. d. Materialismus Winter-but on the other of the finite and thur, 1867, p. 17 foil. It is interesting everywhere constant number of the that recently a Frenchman (A. Blan-elements, whose possible combinations qui, 'L'Eternitfi par les Astros, Hy-must also be finite. This last also is pothese astronomique,' Paris, 1872), an idea of Epikuros (comp. Lucretius, has carried out again, quite seriously, ii. 480-521). the idea that everything possible is M This passage is v. 527-533:—

"Nam quid in hoc mundo sit eorum ponere ccrt-um Difficile est: sed quid possit fiatque per omne In variis mundis, varia ratione creatis, Id doceo, plurisque sequor disponere causas, Motihus astrorum, quae possuit esse per omne; E quibus una tamen siet haeo quoque causa necessest Quae vegeat motum signis: sed quae sit earum Praecipere haut quaquamst pedetentim progredientis." Compare with this Epikuros's letter to Empedokles, Diog. Laert., x. 87 folL

Amongst the most important portions of the whole work we may reckon those sections of the Fifth Book which treat of the gradual development of the human race. With justice, observes Zeller—who is in other respects not entirely fair to Epikuros—that his philosophy established very sound views upon these questions.

Mankind were much stronger in the primeval times, according to Lucretius, than they now are, and had immense bones and strong sinews. Hardened against frost and heat, they lived, like the animals, without any agricultural arts. The fruitful soil offered them spontaneously the means of life, and they quenched their thirst in streams and springs. They dwelt in forests and caves without morality or law. The use of fire, and even a clothing of skins, were unknown. In their contests with the wild animals they generally conquered, and were pursued by few only. Gradually they learnt to build huts, to prepare the soil for crops, and the use of fire; the ties of family life were formed, and men began to grow more gentle. Friendship grew up between neighbours, mercy to women and children was introduced, and though perfect harmony might not yet reign, yet for the most part men lived in peace with one another.

The manifold sounds of speech were struck out by men at the bidding of nature, and their application formed the names of things, very much as their early development leads children to the employment of language, making them point out with their finger what is before them. As the kid feels its horns and tries to butt with them before they are grown up, as the young panthers and lions defend themselves with their claws and mouth although their talons and teeth are scarcely come, as we see birds early trusting themselves upon their wings, so is it with men in the case of speech. It is, therefore, absurd to believe that some one once gave things their names, and that men had thence learned the first words; for why should one suppose that this one man could utter distinctive sounds, and produce the various tones of language, although, at the same time, the others could not do this? and how could this guide and influence the rest to use sounds whose use and meaning were quite unknown to them?

Even the animals utter entirely different sounds when they are in fear, in pain, and in joy. The Molossian hound, which growls and shows its teeth, barks loudly or plays with its young ones, howls when its master leaves it in the house, or whines as it runs from a blow, utters spontaneously the most different tones. And the same thing is true of other animals. How much more, then, concludes the poet, must we suppose that men in primeval times could indicate the various objects by constantly varying sounds.

In the same way he treats the gradual development of the arts. Lucretius admits the force of sentiments and discoveries, but, in strict fidelity to his theory, he assigns the most important share to the more or less unconscious effort. Only after exhausting many false paths did man attain the right, which then maintains itself by its obvious worth. Spinning and weaving were first invented by men, and only later turned over to women, while men applied themselves again to more difficult labours.

In our own day, when the industry of women, step by step—sometimes even with a leap—is forcing its way into vocations devised and hitherto exclusively pursued bymen, this thought is much more pertinent than in the times of Epikuros and Lucretius, when such transferences of whole professions, so far as we know, did not occur.

And thus into the structure of these historico-philosophical considerations are woven also the thoughts of the poet as to the formation of political and religious arrangements. Lucretius thinks that the men who were distinguished by their talents and their courage began to found cities and build themselves castles, and then as kings shared their lands and goods at their-will among the handsomest, strongest, and cleverest of their adherents. Only later, when gold had been found, were those economic conditions produced which soon enabled riches to exalt themselves above might and beauty. But wealth also gains adherents, and allies itself with ambition. Gradually many strive for power and influence. Envy undermines power, kings are overthrown, and the more their sceptre was before dreaded, the more eagerly is it trodden in the dust. Now the rude mob is for some time supreme, until, from an interregnum of anarchy and transition, law and order are developed.

The remarks here and there interwoven bear that character of resignation and of the dislike of political activity which was, generally speaking, characteristic of ancient Materialism. As Lucretius preaches frugality and contentment in place of the chase after wealth, so he is of opinion that it is far better quietly *(quietus!)* to obey, than to wish to exercise mastery over affairs, and to maintain the form of monarchy. We see that the idea of the old civic virtue and genuine republican community of self-government has disappeared. The praise of passive obedience is equivalent to denying the state to be a moral community.

This exclusive assertion of the standpoint of the individual has been unjustly brought into too close connection with the Atomism of the nature-theory. Even the Stoics, whose whole system in other respects brought politics into near relation with moral action, turned with especial distinctness in later times from public business: on the other hand, the community of the wise, which the Stoics ranked so high, is represented among the Epikureans in the narrower and more exclusive form of friendship.

It is much more the exhaustion of the political energy of the peoples of antiquity, the disappearance of freedom, and the rottenness and hopelessness of the political condition of things, that drives the philosophers of this period into quietism.

Religion is traced oy Lucretius to sources that were originally pure. Waking, and still more in dreams, men beheld in spirit the noble and mighty figures of the gods, and assigned to these pictures of fancy life, sensation, and superhuman powers. But, at the same time, they observed the regular change of the seasons, and the risings and settings of the stars. Since they did not know the reason of these things, they transferred the gods into the sky, the abode of light, and ascribed to them, along with all the celestial phenomena, storm also and hail, the lightning flash, and the growling, threatening thunder.

"O hapless race of men, when that they charged the gods with such acts, and coupled with them bitter wrath! What groanings did they then beget for themselves, what wounds for us, what tears for our children's children!" 75

At some length the poet describes how easy it was for man, when he beheld the terrors of the sky, instead of the quiet contemplation of things which is the only real piety to appease the supposed anger of the gods by sacrifice and 'vows, which yet avail nothing.

The last Book of the poem treats, if I may use the expression, of pathology. Here are explained the causes of the heavenly appearances; lightning and thunder, hail and clouds, the overflowing of the Nile and the eruptions of iEtna are discussed. But, as in the previous Book the early history of mankind forms but a part of the cosmogony; so here the diseases of man are interpolated among the wonderful phenomena of the universe, and the whole work is concluded by a deservedly famous description of the plague. Perhaps the poet intentionally finishes his work with an affecting picture of the might of death, as he had begun it with an invocation to the goddess of springing life.

Lib. v. 1194-1197.

Of the more special contents of the Sixth Book, we will only mention the lengthy account of the 'Avernian spots,' and of the phenomena of the loadstone. The former especially challenged the rationalising tendency of the poet, the latter offered a special difficulty to his explanation of nature, which he attempts to overcome by a very careful and involved hypothesis.

'Avernian spots' was the name given by the ancients to such places in the ground as are not seldom found in Italy, Greece, and Asia Minor, in which the ground gives vent to gases which produce stupefaction or death in men and animals. The popular belief naturally supposed that there was a connection between these places and the lower world, the realm of the god of death, and explained the fatal influence by the uprising of spirits and demons of the shadowy realm, who try to drag down with them the souls of the living. The poet then attempts to show, from the various nature of the atoms, how they must be either beneficial or hurtful to different creatures, some to one kind and some to another. He then examines the case of many kinds of poisons, which spread imperceptibly, and mentions, in addition to some superstitious notions, the cases of metal-poisoning by working in mines, and, what is most pertinent to his problem, the fatal action of carbonic vapours. Of course he attributes this, since the ancients were not acquainted with carbonic acid, to malodorous sulphurous vapours. The Tightness of his conclusion to a poisoning of the air by exhalations from the ground in these places may well supply a proof how an orderly and analogical study of nature, even without the application of more stringent methods, must lead to great advances in knowledge.

The explanation of the operation of the magnet, inadequate as it may otherwise be, affords us a view of the exact and consequent carrying out of hypotheses which is characteristic of the whole natural philosophy of the Epikureans. Lucretius reminds us, to begin with, of the continual extremely rapid and tempestuous motions of the subtle atoms which circulate in the pores of all bodies, and stream out from their surfaces. Every body, on this view, is always sending out in every direction streams of such atoms, which produce a ceaseless interchange amongst all the objects in space. It is a theory of universal emanation as against the vibration theory of modern physical science. The relations of these interchanges in themselves, apart from their form, have been in our own days not only demonstrated by experiment, but have had an incomparably greater importance assigned to them in their kind, quantity, and rapidity than the boldest imaginations of the Epikureans could have conceived.

Lucretius tells us that from the magnet there proceeds such a violent stream outwards, that it produces through the driving out of the air a vacuum between the magnet and the iron, into which the iron rushes. That there is no idea here of a mystically acting '*horror vacui*' is, of course, obvious, if we consider the physical philosophy of this school. The result is rather produced because every body is constantly assailed on every hand by blows from atmospheric atoms, and must therefore yield in any direction in which a passage opens itself, unless its weight is too great, or its density is so slight that the air-atoms can make their way unhindered through the pores of the body. And this explains why it is iron of all things that is so violently attracted by the magnet. The poem refers it simply to its structure and its specific gravity; other bodies being partly too heavy, as in the case of gold, to be moved by the streams, and so carried through the void space to the magnet, and partly, as in the case of wood, so porous, that tha streams can fly through them freely without any mechanical collision.

This explanation leaves much still unexplained, but the whole treatment of the subject advantageously contrasts with the hypotheses and theories of the Aristotelian school by its vividness and clearness. We first ask, how is it possible that the currents from the magnet can expel the air without repelling the iron by the same force? And it might have been readily ascertained by an easy experiment that into the void created by rarefied air, not iron alone, but all other bodies, are carried. But the fact that we can raise such objections shows that the attempt at an explanation is a fruitful one, whilst the assumption of secret forces, specific sympathies, and similar devices, is hostile to all further reflection.

This example also shows us, it is true, why this fashion of natural inquiry could make so little progress in antiquity. Almost all the real achievements of physical science among the ancients, are mathematical, and therefore in astronomy, in statics and mechanics, and in the rudiments of optics and acoustics. There was further a valuable mass of materials accumulated by the descriptive sciences; but everywhere, where what was needed was the attainment by the variation and combination of observations to the discovery of laws, the ancients remained in a backward condition. To the Idealist was lacking the sense for and interest in concrete phenomena; the Materialists were always too much inclined to stop short with a single observation, and to content themselves with the first explanation that offered itself, instead of probing the matter to the bottom.

We may compare the well-known and tho plate (Miiller'» Physik., L 9, experiment in which n plate which is 96). Even though we cannot assume held over the opening of a vessel that the Epikureans were acquainted through which a stream of air is flow-with this phenomenon, yet they may ing, is attracted and held fast because have conceived 'in a similar way the the air, which streams rapidly side-expulsion of the air by the currents wards, is rarefied between the vessel proceeding from the stone. *SECOND SECTION.* THE PERIOD OF TRANSITION *SECOND SECTION.* THE PERIOD OP TRANSITION. CHAPTER I. THE MONOTHEISTIC RELIGIONS IN THEIR RELATION

TO MATERIALISM.

The disappearance of the ancient civilisation in the early centuries of the Christian era is an event the serious problems of which are in great part still unexplained.

It is difficult enough to follow the intrioate events of the Eoman Empire in all their extent, and to grasp the important facts; but it is incomparably more difficult to estimate in their full extent the workings of the slight but endlessly multiplied changes in the daily intercourse of nations, in the hearts of the lower orders, by the hearth of humble families, whether in the city or the countryside.

And yet, so much at least is certain, that from the lower and middle strata of the population alone is this mighty revolution to be explained.

A very valuable insight into the physiology of nations has been recently afforded us by the consideration of history from the standpoints of the *natural tcienco* and of *political economy,* and the light thus kindled extends into the poorest hevels; yet it shows us only one side of the matter, and the changes in the *intellectual* condition of peoples remain still covered with darkness, so far as they cannot be explained from the social changes. Liebig's theory of VOL. L the exhaustion of the soil has been carried by Carey (Principles of Social Science, vol. i. chaps, iii. ix., vol. iii. chap, xlvi., &c.) to wrong and exaggerated conclusions, and been fused with entirely absurd doctrines (romp. my essay, Mill's Ansichten iiber die sociale Frage u. d. angebl. UmwalzungderSocialwissensch.durch Carey, Duisb. 1866), but the correctness of this theery in its main features, and its applicability to the civilisation of the old world, cannot be doubted. L

We have, unhappily, been accustomed to regard the socalled law which governs the development of philosophy as a peculiar mysteriously working force, which necessarily leads us from the sunlight of knowledge back into the night of superstition, only to begin its course again from thence under newer and higher forms. It is with this impulse of national development as it is with the lifeforce of organisms. It is there—but there only as the resultant of all the natural forces. To assume it frequently helps our observations; but it veils their uncertainty, and leads to errors if we set it down as a complementary explanation by the side of those elements with the sum of which it is really identical.

The corn-exporting provinces must have gradually become poor and depopulated, while around Rome, and likewise about the subordinate centres, wealth and population led to the most forced system of agriculture, in which heavily-manured and carefully cultivated little gardens produced richer results in fruit, flowers, &c., than extensive holdings in distant neighbourhoods. (Comp. Roscher, Nationalokon. des Ackerbaus, § 46, where it is said, *inter alia,* that single, fruit-trees in the vicinity of Rome produced as much as 15 yearly, while wheat in Italy for the most part produced only fourfold, because only inferior soils were devoted to the growing of wheat.) But the whole concentrated economy of the have come with increasing acceleration, as soon as the pauperisation and depopulation of the provinces was so far gone that, even by means of increased pressure, their contributions could no longer be kept up to their standard. The whole picture of this process would, so far as the Roman Empire is concerned, be much more clearly displayed to us, but that the advantages of a magnificent and powerfully maintained centralising process among the great emperors of the second century counterbalanced the evil, and, in fact, evoked a new period of material splendour at the very brink of the general downfall. It is upon this last brilliant display of the ancient civilisation, the benefits of which fell, of course, for the most rich commercial centre is not only part, to the towns and to certain more sensitive to blows from without than the economy of a country in more moderate circumstances, but it is also dependent upon the productiveness of the circle which delivers to the centre the indispensable necessaries of life. The devastation of a fertile country by war, even though it is accompanied by a decimation of its inhabitants, is speedily compensated by the efforts of nature and of man; while a blow inflicted upon the capital, especially if the resources of the provinces are already diminishing, very easily produces complete ruin, because it hampers the entire system of commercial exchange at its centre, and so suddenly annihilates the exaggerated values enjoyed and created by luxury. But even without such blows from without, the fall must favoured tracts of country, that tbo favourable picture chiefly rests which Gibbon draws of the condition of the Empire in the first chapter of the "History of the Decline and Fall of the Roman Empire." It is evident, however, that the economic evil to which the Empire must ultimately succumb had already attained a serious development. A splendour which rests upon the accumulation and concentration of riches can very easily reach its climax if the means of accumulation are already beginning to disappear, just as the greatest heat of the day occurs when the sun is already setting.

Much earlier must the moral ruin appear in this great process of centralisation, because the subjection and fusion of numerous and utterly ilif ferent peoples and races brings confusion not only into the specific forms of morality, but also into its very principles. Lecky shows quite rightly (History of European Morals from Augustus to Charlemagne, 1869, vol. i. p. 271 foil.) how the Roman virtue, so intimately fused with the local patriotism of the early Romans and the native religion, must inevitably perish through the destruction of the old political forms, and the rise of scepticism and introduction of foreign cults. That the progress of civilisation did not substitute new and superior virtues—" gentler manners and enlarged benevolence"—in place of the old ones, is attributed to three causes: the Empire, slavery, and the gladiatorial games. Does this not involve a confusion of cause and effect? Compare the admirable contrast just before drawn by Lecky himself between the noble sentiments of the Emperor Marcus Aurelius and the character of the masses over whom he ruled. The individual can raise himself with the help of philosophy to ethical principles which are independent of religion and politics; the masses of the people found morality—and that still more in antiquity than in our own days—only in the connection, which had been taught in local traditions, and had become inseparable, of the general and the individual, of the permanently valid and the variable; and accordingly the great centralisation of the world-empire must in this sphere have exercised everywhere, alike amongst conquerors and conquered, a dissolving and disturbing influence. Where, however, is the ' normal condition of society " (Lecky, *loc.* eft., p. 271) which could forthwith replace by new ones the virtues of the perishing social order? Time, above all things, and, as a rule, also the appearance of a new type of people, are needed for the fusion of moral principles with sensational elements and fanciful additions. And so the same process of accumulation and concentration which developed the ancient civilisation to its utmost point appears also as the cause of its fall. In fact, the peculiarly enthusiastic feature of the fermenting process from which mediaeval Christianity finally proceeded seems to find its explanation here; for it distinctly points to an overstraining of the nervous system by the extremes of luxury and abstinence, voluptuousness and suffering,extending through all classes of the population; and this condition, again, is merely a consequence of the accumulation of wealth, although, indeed, slavery lends to its consequences a specially disagreeable colouring. For the facts as to the accumulation in ancient Rome, see Eoscher, Grundl. der Nationalbkon. § 204, and especially Anm. 10; for the seuseless luxury of decaying nations, *ibid.,* § 233 ff., as well as the essay on luxury in Reseller's Ansichten der Volkswirthschaft aua geschichtl. Standpunkte.' The influence of slavery has been specially pointed out by Coutzen, Die Sociale Frage, ihre Geschichte, Lite rat ur u. Eedeut. in d. Gegenw., 2te Anfl., Leipzig, 1872. Compare also the following note.

For our purpose it is well to keep in mind that ignorance cannot be the proper consequence of knowledge, or fantastic caprice the consequence of method; that rationalism does not, and never can of itself, lead us back to superstition. We have seen how in antiquity, amidst the progress of rationalism, of knowledge, of method, the intellectual aristocracy broke away from the masses. The lack of a thorough popular education must have hastened and intensified this separation. Slavery, which was in a sense the basis of the whole civilisation of antiquity, changed its character in imperial times, and became only the more untenable because of the efforts that were made to ameliorate this dangerous institution.2

The increasing intercourse of nations began to produce amongst the superstitious masses a confusion of religions. Oriental mysticism veiled itself in Hellenic forms. At Rome, whither the conquered nations flocked, there was soon no creed that did not find believers, while there was none that was not scoffed at by the majority. To the fanaticism of the deluded multitude was opposed either a lighthearted contempt or a blase indifference: the formation of sharp, well-disciplined parties, amidst the universal division of interests among the higher classes, had become impossible.

Gibbon, Hist. of the Decline, &c., i. 318, rightly distinguishes three chap, ii., describes how the slaves, periods in the position of the slaves: who had become comparatively the earliest, in which they were a part cheaper since the Koman conquests, of the family, and were comparatively rose in value, and were better treated well treated; the second, in which in cousequence, with the falling off their numbers were very largely inin the importation of prisoners of creased, while their treatment grew war, who in the times of the wars of worse; and finally, the third, which conquest had often been sold by begius with the turning-points indithousands at a very cheap rate. It cated by Gibbon. Lecky specially became more and more necessary to points out, too, the influence of ths breed slaves at home, and to promote Stoic philosophy in the milder treatmarriages amongst them. By this ment of the slaves, means the whole mass, which had Slavery no longer reacted in this previously on every estate, often with third period upon the civilisation of the most careful calculation (see the the ancient world by means of the letters of Cato in Contzen, *loc. cit.* , dread of great servile wars, hut did S. 174), been composed of as many so, of course, by the influence which different nationalities as possible, be-the subject class more and more exercame more homogeneous. To this cised on the whole modes of thought was added the ennrmous accumula-of the population. This influence, tion of slaves on the large estates and one diametrically opposed to the in the palaces of the rich;and again, ancient ideals, became especially too, the important part played by marked with the spread of Christian*the frced-men* in the social life of im-ity. Comp. as to this Lecky, Hist. perial times. Lecky, *loc. cit.,* Eur. Morals, ii. 66 foil.

Into these masses there forced a way through the incredible growth of literature, through the desultory studies of officious spirits, through daily intercourse, disjected fragments of scientific discoveries, and produced that state of semi-culture which has been declared, perhaps with less reason, to characterise our own days. We must not, however, forget that this semi-culture was chiefly the condition of the rich and powerful, of the men of influence up to the imperial throne. The fullest social training, elegant social traits in wide command of affairs, are, in a philosophical sense, only too often united with the most pitiable deficiencies, and the dangers which are attributed to the doctrines of philosophers tend to become only too real in those circles where the flexible, unprincipled semi-culture is a slave of natural inclinations or disordered passions.

When Epikuros, with a lofty enthusiasm, flung away the fetters of religion, that he might be righteous and noble, because it was a delight to be so, there came these profligate favourites of the moment, as they are pictured in rich variety by Horace and Juvenal and Petronius, who, with shameless front, rushed into the most unnatural forms of vice; and who was there to protect poor Philosophy when such reprobates claimed the name of Epikuros, if indeed they did not claim that of the Porch?

Contempt of the popular belief was here assumed as a mask for inner hollowness, utter absence of belief and true knowledge. To smile at the idea of immortality was a sign of vice: but the vice was due to the circumstances of the time, and had arisen not through, but in spite of philosophy.

And in these very classes the priests of Isis, the thaumaturgists, and prophets,-with their train of jugglery, found a rich harvest; nay, sometimes even the Jews found a proselyte. The utterly uneducated mob shared in the towns the character of characterlessness with the great in their semi-culture. Thence ensued, then, in those times, in the fullest bloom, that practical Materialism, as it may be called—Materialism of life.

On this point also the prevailing notions require an explanation. There is also a Materialism of life which, reviled by some, prized by others, may, by the side of any other practical tendency, still venture to show its face.

When effort is directed not to transitory enjoyment, but to a real perfecting of our condition; when the energy of material enterprise is guided by a clear calculation, which in all things has ultimate principles in view, and therefore reaches its aim; then there ensues that giant progress which in our own time has made England in two hundred years a mighty people, which in the Athens of Perikles went hand in hand with the highest blossom of intellectual life which any state has ever attained.

But of quite another character was the Materialism of Imperial Home, which repeated itself at Byzantium, Alexandria, and in all the capitals of the Empire. Here also the search for money dominated the distracted multitudes, as we see in the trenchant pictures of Juvenal and Horace; but there were lacking the great principles of the elevation of national power, of the utilisation for the common advantage of national resources, which ennoble a Materialistic tendency, because, though they start from matter, yet they leaven it with force. This would result in the Materialism of prosperity: Eome knew that of decay. Philosophy is compatible with the first, as with all that has principles; she disappears, or has rather already disappeared, when those horrors break in of which we will here forbear to say anything.

Mommsen, History of Rome, fcions ii-ito Rome. "When the Senate
E. T., iv. 560 (chap, xii.), observes: (in 50 B.C.) ordered the temples of Isis
' Unbelief and superstition, different constructed within the ring-wall to be hnes of the same historical phenome- pulled down, no labourer ventured to non, went in the Roman world of that lay the first hand on them, and the day hand in hand, and there was no consul Lucius Paullus was himself lack of individuals who themselves obliged to apply the first stroke of the combined both—who denied the gods axe. A wager might be laid that the with Epikuros, and yet prayed and more lax any woman was, the more sacrificed before every shrine." In piously she worshipped Isis. " the same chapter are some details as Compare further Lecky, Hist. Eur.
to the introduction of Oriental reli- Mjrals, i. 338 folL

Yet we must point out the undeniable fact, that, in the centuries when the abominations of a Nero, a Caligula, or even of a Heliogabalus, polluted the globe, no philosophy was more neglected, none was more foreign to the spirit of the time, than that of all which demanded the coldest blood, the calmest contemplation,the most sober and purelyprosaic inquiry—the philosophy of Demokritos and Epikuros.

The age of Perikles was the blossoming-time of the materialistic and sensationalistic philosophy of antiquity: its fruits ripened in the time of Alexandrian learning, in the two centuries immediately before Christ.

But as the masses under the Empire were drunk with the double intoxication of vice and of the mysteries, no sober disciple was to be found, and philosophy died out. In those times, as everybody knows, prevailed Neo-Platonic and Neo-Pythagorean systems, in which many nobler elements of the past were overpowered by fanaticism and Oriental mysticism. Plotinus was ashamed that he had a body, and would never name his parents. Here we have already in philosophy the height of the anti-Materialistic tendency—an element that was still mightier in the field to which it properly belonged—that of Religion. Never have religions flourished with such wild luxuriance and in such wide variety, from the purest to the most abominable shapes, as in the three first centuries after Christ. No wonder, then, that even the philosophers of this time often appeared as priests and apostles. Stoicism, whose doctrine had naturally a theological turn, first yielded to this tendency, and was therefore the longest respected of the older schools, till it was outbid and supplanted by the ascetic mysteries of Neo-Platonism.5 It is therefore at once unfair and pendent as Draper shows himself in inaccurate when Draper, in his in hisfinaljudgmentsandhiswholemoda many respects valuable "History of of thought, there nevertheless appears the Intellectual Development of Eu-in his account of Epikuros, and per rope," identifies Epikureanism with haps still more in the way in which the hypocritical infidelity of the men he makes Aristotle an experience of the world, to whom society is in-philosopher, the obvious influence of debted for more than half its corruperroneous traditions, tions" (vol. i. pp. 168, 169). Inde

It has been often said that incredulity and superstition further and excite each other; yet we must not allow ourselves to be dazzled by the antithesis. Only by weighing the specific causes and by the severe discrimination of time and circumstance can we see how far it is true.

When a rigorously scientific system, resting upon solid principles, on well-considered grounds excludes faith from science, it will most certainly, and even more entirely, exclude all vague superstitions. In times, however, and under circumstances in which scientific studies are as much disordered and disorganised as the national and primitive forms of faith, this proposition has indeed its application. So was it in imperial times.

Zeller, Phil. d. Griech., iii. I, S. who iesorted to thom for a solution of289, E. T. tr. Keichel (= Stoics, &c.), perplexing cases of practical morals, p. 323: "In a word, Stoicism is not or under the influence of despondency only a philosophic, but also a religious or remorse. " For the extinction of system. As such it was regarded by the Stoic influence, and its supplant its first adherents,... and as such, ing by the Neo-Platonic mysticism, together with Platonism, it afforded comp. Lecky, *loc cit.*, p. 337. in subsequent times, to the best and Zeller, iii. 2, S. 381, observes: "Neo most cultivated men, a substitute for Platonism is a religious system, and declining natural religion, a satisfac-it is so not merely in the sense in tion for religious cravings, and a sup-which Platonism and Stoicism may port for moral life, wherever the in-also be so described: it is not merely flnencc of Greek culture extended." content to apply to the moral duties Lecky, Hist. Eur. Morals, i. 327, and spiritual life of man a philosophy says of the Roman Stoics of the first starting from the idea of God, but two centuries: "On oocasions of nevertheless attained by a scientific family bereavement, when the mind method. But even its scientific view is most susceptible of impressions, of the world reflects from first to last they were habitually called in to con-the religious disposition of man. and sole the survivors. Dying men asked is thoroughly dominated by the wish their comfort and support in the last to meet his religious needs, and to hours of their life. They became the bring him into the most intimate per drectors of the conscience of numbers sonal oommunion with the Deity."

There was then, in truth, no tendency, no need of life which had not a corresponding religious form; but by the side of the wanton festivals of Bacchus, the secret and alluring mysteries of Isis, there silently spread, wider and wider, the love of a strict and self-denying asceticism.

As in the case of individuals who have become blase and enervate after exhausting all pleasures, at last the one charm of novelty remains—that of an austere, selfdenying life; so was it on a large scale in the ancient world; and thus it was only natural that this new tendency, being as it was in sharpest contrast with the cheerful sensuousness of the older world, led men to an extreme of world-avoidance and self-renunciation.

Christianity, with its wonderfully fascinating doctrine of the kingdom that is not of this world, seemed to offer the most admirable support to these views.

The religion of the oppressed and the slave, of the weary and heavy-laden, attracted also the luxurious rich who could no longer be satisfied with luxury and wealth. And so with the principle of renunciation was allied that of universal brotherhood, which contained new spiritual delights for the heart seared by selfishness. The longing of the wandering and isolated spirit after a close tie of community and a positive belief was satisfied; and the firm coherence of the believers, the imposing union of communities ramifying everywhere through the wide world, effected more for the propagation of the new religion than the mass of miracles that was related to willingly believing ears. Miracle was, in short, not so much a missionary instrument as a necessary complement of faith in a time that set no measure to its love or its belief in miracles. In this respect not only did priests of Isis and magicians compete with Christianity, but even philosophers appeared in the character of miracle-workers and Godaccredited prophets. The feats of a Cagliostro and a Gassner in modern times are but a faint copy of the performances of Apollonius of Tyana, the most famous of the prophets, whose miracles and oracles were partly believed even by Lucian and Origen. But the result of all this was to show that only simple and consistent principles can work a lasting miracle—that miracle, at least, which gradually united the scattered nations and creeds around the altar of the Christians. An account of this extreme, as it third century, is to be found in Lccky, uiade itself specially felt after the Hist. Eur. Morals, ii. 107 foil.

Christianity, by preaching the gospel to the poor, unhinged the ancient world. What will appear in the fulness of time as an actual fact, the spirit of faith already apprehended in imagination—the kingdom of love, in which the last are to be first. The stern legal idea of the Romans, which built order upon force, and made property the immovable foundation of human relations, was met by a demand, made with incredible weight, that one should renounce all private claims, should love one's enemies, sacrifice one's treasures, and esteem the malefactor on the scaffold equally with one's self.

As to the spread of Christianity, compare the celehrated fifteenth chapter of Gibbon, which is full of material for the estimation of this fact from the most varied standpoints. More correct views, however, are put forward by Lecky in his "History of European Morals," and in the "History of Rationalism in Europe." As the chief work on the theological side, may be named Eaur, das Christenthum, u. die christliche Kirche der drei ersten Jahrhunderte. From the philosophico-historical standpoint, E. von Lasaulx, der Untergang des Hellenismus u. die Einziehung seiner Tempelgiiter durch die christl.Kaiser, Munchen, 1854. For further literature, see in TJeberweg in the "History of the Patristic Philosophy," a section of his history which unfortunately has not met with the approbation it deserves (comp. my Biographie Ueberwegs, Berlin, 1871, S. 21, 22). On the miracle-mania which marked this period, compare particularly Lecky, Hist. of Eur. Morals, i. 393. Also p. 395 as to miracleworking philosophers: " Christianity floated into the Roman Empire on the wave of credulity that brought with it this long train of Oriental superstitions and legends.... Its miracles were accepted by both friend and foe as the ordinary accompaniments of religious teaching." How much the influence of the Christian care for the poor was felt is shown by the remarkable fact that Julian 'the Apostate,' in his attempt to supplant Christianity by a philosophic Greek State-religion, Ofienly recognised the superiority of Christianity in this respect to the old religion. He recommended, accordingly, in order to rival the Christians in this respect, the establishment in every town of Xenodocheia, in which strangers should be received without respect to creed. For the maintenance of them, and also for distribution to the poor, he devoted considerable sums of money. "For it is disgraceful," he wrote to Arsacius, the high-priest of the Galatians, "that no one of the Jews begs, while the atheistic Galileans not only maintain their own poor, but also any whom we leave helpless.''—Lasaulx, Untergang des Hellenismus, S. 68.

A mysterious awe of these doctrines seized the ancient world, and those in power sought in vain by cruel persecutions to repress a revolution which overturned all existing things, and laughed not only at the prison and the stake, but even at religion and law. In the bold self-sufficiency of the salvation which a Jewish traitor, who had suffered the death of a slave, had brought down from heaven as a gracious gift from the eternal Father, this sect conquered country after country, and was able, while clinging to its main principles, little by little to press into the service of the new creation the superstitious ideas, the sensuous inclinations, the passions, and the legal conceptions of the heathen world, since they could not be wholly destroyed. The place of old Olympus, with its wealth of myth, was occupied by the saints and martvrs. Gnosticism constituted the elements

'Compare Tacitus, Annals, xv. 44, where it is saiil that Nero laid the blame of the burning of Rome upon the Christians. He "inflicted the most exquisite tortures on a class hated for their abominations, called Christians by the populace. Christus, from whom the name had its origin,suffered the extreme penalty during the reign of Tiberius, at the hands of one of our procurators, Pontius Filatus, and a most mischievous superstition, thus checked for the moment, again broke out, not only in Judaea, the first source of the evil, but even in Rome, where all things hideous and shameful from every part of the world find their centre and become popular. Accordingly, an arrest was first made of all who pleaded guilty; then, upon their information, an immense multitude was convioted, not so much of the crime of firing the city, as of hatied against mankind." Their asso ciating amongst themselves, together with their hatred of others, Whs frequently made a subject of reproach to the Jews also. Lasaulx, Untergang des Hellenismus, S. 7 foil., shows the internal necessity of this view of the Romans, and quotes similar judgments froir, Suetonius and the younger l'liny. In the same place, very accuratereferences to theintolerance (strange to Greeks and lloinan.j alike) of the Monotheistic religions, amongst which Christianity particularly from the first took up an *offensive* attitude. Gibbon reckons as one of the chief oauses of the rapid propagation of Christianity its intolerant zoal, and the expectation of another world. For the threatening of the whole human race with the everlasting torments of hell, and the influence of this threat upon the Romans, comp. Lecky, Hist. Eur. Morals, i 447 foil.

of a Christian philosophy. Christian schools of rhetoric were opened for all those who sought to combine the ancient culture with the new belief. From the simple and austere discipline of the early Church were developed the elements of a hierarchy. The bishops gathered unto themselves riches, and led an arrogant and worldly life; the rabble of the great cities became intoxicated with hatred and fanaticism. The care of the poor disappeared, and the usurious rich protected their nefarious gains by a system of police. The festivals speedily resembled in their wantonness and ostentation those of the decaying heathenism, and the piety of devotion in the surge of disordered emotions appeared bent upon destroying the life-germs of the new religion. But it was not so destroyed. Struggling against the foreign forces, it made its way. Even the ancient philosophy, which, from the turbid sources of Neo-Platonism, poured into the Christian world, had to adapt itself to the character of this religion; and whilst cunning, treachery, and cruelty helped to found the Christian state—in itself a contradiction—the thought of the equal calling of all men to a higher existence remained the basis of modern popular development. So, says Schlosser, was the caprice and deceit of mankind one of the means by which the Deity developed a new life from the mouldering ruins of the ancient world.10

It now becomes our duty to examine the influence that the carrying out of the Christian principle must have exercised upon the history of Materialism, and with this we will connect the consideration of Judaism and of Mohammedanism, which latter is of special importance.

What these three religions have in common is Monotheism.

When the heathen regards everything as full of gods, and has become accustomed to treat every individual event as the special sphere of some daemonic influence, the difficulties which are thus opposed to a Materialistic explanation of the universe are as thousandfold as the ranks of the divine community. If some inquirer conceives the mighty thought of explaining everything that happens out of necessity, of the reign of laws, and of an eternal matter whose conduct is governed by rules, there is no more any reconciliation possible with religion. Epikuros's forced attempt at mediation is but a weakly effort, therefore, and more consistent were those philosophers who denied the existence of the gods. But the Monotheist occupies a different position in relation to science. We admit that even Monotheism admits of a low and sensuous interpretation, in which every particular event is again attributed to the special and local activity of God in anthropomorphic fashion. And this is the more possible because every man naturally thinks only of himself and his own surroundings. The idea of omnipresence remains a mere empty formula, and one has really again a multiplicity of gods, with the tacit proviso that we shall conceive them all as one and the same.

Schloaser, Weltgesch. f. J. deutsche Volk, bearb. v. Kriegk, *ir.* 426 Geach. der Bomer, liv. 7).

From this standpoint, which is peculiarly that of the charcoal-burner's creed, science remains as impossible as it was in the case of the heathen creed.

Only when we have a liberal theory of the harmonious guidance of the whole universe of things by one God, does the cause and effect connection between things become not only conceivable, but is, in fact, a necessary consequence of the theory. For if I were to see anywhere thousands upon thousands of wheels in motion, and supposed that there was one who appeared to direct them all, I should be compelled to suppose that I had before me a mechanism in which the movements of all the smallest parts are unalterably determined by the plan of the whole. But if I suppose this, then I must be able to discover the structure of the machine, at least partially to understand its working, and so a way is opened on which science may freely enter.

For this very reason developments might go on for centuries, and enrich science with positive material, before it would be necessary to suppose that this machine was a *perpetuum mobile.* But when once entertained, this conclusion must appear with a weight of facts by the side of which the apparatus of the old Sophists appears to us utterly weak and inadequate.

And here, therefore, we may compare the working of Monotheism to a mighty lake, which gathers the floods of science together, until they suddenly begin to break through the dam.

But then there came into view a fresh trait of Monotheism. The main idea of Monotheism possesses a dogmatic ductility and a speculative ambiguity which specially adapt it, amid the changing circumstances of civilisation, and in the greatest advances of scientific culture, to serve as the support of religious life. The theory of a recurrent or independent regulation of the uuiverse, in pursuance of eternal laws, did not, as might have been expected, lead at once to a mortal struggle between religion and science; but, on the contrary, there arose an attempt to compare the relation between God and the world to that of body and soul. The three great Monotheistic religions have therefore all, in the period of the highest intellectual development of their disciples, tended to Pantheism. And even this involves hostility to tradition; but the strife is very far from being mortal.

It is the Mosaic creed which was the first of all religions to conceive the idea of creation as a creation out of nothing.

Let us call to mind how the young Epikuros, according to the story, while yet at school, began to devote hiinself to philosophy, when he was obliged to learn that all things arose from chaos, and when none of his teachers could tell him what then was the origin of chaos.

There are peoples which believe that the earth rests upon a tortoise, but you must not ask on what the tortoise rests. So easily is mankind for many generations contented with a solution which no one could find really satisfactory.

This in modern times refers espe-the popularising of Newton's system daily to the turning-point made by of the universe by Voltaire.

By the side of such fantasies the creation of the world from nothing is at least a clear and honest theory. It contains so open and direct a contradiction of all thought, that all weaker and more reserved contradictions must feel ashamed beside it.

But what is more: even this idea is capable of transformation; it too has a share of the elasticity which characterises Monotheism; the attempt was ventured to make the priority of a worldless God one purely of conception, and the days of creation became aeons of development.

In addition to these features, which had already belonged to Judaism, it is important that Christianity first requires that God shall be conceived as free from any physical shape, and strictly as an invisible spirit. Anthropomorphism is thus set aside, but returns first in the turbid popular conception, and then a hundredfold in the broad historical development of the dogma.

We might suppose, since these are the prominent traits of Christianity, that, when it gained its victory, a new science might have blossomed more luxuriantly; but it is easy to see why that was not the case. On the one hand we must bear in mind that Christianity was a popular religion, which had developed and spread from beneath upwards until the point at which it became the religion of the State. But the philosophers were just the people who stood furthest removed from it, and the more so as they were the less inclined to pietism or the mystical treatment of philosophy. Christianity extended itself to new peoples hitherto inaccessible to civilisation, and it is no wondei that in a school beginning again from the foundations, all those preliminary steps had again to be made which ancient Greece and Italy had been through since the period of the earliest colonisations. Above all, however, wc must bear in mind that the emphasis of the Christian doctrine by no means rested originally on its great theological principles, but much rather on the sphere of moral purification through the renunciation of worldly desires, on the theory of redemption, and on the hope of the advent of Christ.

It is interesting to observe how, It is true, indeed, that the mystic in Mo-

hammedan orthodoxy, recourse Neo-Platonists such as Plotinus nnd is had to atoms to render more intel-Porphyry were decided opponents of ligible the transcendental creation by Christianity (Porphyry wrote fifteen a God who is outside the universe, books against the Christians), but iu
Compare Kenan, Averroes et l'Avcr-ternally they stood very near to the roume, Paris, 1S52, p. So. Christian doctrine, just as it cannot be doubted that they acquired great sceptics of the school of Aenesidemus

Moreover, it was a psychological necessity that as soon as this immense success had restored religion generally to its ancient privileges, heathen elements in mass forced their way into Christianity, so that it speedily acquired a rich mythology of its own. And so, not merely Materialism, but all consistent monistic philosophy, became, for hundreds of years to come, an impossibility.

But a dark shadow fell especially upon Materialism. The dualistic tendency of the religion of the Zend-Avesta, in which the world and matter represent the evil principle, God and light the good, is related to Christianity in its fundamental idea, and especially in its historical development. Nothing, therefore, could appear more repugnant than that tendency of the ancient philosophy, which not only assumed an eternal matter, but went so far as to make this the only really existing substance. If we add the Epikurean moral principle, however purely it may be conceived, the true antithesis of the Christian theory is complete, and we can comprehend the perverse condemnation of this system which prevailed in the Middle Ages.1
influence over the late development and the "empirical physicians" of Christian philosophy. Much fur-(Zeller, iii. *a,* 2 Aufl. S. 1 foil.), eepe ther really stood Galen and Celsus cially Sextus Empiricus.
(although he, too, is not, as was for-From a very early period, there merly believed, an Epikurean, but a fore, dates the vulgarisation of the
Platonist: See TJeberweg's Hist. of no-tions of 'Epikurean' and 'Epiku rhil. S 65). Furthest removed are the reanism' in the sense of absolute opposition to the transcendental theism and Dante describes as lying in fiery-pits

In this last point, the third of the great monotheistic religions, Mohammedanism, is more favourable to Materialism. This, the youngest of them, was also the first to develop, in connection with the brilliant outburst of Arabian civilisation, a free philosophical spirit, which exercised a powerful influence primarily upon the Jews of the middle ages, and so indirectly upon the Christians of the West.

Even before the communication of Greek philosophy to the Arabians, Islam had produced numerous sects and theological schools, some of which entertained so abstract a notion of God that no philosophical speculation could proceed further in this direction, whilst others believed nothing but what could be understood and demonstrated; others, again, combined fanaticism and incredulity into fantastic systems. In the high school at Basra there arose, under the protection of the Abbassides, a school of rationalists which sought to reconcile reason and faith.15

By the side of this rich stream of purely Islamitic theology and philosophy, which has not unjustly been compared with the Christian Scholasticism, the Peripatetics of whom we usually think when the Arabian medieval philosophy is mentioned, form but a relatively unimportant branch, with little internal variety; and Averroes, whose name was, next to that of Aristotle, the most frequently mentioned in the West, is by no means a star of the first magnitude in the heavens of the Mohammedan philosophy. His true importance lies much rather in the fact that it was he who gathered together the results of the ArabicoAristotelian philosophy as the last of its great representatives, and delivered them to the West in a wide range of literary activity, and especially by his commentaries on Aristotle. This philosophy was developed, like the Christian Scholasticism, from a Neo-Platonically coloured interpretation of Aristotle; only that while the Scholastics of the first period possessed a very slender stock of Peripatetic traditions, and those thoroughly intermingled and controlled by the Christian theology, the springs flowed to the Arabians through the channel of the Syrian schools in much greater abundance, and thought was with them developed with greater freedom from the influence of theology, which pursued its own paths of speculation. So it resulted that the naturalistic side of the Aristotelian system *(cf.* above, p. 85) could develop itself amongst the Arabians in a manner which remained quite foreign to the earlier Scholasticism, and which later made the Christian Church regard Averroism as a source of the most arrant heresies. There are three points in particular here to be regarded: the eternity of the world and of matter in its opposition to the Christian doctrine of creation; the relation of God to the world, according to which he influences either only the outermost sphere of the fixed stars, and all earthly things are only indirectly governed by God through the power of the stars, or God and the world run into each other in pantheistic fashion; finally, the doctrine of the unity of the reason, which is the only immortal part of man—a doctrine which denies individual immortality, since the reason is only the one divine light which shines in upon the soul of man, and makes knowledge possible. ascetic dogmatism. While the Epiku-(comp. Renan, Averroes, pp. 123 and rean school (see above, p. 125), among 227). A similar vulgarisation has, of all the ancient philosophical schools, course, befallen also the name of the preserved the most distinctive stamp 'Stoics.' and the most self-contained system Eenan, Averroes, p. 76 ff., shows of doctrines, the Talmud already how the most abstract shape of the describes Sadducees and Free-thinkers idea of God was essentially promoted generally as Epikureans. In the by the opposition waged against the twelfth century there appears in Christian doctrines of the Trinity and

Florence a sect of 'Epikureans,' the incarnation of the Deity. Tho which can scarcely be considered so mediatising

school of the 'Motaze in the strict Scholastic sense, any lites' is compared by Renan with tha more than the Epikureans whom school of Schleienu-acher.
VOL. I. M To the first of these views Avi-soon us we place ourselves at the cenna gave his adhesion, while the standpoint of eternity, the distinction second, according to an opinion start-between potentiality and actuality ed by Averroes, is supposed to have disappears, since in the course of eter been his real view. Averroes himself nity all potentialities become actunli makes all change and movement in ties. But thus disappears also from the world, and especially the becoming the highest standpoint of observation and perishing of organisms, poten-the opposition, too, of God and the tially inherent in matter, and God world. *Cf.* Renan, Averroes, pp. 73 has nothing to do but to turn this and 82 foil, potentiality into actuality. But as
It is intelligible enough that such doctrines must have exercised a mischievous interference in the world under the sway of Christian dogma, and that in this way, as well as through its naturalistic elements, Averroism prepared the way for the new Materialism. For all that, the two tendencies are fundamentally different, and Averroism became a chief pillar of that Scholasticism which, by the unconditional reverence for Aristotle, and by the strengthening of those principles which we shall examine more closely in the following chapter, rendered so long impossible a Materialistic consideration of things.

But besides its philosophy, we have to thank the Arabian civilisation of the middle ages for still another element, which stands perhaps in yet closer relation to the history of Materialism; that is, its achievements in the sphere of positive inquiry, of mathematics and the natural sciences, in the broadest sense of the term. The brilliant services of the Arabians in the field of astronomy and of mathematics are sufficiently known. And it was these studies particularly which, connecting themselves with Greek traditions, again made room for the idea of the regularity and subjection to law of the course of nature. This happened at a time when the degeneracy of belief in the Christian world had brought more disorder into the moral and logical order of things than had been the case at any period of Greeco-Eoman heathenism; at a time when everything was regarded as possible and nothing as necessary, and an unlimited field was allowed for the discretion of beings, which were ever endowed by the imagination with fresh properties.
This view, which rests upon the *tf.* 582. Draper, Intellectual DeveAristotelian theory of the *vovs xoirj*-lopment of Europe (ed. 1875), ii. 36 *rucit* (De Anima, iii. 5), has been de-foil. The author, who is best qualisignnted "Monopsychism," that is, fied to speak in the matter of natuml the doctrine that the immortal soul science (i-/. above, note 4), complains (in distinction from the perishable (p. 42) of "the systeiuatio manner in animal soul) in all beings that partake which the literature of Europe has of a soul is one and the same. contrived to put out of sight our Comp. Humboldt's Kosmos, it scientific obligations to the Moham.s;3 foil. E. T.; Bonn's ed. , ii. 593, medans."
The mingling of astronomy with the fantasies of astrology was, for this very reason, not so disadvantageous as might be supposed. Astrology, as well as the essentially related alchemy, possessed in every respect the regular form of sciences, and were, in the purer shape in which they were practised by the Arabian and the Christian savants of the middle ages, far removed from the measureless charlatanry which made its appearance in the sixteenth and especially in the seventeenth century, and after austerer science had rejected these fanciful elements. Apart from the fact that the impulse to inquiry into important and unfathomable secrets through that early connection came to the aid of the scientific discoveries in astronomy and chemistry, in those deep mysterious studies themselves was implied, as a necessary presupposition, the belief in a regular progress of events following eternal laws. And this belief has formed one of the most powerful springs in the whole development of culture from the middle ages to modern times.

'» Cotnp. Liebig, Chemische Briefe, 3 and 4 Br. The remark, " Alchemy was never anything more than chemistry," goes, of course, a little too far. As to the caution against confounding it with the gold-making art of the sixteenth and seventeenth centuries, it must not escape us that this is only alchemy run wild, just as the nativity delusion of the same period is astrology run wild. The most important contrast between the spirit of modern chemistry and of medieval alchemy may be most clearly shown in the relation between theory and experiment. With the alchemists the theory in all its main features stood unshakably firm; it was ranked above experiment; and if this gave an unexpected result, this was forced into an artificial conformity with the theory, which was of aprioristic origin. It was therefore essentially directed to the production of this previously anticipated result rather than to free investigation. This tendency of experiment is indeed still active enough in our modern chemistry, and the authority of general theories, if not in our own days, at all events in a period not very far behind us, was very great. Yet the real principle of modern chemistry is the empirical; that of alchemy, despite its empirical results, was the Aristotelo-scholastic. The scientific form of alchemy as well as of astrology rests upon the consistent carrying out of certain axioms as to the nature of all bodies and their mutual relations—axioms simple in themselves, but capable of the utmost varieties in their combinations. As to the furtherance of the scientific spirit by means of astrology in its purer forms, compare, further, Lecky, Hist. of Rationalism in Europe, i. 302 foil.; where also, in note 2 to p. 303, several instances are given of the bold ideas of astrological freethinkers. Compare also Humboldt's Kosmos, ii. 256 foil.

We must here also have special regard to medicine, which in our days has become in a certain measure the theology of Materialists. This science was treated by the Arabs with especial zeal. Here too, whilst attaching themselves chiefly to Greek traditions, they nevertheless set to work with an independent feeling for exact observation, and developed especially the doctrine of life, which stands in so close a connection with the problems of Materialism. In the case of man, as well as in those of the animal and vegetable worlds, everywhere, in short, in organic nature, the fine sense of the Arabians traced not only the particularities of the given object, but its development, its generation, and decay—just those departments, therefore, in winch the mystic theory of life finds its foundation.

Every one has heard of the early rise of schools of medicine on the soil of Lower Italy, where Saracens and the more cultivated Christian races came into such close contact. As early as the tenth century, the monk Constantine taught in the monastery of Monte Cassino, the man whom his contemporaries named the second Hippokrates, and who, after wandering through all the East, dedicated his leisure to the translation from the Arabic of medical works. At Monte Cassino, and later at Salerno and Naples, arose those famous schools of medicine, to which the seekers for knowledge streamed from the whole "Western world. 21 Draper, Intell. Develp. of Eu-cales (Paris, 1870). Yet their great rope, i. 384 foil. Less favourable activity in this department is shown judgments of Arabian medicine will clearly enough even in these ac be found in Hascr, Gesch. d. Med. counts. (2 Aufl., Jena, 1853), 173 foil., and in Comp. Wachler, Handb. dor IJarem-berg, Hist, des Sciences Medi-Gesch. d. Liter., ii. S. 87. Meincrs,

Let us observe, that it was upon the same territory that the spirit of freedom first took its rise in Europe—a spirit which we must not indeed confound with complete Materialism, but which is at all events closely related to it. For that strip of land in Lower Italy, and especially that in Sicily, where to-day blind superstition and mad fanaticism are at their height, was then the native home of enlightened minds and the cradle of the idea of toleration.

Whether the Emperor Frederick II., the highly cultivated friend of the Saracens, the scientific protector of the positive sciences, really littered the famous expression about the three impostors, Moses, Mohammed, and Christ,22 this time and place at least produced such opinions. Not without reason did Dante count by thousands the bold doubters who, resting in their fiery graves, ever preserve their contempt for hell. In that close contact of the different monotheistic religions—for at that time the Jews were there very numerous, and were in point of culture scarcely behind the Arabians—it was inevitable that, as soon as intellectual intercourse took place, the reverence for specific forms should be blunted; and yet it is in the specific that the force of religion lies, as the force of poetry lies in the individual.

Hist. Vergleich der Sitten u. s. w. hatred and suspicion upon persons of des Mittelalters mit d. unsr. Jahrh., freethinking tendency. Later a book ft. 413 foil. Daremberg, Hist, des on the Three Impostors became the

Sciences M6d., i. 259 foil., shows subject of this fabulous story, and a that the importance of Salerno in long series of liberal men (see the list medicine is older than the influence of them in Gen-the, De Impostura Re of the Arabians, and that here pro-ligionum, Leipz. 1833, p. 10 sq., as bably ancient traditions had survived, well as in Renan, A vermes, p. 235)

Yet the school certainly received a were accused of having written s great impulse through the Emperor book which did not even exist, until

Frederick II. at length the zeal with which the The assertion that Averroes, or question of its existence was debated the Emperor Frederick II., or some led certain industrious forgers to the other insolent freethinker, spoke of fabrication of such writings, which,

Mohammed, Christ, and Moses as the however, turned out very feeble

'three impostors/appears in the mid-productions. For further details see die ages to have been merely unfound-Gen-the, *loc. tit.* ed calumny, and a means of drawing

How much Frederick II. was distrusted is shown hy the accusation that he was in complicity with the Assassins, those murdering Jesuits of Mohammedanism, who are said to have had a secret doctrine which openly and freely expressed to the utmost a complete atheism, with all the logical consequences of an egoism seeking to gratify its lust of pleasure and power. If the tradition of the doctrines of the Assassins were true, we should have to pay this sect more respect than that of this incidental mention. The Assassins of the highest type would then represent the model of a Materialist such as the ignorant and fanatical partisans of our day love to imagine him in order to be able to urge a successful contest with him. The Assassins would be the solitary historical example of a combination of Materialistic philosophy with cruelty, lust of power, and systematic crime.

Let us not forget, however, that all our information as to this sect proceeds from their bitterest foes. It amounts to the highest degree of internal improbability that from the most harmless of all theories of the universe should have proceeded an energy so fearful that it demands the utmost strain of all the forces of the soul—an energy which in all other cases we find only in union with religious ideas. They are also, in their awful sublimity and transporting charm, the one element in the world's history to which we can pardon even the extremest abominations of fanaticism from the highest standpoint; and this is rooted deep in human nature. We would not venture, in the face of tradition, to build a conjecture upon purely internal grounds, that religious ideas were in the utmost activity amongst the Assassins, unless the sources of our knowledge of the Assassins afforded room for such consideration That a high degree of freethinking may be combined with the fanatical conception of a religious idea, is proved by the case of the Jesuits, with whose whole being that of the Assassins has a striking similarity.

- Hammer, in his book, based upon and deluded, and in the highest grades

Oriental sources," The History of the fi-uds nothing but cold-blooded calcu

Assassins," Stutt. and Tub. 1818, E. lation, absolute unbelief, and the

T. 1835, is entirely of the view which most vicious egotism. Enough, in di-vides tne Assassins into deluders deed, to this effect can be found in the sources; and yet we must not the tongue, the pen, or the sword,

To return to the natural science of the Arabians, we cannot, in conclusion, avoid quoting the bold expression of Humboldt, that the Arabians are to be considered the proper founders of the physical sciences, " in the signification of the term which we are now accus-tomed to give it." Experiment and mea-surement are the great instruments with the aid of which they made a path for progress, and raised themselves to a po-sition which is to be placed between the achievements of the brief inductive pe-riod of Greece, and those of the more modern natural sciences.

That Mohammedanism exhibits most of that furtherance of natural study which we assign to the Monotheistic principle, falls in with the talents of the Arabians with their historical and local relation to Greek traditions, without doubt, however, also with the circum-stance that the Monotheism of Mo-hammed was the most absolute, and comparatively the freest from mythical adulterations. Finally, let us place among the new elements of culture which might react upon a Materialistic theory of nature this further one, which is handled at length hy Humboldt in the second volume of his Kosmos—the de-velopment of the aesthetical contempla-tion of nature under the influence of Monotheism and of Semitic culture.
forget that this is the usual way in which have overturned the throne, which vic-torious orthodoxy deals and shaken the altar to its base, am with defeated sects. It is really bition is the first and might-iest. It here, apart from the frequent in-uses crime as a means, virtue as a stances of malicious misrepre-mask. It respects nothing sacred, sentation, just as it is with our and yet it has recourse to that which judgment of so-called 'hyp-ocrites' is most beloved, because the most in private life. Unusual piety is in secure, that of all held most sacred the popular eyes either genuine saint-by man—religion. Hence the history ship or a wicked cloak of all that is of re-ligion is never more tempestuous vile. For the psychological subtlety and san-guinary than when the tiara, of the mix-ture of genuine religious united to the diadem, imparts and emotions with coarse selfishness and receives an in-creased power." But vicious habits the ordinary mind has when was there ever a priesthood no appreciation. Hammer sets forth which was *not* ambitious; and how his own view of the psychological can religion be the most sacred ele ex-planation of the Assassin move-ment of humanity if its first servants ment in the following words (S. 20, find in it only a means to satisfy their
E. T. p. 13):—"Of all the passions am-bition? And why is ambition so which have ever called into action common and so dangerous a passion, since for the most part it only leads, very near to the Assassins, as Hammer

The ancients had carried personifica-tion to the utmost pitch, and seldom got so far as to regard or to represent nature simply as nature. A man crowned with reeds represented the ocean, a nymph the fountain, a faun or Pan the plain and the grove. When the landscape was robbed of its gods, then began the true observation of nature, and joy at the mere greatness and beauty of natural phenomena.

"It is a characteristic," says Hum-boldt, " of the poetry of the Hebrews, that, as a reflex of Monotheism, it al-ways embraces the universe in its unity, comprising both terrestrial life and the luminous realms of space. It dwells but rarely on the individual phenomenon, preferring the contemplation of great masses.... It might be said that one sin-gle psalm (Ps. civ.) represents the image of the whole kosmos: The Lord,'who coverest thyself with light as with a gar-ment; who stretchest out the heavens like a curtain; who laid the foundations of the earth, that it should not be re-moved for ever. He sendeth the springs into the valleys, which run among the hills: thou hast set a hound that they may not pass over; that they turn not again to cover the earth. They give drink to every beast of the field. By them shall the fowls of the aii have their habitation, which sing among the branches. The trees of the Lord are full of sap; the cedars of Lebanon which he hath planted, where the birds make their nests; as for the stork, the fir-trees are her house.'" by a very thorny and extremely un-represents them; while, at the same certain way, to that life of pleasure time, they would scarcely have been which is regarded as the object of able to establish their power in the every sel6sh man? There is obviously souls of believers without the help of acting, of-ten at least, and almost genuine fanati-cism. Hammer often always in the great events of world-adduces them, and cer-tainly with history, in connection with ambition, justice, as a parallel to the case of an ideal which is partly in itself the Assassins (S. 337, *ct passim,* over-prized, but partly passes into a E.T. 216); but when he thinks the one-sided relation to the particular regicides of the French Revolution person regarded as its special bearer, worthy to have been satellites of the

And this is the reason why it is *reli-* 'old man of the mountain,' this shows *pious* ambition especially that is so how easily such generalisations may fre-quent, for the cases in which reli-lead to a misapprehension of peculiar gion is employed by an ambitious historical phenomena. It is certain but not reli-gious person as a valuablo that the po-litical fanaticism of the means must be very rare in history. French 'men of tenor' was, on the

These considerations apply also whole, very sincere, and by no means to the Jesuits, who at certain periods hyp-ocritical, of their history have certainly come 1 Kosmos, E. T., Bohn's ed., ii. 412, 413.

To the times of the Christian an-chorites belongs a letter of Basil the Great, which in Humboldt's translation affords a magnificent and feeling de-scription of the lonely forest in which stood the hermit's hut.

So the sources flowed on all sides to form the mighty stream of modern intellectual life, in which, under numerous modifications, we have again to seek for tho object oi our inquiry, Materialism.

CHAPTER IT. SCHOLASTICISM AND THE PREDOMINANCE OF THE ARISTOTELIAN NOTIONS OF MATTER AND FORM.

While the Arabians, as we saw in the previous chapter, drew their knowledge of Aristotle from abundant though much polluted sources, the Scholastic philosophy of the West began by dealing with extremely scanty, and, at the same time, much corrupted traditions. The chief portion of these materials consisted of Aristotle's work on the 'Categories,' and an introduction to it by Porphyry in which the " five words" are discussed. These five words, which form the entrance to the whole Scholastic philosophy, are genus, species, difference, property, and accident. The ten categories are substance, quantity, quality, relation, place, time, position, possession, action, and passion.

It is well known that there is a large and still steadily increasing body of literature on the question what Aristotle exactly meant by his categories, that is, predications, or species of predication. And this object would have been sooner attained if men had only begun by making up their minds to treat as such all that is crudo and uncertain in the Aristotelian notions, instead of seeking behind every unintelligible expression for some mystery of the profoundest wisdom. It may now, however, be regarded as settled that the categories were an attempt on the part of Aristotle to determine in how many main ways we can say of any object what it is, and that he allowed himself to be misled by the authority of language into identifying modes of predication and modes of existence. 4 Prantl, Gesch. der Logik im division into the three periods of the

Abendlande, ii. 4, finds in Scholas- incomplete, the complete, and the t icism only theology and logic, but no again inadequate accommodation of trace at all of philosophy.' It is Aristotelianism to eoclesiastical doo quite correct, however, to say that trines, is untenable). In the same the different periods of Scholasticism place will be found a complete enu oan only be distinguished according meration of the Scholastic material to the varying influence of the gradu-which the middle ages had at their ally increasing Scholastic material disposition, (and so, for example, even Ueberweg's

Without entering here upon the question how far we can justify *e.g.,* with' Ueberweg's logic, or in the sense of Schleiermacher and Trendelenburg) the exhibition of forms of being and forms of thought as parallel, and the assumption of a more or less exact correspondence between them, we must at once point out, what will be made clearer further on, that the confusion of *subjective* and *objective* elements in our conception of things is one of the most essential features of Aristotelian thought, and that this very confusion, for the most part in its clumsiest shape, became the foundation of Scholasticism.

Aristotle, indeed, did not introduce this confusion into philosophy, but, on the contrary, made the *jirst* attempt to distinguish what the unscientific consciousness is always inclined to identify. But Aristotle never got beyond extremely imperfect attempts to make this distinction; and yet precisely that element in his logic and metaphysic, which is in consequence especially perverse and immature, was regarded by the rude nations of the West as the corner-stone of their wisdom, because it best suited their undeveloped understanding. We find an interesting example of this in Fredegisus, a pupil of Alcuin's, who honoured Charles the Great with a theological epistle 'De Nihilo et Tenebris,' in which that ' Nothing' out of which God created the world is explained as an actually *existing entity,* and that for the extremely simple reason that every name refers to some corresponding thing. This latter point is very well this controversy, which it would here shown by Dr. Schuppe in his work, lead us too far to discuss. According

"The Aristotelian Categories," Ber-to Prantl, Gesch. der Logik, i. 192, lin, 1871. Less forcible seems to me what actually exists receives its the argument against lion it z, with re-full concreto determination by ir.eans gard to the meaning of the expres-of the elements expressed in the sion *Karriyoplai* Toc *ivros.* The phrase categories, employed in the text seeks to avoid

A much higher position was taken by Scotus Erigena, who declares ' darkness,' 'silence, ' and similar expressions, to be notions of the thinking subject; only, of course, Scotus also thinks that the ' absentia' of a thing and the thing itself are of *the like kind:* so therefore are light and darkness, sound and silence. I have, then, at one time a notion of the thing, at another a notion of the absence of the thing, in a precisely similar manner. The ' absence,' therefore, is also objectively given: it is something real.

This is an error which we find also in Aristotle himself. Negation in a proposition *(airofaais)* he correctly explained as an act of the thinking subject: 'Privation' *(crrepr)(7t;),* for example, the blindness of a creature that naturally sees, he regards, however, as a property of the object. And yet, as a matter of fact, we find, instead of the eyes in such a creature, some degenerate form which has nevertheless only positive qualities: we find, it may be, that the creature moves only with much groping and difficulty, but in the motions themselves everything is in its way fixed and positive. It is only our comparison of this oreature with others that, on the ground of our experience, we call normal, that gives us the notion of blindness. Sight is wanting only in our conception. The thing, regarded in itself, is as it is, without any reference to seeing or not seeing.

It is easy to perceive that serious blunders like this are to be found also in the Aristotelian enumeration of the categories; most conspicuously in the category of relation (7r/3o? Tt), as, *e. g.,* 'double,' 'half,' 'greater,' where no one will seriously maintain that such expressions can be applied to things except in so far as they may be compared by the thinking subject.

Prantl, Gesch. der Logik, ii. 17 foil., esp. Anm. 75.

Much more important, however, became the vagueness as to the relation of word and thing in dealing with the notion of substance and the species.

We have seen how, on the threshold of all philosophy, appear the 'five words' of Porphyry—a selection from the logical writings of Aristotle, intended to supply to the student, in a convenient form, what he chiefly needs at starting. At the head of these expositions stand those of 'genus' and ' species;' and at the very introduction of this introduction stand the eventful words which probably aroused the great medieval controversy about universals. Porphyry mentions the great question whether the genera and species have an independent existence, or whether they are merely in the mind; whether they are corporeal or incorporeal substances; whether they are separate from sensible objects, or exist only in and through them? The decision of the problem so solemnly propounded is postponed, because it is one of the highest problems. Yet we see enough to perceive that the position of the 'five words' at the entrance to philosophy is quite in accordance with the speculative importance of the notions of genus and species, and the expression betrays clearly enough the Platonic sympathies of the writer, although he suspends his judgment.

The Platonic view of the notions of genus and species (comp. p. 74 ff.) was, therefore, in spite of all inclination towards Aristotle, the prevailing view of earlier medieval times. The Peripatetic school had received a Platonic portico, and the young disciple on his entrance into the halls of philosophy was at once greeted with a Platonic consecration; perhaps, at the same time, with an intentional counterbalance to a dangerous feature of the Aristotelian categories. For in the discussion of substance *(ovaia),* he declares that, in the primary and strict sense, the concrete particulars, such as this particular man, this horse standing here, are substances. This is, of course scarcely in accordance with the Platonic contempt for the concrete, and we must not be surprised at the rejection of this doctrine by Scotus Erigena. Aristotle calls the species substances only of the second order, and it is only by the mediation of the species that the genus also has a certain substantiality. Here then was opened, at the very outset of philosophical studies, a wide source of school controversy, although on the whole the Platonic view (Realism, because the universals are regarded as 'res') remained, until nearly the close of the middle ages, the prevailing, and, at the same time, the orthodox doctrine. It is, therefore, the most absolute antithesis to Materialism produced by all antiquity that controls from the first the philosophical development of the middle ages; and even at the dawnings of Nominalism there appeared for many centuries scarcely any tendency to start from the concrete phenomena which could in any degree remind us of Materialism. The whole era was swayed by the name, by the thought-thing, and by an utter confusion as to the meaning of sensible phenomena, which passed like dream-pictures through the miracle-loving brain of philosophising priests.

Things changed, however, more and more after the influence of Arabian and Jewish philosophers had become observable, from the middle of the twelfth century, and gradually a fuller knowledge of Aristotle had been spread by means of translations, first from the Arabic, and later also from the Greek originals preserved at Byzantium. But, simultaneously, the principles of the Aristotelian metaphysic became only more and more fully and deeply rooted.

These principles are, however, of importance for us, not only because of the negative part which they play in the history of Materialism, but also as indispensable contributions to the criticism of Materialism; not indeed as though we must still measure and try the Materialism of to-day by them, but because only by their assistance can we thoroughly overcome the misunderstandings which constantly threaten us in the discussion of this subject. One portion of the question here concerned has been already decided, what is right and what is wrong in Materialism being already shewn, as soon as the notions with which we have here constantly to deal are made clear; and further, it is essential that we should take them at their immediate source, and observe the gradual modifications they undergo.

Aristotle is the creator of metaphysic, which, as everybody knows, is indebted for its unmeaning name merely to the position of these books in the series of Aristotle's writings. The object of this science is the investigation of the principles common to all existence, and Aristotle therefore calls it the ' first philosophy'—that is, the general philosophy, which has not yet devoted itself to a special branch. The idea of the necessity of such a philosophy was correct enough, but the solution of the problem could not even be approached until it was recognised that the universal is above all that which lies in the nature of our mind, and through which it is that we receive all knowledge. The failure to separate the subject and the object, the phenomenon and the thing-in-itself, is here therefore especially noticeable, as, owing to this failure, the Aristoteban philosophy becomes an inexhaustible source of self-delusion. And the middle ages were especially inclined eagerly to embrace the very worst delusions of this kind; and these are at the same time of special importance for our subject: they lie in the notions of matter and potentiality, as related to form and actuality.

Aristotle mentions four universal principles of all existence: form (or essence), matter *(yr), materia,* as it was rendered by the Latin translators), the efficient cause, and the end.27 We are here chiefly concerned with the first two.

Ueberweg, Hist. of Phil., 4 references there given are quite enough Aufl., i. 172-175, E. T. i. 157-159-The for our purpose, as we are not here concerned with a n?w view of the nised Aristotelian notions and docAristotelian metaphysie, but merely trines. with a critical exposition of recog

The notion of matter is, in the first place, entirely different from what we nowadays understand by 'matter.' While our thought retains in so many departments the stamp of Aristotelian conceptions, on this point, through the influence of natural science, a Materialistic element has forced itself into our modes of thinking. With or without Atomism, we conceive of matter as a corporeal thing distributed universally, save where there is a vacuum, and of an essentially uniform nature, although subject to certain modifications.

In Aristotle the notion of matter is *relative;* it is matter in relation to that which is to result from it through the accession of form. Without form the thing cannot be what it is; through form the thing becomes what it is in reality; whilst previously matter had only supplied the potentiality of the thing. Matter has, nevertheless, to begin with a form of its own, though of but a low order, and one quite indifferent in relation to the thing which is to result.

The bronze of a statue,for example, is the matter; the idea of the work is the form; and from the union of the two results the actual statue. Yet the bronze was not the matter in the sense of this particular piece of metal (for as such it had a form which had nothing to do with the statue), but as bronze in general, *i.e.,* as something having no reality in itself, but which 'can' only become something. And so matter also is only potentially existing *(Swdpet Op),* form only in reality or in actuality *(ivepyela. 6v* or *ivreKejfeia ov).* The passing of the possible into actuality is Becoming, and this is, therefore, the moulding of matter by form.

As we see, there is here no question whatever of an independent corporeal substrate of all things. The concrete, phenomenal thing itself, as it here or there exists—*e.g.,* a log of wood lying yonder—is at one time 'substance,' that is, an actualised thing consisting of form and matter, at another time is merely matter. The log is 'substance,' a complete thing, as a log having received from nature the form of a log; but it is 'matter' with regard to the rafter, or the carving which is to be made from it. We have only to add the qualifying words, "in so far as we regard it as matter" *(i.e.,* material). Then everything would be clear, but the conception would no longer be strictly Aristotelian, for Aristotle, in fact, transfers to the things themselves these relations to our thought.

VOL. I. N

Besides matter and form, Aristotle further regards efficient causes and ends as grounds of all existence, the last of which, in the nature of things, coincides with the form. As the form is the end of the statue, so also Aristotle regards in nature the form that realises itself in matter as the end, or the final cause, in which Becoming finds its natural consummation.

But while this manner of regarding things is consistent enough in its own way, it was completely lost from view that the related notions are throughout of such a kind that they cannot, without producing error, be assumed as actually recognised properties of the objective world, though they may supply a well-articulated system from a subjective standpoint. And it is therefore of the more importance that we should make this clear, because only a very few of the keenest thinkers, such as Leibniz, Kant, and Herbart have entirely avoided this rock, simple as the matter really is.

The underlying error consists in this, that the notion of the possible, of the *Swdfiei 6v,* which is in its nature a purely subjective assumption, is transferred to things.

It is undeniable that matter and form are but two sides from which we may contemplate the essence of things; and even Aristotle was cautious enough not to say that the essence was compounded from these two, as if they were separable parts; but if we refer the becoming and actually happening to the interpenetration of matter and form, of potentiality and actuality, the error we have just avoided meets us at this point with redoubled force.

It must much rather be indisputably concluded that if there is no formless matter, even though this can be only assumed and not imagined, then there exists also no potentiality in things. The *Svvdpet ov,* the potentially existing, is, as soon as we leave the sphere of fiction, a pure nonentity, no longer to be found. In external nature there is only actuality and no potentiality.

Aristotle regards, for example, the general who has won a battle as an actual conqueror. This actual conqueror, however, was a conqueror before the battle, yet only *Swa/Met, potentia,* potentially. So much we may readily concede, that there lay even before the battle in his person, in the strength and disposition of his army, and so on, conditions which brought about his victory—his victory was possible; but this whole employment of the notion of potentiality rests upon this, that we mortals can never see more than a portion of the causes in action: if we could view all, we should find out that the victory was not' potential,' but that it was 'necessary;' since the incidental and contributory circumstances stand also in a fixed causal connection, which is so ordered that a particular consequence will result, and no other.

It might be objected that this is quite in harmony with the Aristotelian assumptions; for the general who is necessarily victorious is in a certain way already the conqueror, and still he is not yet actually so, but only 'potentia.'

Here we should have an admirable example of the confusion of notions and of objects. Whether I call the general conqueror or not, he is what he is—a real person, standing at a certain point of time in the course of inner and outer properties and events. The circumstances that have not yet come into play have for him as yet no existence at all; he has only a certain plan in his conceptions, a certain strength in his arm and voice, certain moral relations to his army, certain feelings of hope and apprehension; he is, in short, conditioned on every hand. That from these conditions, in connection with other conditions on the side of his opponent, of the ground, of the armies, of the weather, his victory will result, is a relation which, if conceived by our thought, produces the notion of the possibility, or even of the necessity, of a result, without thereby taking anything from him or adding anything to him. No addition is necessary to this notional possibility in order to turn it into actuality, except in our thought.

"A hundred actual thalers," says Kant, "contain no whit more than a hundred potential thalers." Kant's Kritik d. T. Vemunft, Elementar., II. Thl. 2 Abth. 2 Buoh. Haupst. 4 Abschn., E. T. Meiklejohu, p. 368, ed. Hartenatein, 409.

Kant is there discussing the impossibility of an ontological proof of the existence of God, and shows that 'existence' is not a real predicate at all, that is, not a "conception of something which is added to the conception of some other thing." And so, therefore, the real contains no more (in its conception) than the merely possible, and reality is the existence *of the tame thing* as an *object,* of which the (merely logical) possibility gave me only the conception. In order to explain this relation Kant employs the following example: "A hundred real dollars contain no more than a hundred possible dollars. For, as the latter indicate the conception, and the former the object, on the supposition that the content of the former was greater than that of the latter, my conception would not be an expression of the whole object, and would consequently be an inadequate conception of it. In another sense, however, it may be said that there Ib more in a hundred real dollars than in a hundred possible dollars— that is, in the mere conception of them. For the real object—the dollars —is not analytically contained in my conception, but forms a synthetical addition to my conception (which is merely a determination of my mental state), although this objective reality — this existence — apart from my conception, does not in the least degree increase the aforesaid hundred dollars." The illustration of a treasury-bill, added in the text, attempts to make the matter still clearer, since, in addition to the, merely logical possibility (the idea of a hundred dollars) an additional ground of probability is brought into play, which rests upon a partial view of the conditions influencing the actual payment of a hundred dollars. These conditions (partially recognised) are what Ueberweg *(apropos* of Trendelenburg; comp. Ueberweg's Logik, 3 Aufl. S. 167, § 69) calls "real or objective possibility." The appearance of a problematical relation is due to this fact, that we transfer to the object the *relation* which is conceived by our mind between the mere actual presence of the conditions, and the later, also actual existence of the condiditioned.

This proposition would appear to a financier doubtful, if not absurd. A few years after Kant's death (July 1808), a treasury-bill for a hundred thalers sold in Konigsberg for scarcely twenty-five. So that in the birthplace of the great philosopher, a hundred actual thalers were worth more than four hundred merely potential thalers; and this might be regarded as a brilliant justification of Aristotle and all the Scholastics down to Wolff and Baumgarten. The treasury-bill which is to be obtained for twenty-five actual thalers represents a hundred potential thalers. If we look a little more closely, we see, of course, that what we really get for twenty-five thalers is the very doubtful prospect of the payment at some future time of the hundred thalers; and this is the actual value of the prospect in question, and therefore, of course, the actual value of the bill, which carries the chance with it. But the thing of which we possess the chance is, as before, the full hundred thalers of the nominal value. This nominal value represents the amount of that which is regarded as potentially to be obtained, with a probability, however, of only one-fourth in its favour. The actual value has nothing to do with the amount of the potential sum; and so far Kant was entirely right.

Kant, however, meant by this illustration something more than this, and here again he was right. For when our financier, after the 13th January 1816, had his hundred thalers paid to him in full, nothing was added to the potentiality, so that it became an actuality. The potentiality, as the merely conceived in thought, can never pass into actuality, but actuality arises out of preceding actual circumstances by which it is entirely conditioned. Besides the restoration of the national credit and other circumstances, there is also necessary the presentation of an actual treasury-bill—not of a 'potential' hundred thalers; for these exist only in the brain of the speculator, who represents to himself one portion of the circumstances which influence the conversion of the paper notes into silver, and makes this the subject of his hopes, and his fears, and his thoughts.

Perhaps we shall be pardoned the length of these remarks, if we again very briefly point out that the notion of potentiality is the source of most of the worst metaphysical fallacies. Aristotle, of course, cannot be blamed for this, since the primary error is grounded deep in our organisation; and this must inevitably be doubly fatal in a system which, more than any previous one, based metaphysics upon dialectical discussion; and the high esteem which Aristotle gained through this very procedure, in other respects so fertile, appeared as though it would perpetuate this misfortune.

After Aristotle, then, had so unhappily explained becoming and motion generally, as results of purely potential matter, and the actualising of form, it was a logical consequence that the form or the end of things must be the true source of motion; and as the soul moves the body, so is God as Form and End of the world the first cause of all motion. It could not be expected that Aristotle should regard matter as moved in itself, since all that he ever allows to it is the negative determination, the potentiality of becoming anything or everything.

The same false conception of potentiality which exercises this corrupting influence on the notion of matter, meets us once more in the relation of the permanent thing to its changing circumstances, or, to keep within the vocabulary of the system, in the relation between substance and accident. The substance is the self-existent essence of the thing, the accident a casual property which is only ' potentially' in the substance. There is really, however, nothing casual in things, although, out of ignorance of the causes, some of them I am obliged to describe as casual.

Just as little can the potentiality of any property or attribute be latent in a thing. This is only a creature of our combining imagination. Nor, again, can any property be 'potentially' in things, since this is not a form of existence but a form of thought. The seed-corn is not a potential halm, but a seed-corn. If a cloth is wet, this wetness for the moment in which it is, is as much there as a necessary result of general laws, as any other property of the cloth; and if it can be thought of previously as potential, yet the cloth which I shall later dip in water has absolutely no other qualities than another cloth which is to be subjected to no such experiment.

The separation in thought of substance and accident is indeed a convenient, perhaps an indispensable, assistance to us in taking our bearings, but as soon as we begin to go more deeply into the essence of things, we must admit that the distinction between substance and accident likewise disappears. A thing has, it is true, certain qualities which stand in a more durable relation to it than others; but none is absolutely permanent, and at bottom all are in constant change. If we once conceive, then, of substance as a single object, not as a species, nor as a universal corporeal substrate, we must, in order to determine fully its form, limit the consideration of it to a certain period of time, and within this regard all the properties in their mutual interpenetration as the substantial form, and this again as the only essence of the thing.

If we speak, on the other hand, with Aristotle, of the notional *(to Tc ty elvai)* in things as their true substance, we find ourselves already in the field of abstraction; for the logical abstracting process is eventually the same, whether we frame a generic notion from our experience of a dozen cats, or whether we follow our own domestic cat through its life history, through all its changes and vicissitudes, regarding it as one and the same being. Only in the sphere of abstraction has the opposition of substance and accident its importance. For taking our bearings for the practical treatment of things, we shall never be able to dispense entirely with the antithesis worked out by Aristotle with masterly acuteness of the potential and the actual, of form and matter, of substance and accident. It is equally certain, however, that in positive inquiry we are always led astray by these notions, as soon as we lose sight of their subjective nature and relative validity, and of their consequent inability to help us to see further into the objective essence of things.

The standpoint of ordinary empirical thought, which in the main remains that of modern Materialism, is by no means free from these defects of the Aristotelian system, since it maintains more firmly and obstinately, if possible, the false antithesis, though in an opposite direction. We ascribe the true being to stuff or matter, which, however, only represents a notion reached by abstraction: we are inclined to regard the matter of things as their substance, and the form as a mere accident. The block out of which a statue is to come every one holds to be real; the form which it is to receive we look upon as merely potential. Nevertheless, it is easy to see that this is only true in so far as the block has a form, which I leave out of consideration, namely, the form in which it came from the quarry. The block as material of the statue, on the other hand, is only so in thought, whilst the idea of the statue, so far as it is conceived by the artist, at least as a conception, possesses a kind of actuality. So far, then, Aristotle was right as against the ordinary empiricism. His mistake lies only in this, that he transfers what is actually the idea of a thinking being to a foreign object, which is the subject of this being's thought, as a potentially present property of the same.

The Aristotelian definitions of substance, form, matter, and so on, prevailed so far as they were understood, so long as Scholasticism reigned alone—that is, in our own country of Germany, until after the time of Cartesius.

If, however, Aristotle had already treated matter somewhat depreciatingly, and in particular had denied to it any motion of its own, this depreciation of matter must have been increased through the influence of Christianity, which we have sketched in the previous chapter. Men did not reflect that everything by which matter can be anything determinate—for example, evil or sinful—must be form in the Aristotelian sense; the system had not been so far modified that matter was distinguished as the bad or evil principle, but they were still fond of representing it as absolutely passive; and this they conceived to be an imperfection, without reflecting that the perfection of every being consists in its answering to its end, and that, therefore, if we are childish enough to play the censor over the last grounds of all existence, it must much rather redound to the praise of matter, that it keeps so beautifully quiet. When, later, Wolff endowed matter with the *vis inertim,* and the physicists empirically transferred the properties of weight and impenetrability to matter, while these must in themselves be forms, the melancholy picture was soon complete.

"Matter is a dark, inert, rigid, and absolutely passive substance."

"And this substance is to think?" asked the one party, while the others complain that there ought to be immaterial substances, because meanwhile the notion of substance in colloquial usage has become identical with that of matter.

Modern Materialism has, of course, not been without influence on these modifications of the notions, although the reaction of the Aristotelian views and the authority of religion were strong enough to turn the effects of this influence into quite another course. The two men who have exercised the greatest influence in the modelling of the notion of matter are certainly Descartes and Newton. Both occupy in the main the ground of the Atomism which Gassendi had revived (although Descartes, by his denial of vacuum, seeks as far as possible to conceal this); yet in this both are distinguished from Demokritos and Epikuros, that they separate motion from matter, and make it arise through the will of God, who first creates matter, and then, by an act which may, at least in thought, be regarded as separate, brings motion into it.

For the rest, however, the Aristotelian view lingered longest, and with a comparative exclusiveness in that particular department for which the questions of Materialism have an especially critical importance—in the sphere of psychology. The foundation of this theory of the soul rests upon the delusion of potentiality and actuality. For Aristotle defines the soul as the actualisation of an organic body possessing a ' potential' life. This expression is in itself neither so puzzling nor so ambiguous as many have found it. 'Actualisation,' or ' consummation,' is rendered by *evrekkyeia,* and it is difficult to say how much has been imported into this expression. In Aristotle it indicates the well-known antithesis to *Bwafm;* what further force it may have has crept into it. The organic body possesses life only potentially. The actualisation of this potentiality comes from without, and that is all. The internal untruth of the whole theory is even more obvious than in the relation of form and matter, although the antithesis of the two pairs of notions is exactly parallel. That the organic body as the mere potentiality of a human being is in no way conceivable without human form, which, again, on its side, presupposes the active realisation of a human being in plastic material, the soul, that is, is a sunken rock in the orthodox Aristotelian view, which, it cannot be doubted, essentially contributed to the extensive development of Stratonism. Aristotle, in order to avoid this rock, fell back upon the act of generation, as though here at least a formless material, through the psychical energy of the generator, received its actualisation as a human creature; but this is only to transfer the separation of form and matter, actualisation and potentiality which is demanded by the system, into the twilight of an unfamiliar process, and so to fish in troubled waters. *i* The full definition (De Anima, ii. i) runs: *TJ/vxJl tarw ivriix V rpwTTi* trayiaros cWc/coO funy *£xs Svvdfiei Toio6tov be 8 hv fj 6pyayac6p.* Comp. V. Kirchmann's translation (Phil.Bibl.Band.43). The commentary then is, on the whole, excellent; but when v. Kirchmann says (S. 58), that this definition is no definition at all of the soul in the modern sense, hut only a definition of the *organic force* which is common to man with animals and plants, this cannot be right, for Aristotle has already premised the explanation that he proposes to give a *vnivertal* idea of the soul, and accordingly one which embraces all kinds of souls. This cannot mean, however, as Kirchmann supposes, the idea of a kind of soul which is common to all animated beings, but, in addition to which, a portion of these beings may have still another kind of soul, and one not included in the definition. The definition must rather embrace the *whole* human soul, including its higher faculties, just as much as, *e.g.,* the plant-soul, and this in fact it does. For according to Aristotle, the human body as an organism is adapted for a *rational* soul; and this soul, therefore, constitutes its actualisation, including within itself the lower faculties.
Fortlage, System der Psychologic, 1855, L S. 24, says: "Die negative Grosse eines Immateriellen, von welcher die Sphare des ausseren Sinnes beherrscht sei, wurde von Aristotles durch den rathselhaften und vieldeutigen, durum tiefsinnig scheinendenAusdruckder &rcXlxctafixirt, und gleichsam aus nichts zu etwa gemacht." Herethe latter statements undoubtedly true that Aristotle, in the doctrine of the entolechy, has made an apparent entity out of nothing. But this applies not merely to the idea of thesoul. but to the whole application of the word *iyrtix,* ' moreover, to the entire Aristotelian doctrine of potentiality and actuality. In things there is from first to last nothing but complete actuality. Each thing, conidered in itself, is entelechy, and also into the notion of the entelechy, in when we imagine a thing and its en-which it could then indeed admirably telechy side by side, this is in effect luxuriate. nothing but a mere tautology. And Comp. De An. ii. 1, v. Kirchthe case of the soul differs in no re-mann's Translation, S. 61: "Auch spect at all from any other case. *The* ist nicht das, was seine Seele verloren *Moul of the man, according to Arit-*hat, das dem Vermogen nach Leben*totle,* u *the man.* This tautology only dige, sondern das, was sie hat; dagogen acquires a deeper significance within ist der Same und die Frucht ein solthe system because (1) the deoeptive chor Korper dem Vermogen nach." Iihenomenon of the body as a merely Here Aristotle is endeavouring to potential man is opposed to the actual avoid the very proper objection that and perfect man (comp. further the on his system every man must arise following note); (2) the actual and out of a dead body by the accession perfect being is then subsequently of the entelechy. He may then quite again confused with the essential or rightly maintain that the corpse is no logical portion of the being, with the longer in a proper condition for this, same equivocalness which is so strik- because it is no longer a perfect ing in the notion of the *ovala.* And organisation (although there is still Bo Aristotle has not fixed "die nega-some doubt whether Aristotle's ideas tive Grosseeines Immateriellen" any were so advanced; comp. Kirchmore in his notiou of the soul than in mann's note on the passage); but, tho notion of form generally. It was then, it becomes impossible to adduce theNco-Platonioviewofthesupersen-any oase in which the 'potentially' suous that first brought mysticism living tiody would differ from the actually living body, and so Aristotle only, and hastily pass over the set of
The medieval philosophers were able to make good use of this doctrine, however, and brought it into admirable harmony with dogma.

Of much greater value is the profound doctrine of the Stagirite, that man, as the highest product of creation, carries within himself the nature of all the lower stages. The function of plants is to grow and to multiply; the essence of the plant soul is therefore of vegetation. In an animal arise, besides, sensation, motion, appetite; the vegetative life has here entered into the service of the higher or sensitive life. Finally, in man appears the highest principle, that of intellect *(voW),* and dominates the others. By a certain mechanical process, to which Scholasticism was prone, there were made from these elements of human existence three almost completely independent souls—the *anima vegetativa,* the *anima sensitiva,* and the *anima rationalis,* of which man has the first in common with the animal and the plant; the second at least in common with the animal; while the last is alone immortal, and of divine origin, and includes all the higher intellectual faculties which are denied to the beasts.33 From this separation proceeded the favourite distinction of Christian dogmatists between soul and spirit, the two higher forces, while the lowest, or *anima vegetativa,* became the foundation of the later doctrine of vital force.

has recourse to seeds and fruit. In realisation. But if we pursue this them he finds the appearance of a method, and follow it through the justification of his antithesis, but separate steps, the whole delusion only the appearance, for seeds and breaks up into nothing; for Aristotle fruit are themselves living things, can scarcely have meant to say that and have a form corresponding to the youth is the body of the man, the nature of man. But suppose we because he is his potentiality, were to apply the relativity explained Tho separation of the *anima* in the text and say: The embryo has *ralionalit* from the lower faculties of indeed the form (and therefore the the soul was indeed denied by the entolechy) of the embryo, but in rela-Church, and the converse doctrine tion to the *developed man* it is only was raised to the dignity of a dogma a *potentiality,* and therefore matter, in the Council of Vienne (1311): but

That sounds well enough so long as the more convenient and more Aris we keep our eyes upon the extremes totelian view steadily returned.

There is no room for doubt that Aristotle only mentally separated these forces in man. As the human body has its animal nature, not by the side of the specific human nature, but *in* it, it is a complete animal body of the noblest kind, that, nevertheless, in its particular conformation is specially and thoroughly human; so, according to him, we must conceive the relation of the gradations of the soul. The human form contains the spiritual being in complete interpenetration with the sensitive and appetitive faculties, as these constitute in the animal one and the same thing with the merely vital principle. Only in the doctrine of the 'inseparable' reason—that doctrine upon which rest the Averroistic monopsychism on the one hand, and the Scholastic doctrine of immortality on the other, is the unity abandoned, but even here not without obvious violence to the main features of the system. This unity, which makes the form of man, uniting all lower forms in itself, his soul, was broken up by the Scholastics. For doing this, quite apart from the 'separable reason,' they could rely upon many an expression of the great philosopher, who everywhere in his system unites with the keenest consistency in certain main features a striking hesitation in its development. So particularly with the doctrine of immortality, which, like that of the existence of God, adheres very locsely to the system, and in many points contradicts it.

From the Aristotelian philosophy are to be explained many more of the assumptions of the older metaphysic which the Materialists are fond of rejecting as simply absurd. Of this class is especially the assertion that the soul is not only distributed through the whole body, but that it is also wholly present in every part of it. Thomas of Aquin expressly taught that it is not only potentially but actually present in every part of the body, with its one and indivisible essence. This, to many Materialists, was the height of absurdity, but within the Aristotelian system it is at least as rational as if we say that the principle of the circle, expressed by the one indivisible proposition, a; + y = r, is actualised in any particular portion of a given circle of the radius *r* whose centre falls at the springing of the co-ordinates.

The contradiction in the doctrine Ueberweg, Grand., 1. 4 Aufl., p. 182, of coOs in relation to the doctrine of E. T. 168. For the rent, compare note immortality is recognised also by 55 to the first section.

Let us compare the formal principle of the human body with the equation of the circle, and we shall perhaps understand the root-idea of the Stagirite more purely and clearly than he knew how himself to express it. The question is a quite different one as to the seat of the conscious functions of sensation and appetite. This Aristotle places in the heart; the Scholastics, following Galen, in the brain. Aristotle, however, quite consistently leaves to these functions their physical nature, and hence agrees in one very important point with the Materialists *(cf.* note 31). There, however, the Scholastics would, of course, not follow him, as it cannot be denied that the later metaphysic in many ways introduced a mysterious confusion into their, in themselves, simple and intelligible formuhe, a confusion more akin to utter absurdity than to clear thought.

But if we are here to fully understand the opposition of Materialism to metaphysic, we need only go back to that confusion of existence and thought which had such momentous consequences in the case of the notion of potentiality. We maintain firmly that this confusion had originally the character of vulgar error. It was reserved for modern philosophers to make a virtue of their inability to free themselves from the chains worn for thousands of years, and to erect into a principle this very unestablished identity of being and thought.

If, by the aid of a mathematical construction, I describe a circle with chalk, the form of the local disposition of the chalk particles is first present, of course, in my mind as end. The end becomes the moving cause, the form becomes the realisation of the principle in the material parts. But where, then, is the principle? In the chalk? Obviously not in the individual particles; nor, again, in their sum. But it is in their 'disposition,' *i.e.*

, in an abstraction. The principle is, and remains, in the human thought. Who, then, gives us the right to transfer such a previously existing principle into those things which do not come to pass through human ingenuity, as, for example, the form of the human body? Is this form anything? Certainly in our conception. It is the way in which matter manifests itself, that is, the fashion in which it appears to us. Only, can this way in which the thing appears exist previously to the thing itself? Can it be separated from it?

As we see the opposition of form and matter, as soon as we go to the root of the matter, leads us back to the question of the existence of universals, for only as a universal could the form in general be regarded as having an existence of its own outside man's thinking faculty. And these Aristotelian modes of thought everywhere lead us back when we go thoroughly into things to Platonism, and as often as we find an opposition between Aristotelian empiricism and Platonic idealism, we have also a point before us in which Aristotle contradicts himself. Thus, in the doctrine of substance, Aristotle begins quite empirically with the substantiality of the individual concrete things. This notion is immediately refined away into the theory that the notional in the things, or the form, is substance. But the notional is the universal, and it is yet the determining element in its relation with the in itself quite undetermined matter. This is sensible enough in riatonism, which regards the individual things as futile appearances; but in Aristotle it remains an utter inconsistency, and is, therefore, of course, just as puzzling to the wise as to the foolish.35

If we now apply these remarks to the controversy between the Nominalists and the Realists *(cf.* above p. 85 foil.), we understand that the origin of the individual must to the Realist have presented especial difficulties. The form as universal can produce no individual out of matter; whence therefore do we get a *principium individuationis,* to use scholastic language? Aristotle never gives us the answer to which we are entitled. Avicenna attempted to shift on to matter the principle of individuation, and that, therefore, whereby, from the notion of dog, this particular dog is produced—a device which involves either the fall of the whole Aristotelian notion of matter (and previously, of course, the Platonic), or the Platonic subversion of the individual. Here stumbled even St. Thomas, who otherwise contrived so carefully to avoid the errors of the Arabian commentators while employing their works. He laid the principle of individuation in *See* Trantl, Geach. d. Logik im Abend, iv. 184.
matter and became a heretic; for, as was shown by

Bishop Etienne Tempier, this view conflicts with the doctrine of immaterial individuals, as the angels and departed souls.

Duns Scotus tried to help himself by the device of the notorious *Haccceitas,* which is often cited without much regard to the connection of the notions as the height of Scholastic absurdity. It does, in fact, seem an absurd idea to make the individuality in turn merely the effect or result of a universal *ad hoc;* and yet this solution of the difficulty is, of all the expedients that have been proposed, the one most in harmony—or, let us rather say, the one least inconsistent—with the collective Aristotelian doctrine.

The Nominalists, however, found no great difficulty here. Occam very calmly explains that the principle of individuation lies in the individuals themselves, and this harmonises excellently with the Aristotle who makes individuals substances, but all the worse with the Platonising Aristotle, who invented the 'second substances' (notions of species and genus) and substantial forms. To take the first Aristotle literally, means to reject the second Aristotle altogether. But the second is the reigning one, and that not only in Scholasticism, amongst the Arabians and the old commentators, but also in the genuine unadulterated Aristotelian system. And therefore, we may in fact regard Nominalism, and especially the Nominalism of the second Scholastic period, as the beginning of the end of Scholasticism. In the history of Materialism, however, Nominalism is of importance not only through its general opposition to Platonism and its recognition of the concrete, but also through perfectly distinct historical traces, which indicate that Nominalism did actually prepare the way for Materialism, and that it was chiefly and most strongly cultivated above all in England, where Materialism also later found its most vigorous development.

If the older Nominalism connects itself with the tenor of the Aristotelian categories against the Neo-Platonic commentators, it cannot be doubted that the spread of the whole body of Aristotle's writings had a very great influence on the origin and extension of the later Nominalism. Once freed from the leading strings of Neo-Platonic tradition, and launched out on the high sea of the Aristotelian system, the Scholastics must soon have discovered so many difficulties in the doctrine of the universal, or, more fully expressed, the doctrine of word, notion, and thing, that innumerable attempts were made to solve the great problem. In fact, as Prantl has shown in his "Gesch. der Logik im Abendlande," instead of the three main conceptions *(universalia ante rem, post rem,* or *in re),* there appear the most manifold combinations and attempts at reconciliation; and the opinion that the 'universalia,' in fact, have their first origin in the human mind, is found isolated in writers who, on the whole, distinctly belong to Realism.37 Comp. on this point, besides developed Nominalism is traced in n

Prantl, in particular Barach, Zur manuscript of the tenth century.

Gesch. des Nominalism, ror Roscel-So also in isolated passages Alber lin, Wien, 1866, where a very fully tus Magnus; comp. Prantl, iii. 97 *S.* VOL. I. O

Besides the spread of Aristotle's writings, Averroism also may have had some influence, although, as the forerunner of Materialism, it is chiefly to be regarded from the standpoint of freethought; for the Arabian philosophy is, in spite of its leaning to naturalism, yet essentially realistic in the sense of the medieval factions, *i.e.,* it Platonises; and even its naturalism is fain to adopt a mystic colouring. But in so far as the Arabian commentators energetically raised the questions with which we are here concerned, and in general compelled men to increased independence of thought, they must indirectly have furthered Nominalism. The main influence nevertheless came from a quarter from which one at first sight would least expect it—from that Byzantine logic which has been so much decried on account of its abstract subtleties.8

It cannot indeed but surprise us that the very extreme of Scholasticism, that ultra-formal logic of the schools and of the sophistical dialectic, should be connected with that reawakening empiricism which ended by sweeping Scholasticism away; and yet we have traces of this connection lasting down to the present time. The most distinct empiricist among the chief logicians of our time, John Stuart Mill, opens his "System of Logic" with two utterances of Condorcet and Sir W. Hamilton bestowing hish praise upon the Scholastics for the subtlety and precision -which they have lent to the expression of thought in language. Mill himself adopts into his "Logic" several distinctions of various kinds in the signification of words which belong to the Scholasticism of those last centuries of the middle ages, which we are wont to regard as an unbroken chain of absurdities.

The proof of the connection be-nies to 'universalia' the name of tween the spread of the Byzantine things. With Occam they are, of logic in the West and the victory of course, not 'names' but 'termini,' Nominalism is one of the most valua-which represent the things compreblcresultsof Prantl's "Geschicht-eder bended in them. The 'terminus'is Logik im Abendlande." ThatPrantl ono element of a mentally formed himself designates the tendency of judgment; it has no existence w batOccam, not as 'Nominalism,' but as ever outside the soul, but it is also 'Terminism' (from the logical 'ter-not purely arbitrary, like the word minus,' the chief implement of this by which it may be expressed, but it school), is irrelevant to our purpose, arises by a natural necessity in the as we only just touch the subject, contact of the mind with things. Accordingly we still use 'Nomina-Comp. Prautl, iii. S. 344 ff. esp. lism' in the wider sense of that body Anm. 78 of opposition to Platonism which de

The riddle is, however, soon solved if we start with the consideration that it was a.principal service of English philosophy since Hobbes and Locke to deliver us from the usurpation of idle words in speculation, and to connect our thoughts more with things than traditional expressions. But in order to attain this, the doctrine of the significance of words must be thoroughly comprehended, and be begun with a keen criticism of the relation of the word and its meaning. And to this end the Byzantine logic, in the development which it had attained in the West, and especially in the school of Occam, exhibits preliminary efforts which are still of positive interest.

That empiricism and logical formalism go hand in hand is in other respects, apart from this, by no means a rare phenomenon. The more our efforts are directed to allow of things acting on us as freely as possible, and to making experience and natural science the foundation of our views, the more shall we feel the necessity of connecting our conclusions with accurately defined signs for the things we mean to express, instead of allowing the ordinary forms of expression to bring in with them into our opinions the prejudices of past centuries and of the childish stages in the development of the human spirit.

It was not, of course, that the whole body of the Byzantine logic had originally been worked out as a conscious emancipation from the forms of language, but much rather as an attempt to follow to its consequences the supposititious identity of speech and thought. Yet the result could not but end in the emancipation of the precise expression of thought from the forms of speech. He who is still in these days disposed, with Trendelenburg, K F. Becker, and Ueberweg, to identify grammar and logic, might certainly have learnt much from the logicians of those ages, for they made earnest efforts at a logical analysis of all grammar, and in doing so at least succeeded in creating a new language, at whose barbarism the Humanists could never express sufficient horror.

In Aristotle the identification of grammar and logic is still naive, because in this case, as Trendelenburg has very rightly observed, both sciences sprang up from a common root: indeed, to Aristotle came certain penetrating gleams of light upon the distinction of word and notion, though they are not as yet sufficient to scatter the general darknessThere appear in his logic always only subject and predicate, considered as parts of speech, noun and verb, or the adjective and copula instead of the verb; in addition negation, the words that indicate the extent to which the predi-: cate applies to the subject, as 'all,' 'some,' and certain auxiliaries used to express the modality of judgments. The Byzantine logic, on the other hand, such as it was, as it spread in the thirteenth century over the West, had not only brought the adverb into play, enlarged the circle of auxiliary verbs used in logic, and treated the signification of the cases of the noun, but had above all things perceived and endeavoured to overcome the ambiguities which are brought in by the relation of the noun to the group of ideas that it denotes. These ambiguities are in Latin, which possesses no article, much more numerous than in German; as, for example, in the well-known example in which a drunken student says that he has not drunk 'vinum,' because he avails himself of the *rescrvalio mentalis* of understanding by ' vinum,' wine in its full extent, that is, all the wine that exists, and the wine that exists in India, or even in his neighbour's glass, he has, of course, not drunk. Such sophisms, indeed, formed the regular business of the late Scholastic logic, and its extravagance in this respect, as well as in the subtle application of the Scholastic distinctions, has rightly been condemned, and bos often enough helped the Humanists to victory in their contest with the Scholastics. Yet the main motive to this activity was a very serious one, and the whole problem will, perhaps, sooner or later, have to be taken up again—of course in another connection, and with another ultimate purpose.

The result of the great experiment was so far negative, that a perfect logic was not to be reached by this path, and a natural reaction against the extravagance of its artificiality soon caused the child to be thrown away together with the bath. And yet there was attained not merely a habit of precision in the expression of thought which had been 'unknown to the ancients,' as Condorcet says, but also a view of the nature of language admirably harmonising with empiricism.

Sokrates had thought that all words must originally have expressed as completely as possible the true nature of the things they denoted; Aristotle, in a moment of his empiricism, declared language to be conventional; the school of Occam tended, though it may have been without a full consciousness of it, to make the language of science conventional, that is, by an arbitrary fixing of the notions, to free it from the type of expressions that had become historical, and so to get rid of innumerable ambiguities and confusing by-notions. This whole process was, however, necessary if a science was to arise which, instead' of creating everything out of the subject, should allow the things themselves to speak, whose language is often quite other than that of our grammars and dictionaries. This one circumstance alone makes Occam a most important forerunner of a Bacon, a Hobbes, and a Locke. This he was, moreover, by the greater activity of independent speculation, instead of mere repetition, which was part of his tendency; but above all, by the natural harmony of his logical activity with the bases of the old Nominalism, which in all' universals' finds comprehensive terms only for the only substantial things, the concrete, individual, sensible things that alone exist outside-human thought.

Nominalism was, for the rest, more than a mere opinion of the schools, like any other. It was really the principle of scepticism asserting itself against the whole medieval love of authority. Cultivated by the Franciscans in their standpoint of opposition, it turned the edge of its analytical modes of thought against the edifice of the hierarchy in the Church's constitution, just as it attacked the hierarchy of the intellectual world; and therefore we must not be surprised that Occam demanded freedom of thought, that in religion he held fast to the practical side, and that he, as did later his countryman Hobbes, threw the whole of theology overboard by declaring the doctrines of the faith to be incapable of proof. His doctrine that science, in the last line, has no other subject-matter than the sensible particular, is in our day the foundation of Stuart Mill's " Logic;" and thus he expresses generally the opposition of the healthy human reason to Platonism, with a keenness which gives him a lasting significance. Prantl, iii. 328. The demand At the same time Occam by no for freedom of thought applies indeed means mistakes the value of uni only to philosophical principles (comp. versnl propositions. He tenches ex tho remarks in the following chapter pressly that science is concerned with about twofold truth in the middle universals (and not directly with in ages); but as theology remains essen-dividual things), but yet it does not tiully only a province of belief, and treat of universals as such, but merely not of knowledge, the demand ap-as the expression of the particulars

'plies to the whole sphere of scientific included in them. Prantl, iii. 332 thought. folL esp. note 75a CHAPTER IIL THE RETURN OF MATERIALISTIC THEORIES WITH THE REGENERATION OF THE SCIENCES.

In the place of positive achievements, the domination of Scholasticism in the sphere of the sciences resulted only in a system of notions and terms, which was deeply rooted, and consecrated by many centuries. Progress had indeed to commence its work by shattering this system, in which were embodied the prejudices and fundamental errors of the traditional philosophy. Nevertheless, even the fetters of Scholasticism in their time rendered important services to the intellectual development of humanity. Like the theological Latin of the same period, so the formulas of Scholasticism formed a common element of intellectual intercourse for the whole of Europe. Apart from the formal exercise of thought, which remained very important and real even in the most degenerate form of the Aristotelian philosophy, this community of thought, which the old system had created, soon became an excellent medium for the propagation of new ideas. The period of the renascence of the sciences formed a connection among the learned men of Europe such as has never existed since. The fame of a discovery, of an important book, of a literary controversy, spread, if not quicker, at all events more generally and thoroughly, than in our own days, through all civilised countries.

If we reckon the whole course of the regenerative movement, whose beginning and end are difficult to fix, as from the middle of the fifteenth to the middle of the seventeenth century, we may then distinguish within this term of two centuries four epochs, which, although not sharply marked off from each other, are nevertheless in their main features clearly distinguishahle from each other. The first of them concentrates the chief interest of Europe upon philology. It was the age of Laurentius Valla, of Angelo Politiano, and of the great Erasmus, who forms the transition to the theological epoch. The dominion of theology is sufficiently indicated by the storms of the Reformation era: it suppressed for a long time almost all other scientific interests, especially in Germany. Then the natural sciences, which had been gaining strength since the beginning of the renascence in the quiet workshops of inquirers, in the brilliant era of Kepler and Galilei, first took up a commanding and prominent position. Only in the fourth line came philosophy, although the culminating point of Bacon's and Descartes' activity in establishing principles falls not much later than the great discoveries of Kepler. All these epochs of creative labour were still exercising an unslackening influence upon their contemporaries, when the materialistic physic was again systematically developed, about the middle of the seventeenth century, by Gassendi and Hobbes.

In placing the regeneration of philosophy at the conclusion of this course, we shall scarcely meet with any serious objection if we take the ' renascence,' the 'revival of antiquity,' not in a mere literal sense, but in the sense of the true character which belongs to this great and essentially homogeneous movement. It is a time which enthusiastically clings to the efforts and traditions of antiquity, but in which, at the same time, there are everywhere present the germs of a new, a great, and an independent period of thought. It might indeed be possible to separate from the ' renascence,' in the strict sense, this character of 'independence,' and the appearance of new and completely modern efforts and aims, and, with the names of Galilei and Kepler, Bacon and Descartes, to begin an entirely new period; but, as in all attempts to mark off historical periods, we everywhere come upon intersecting threads and overlapping characteristics. Thus, as we shall see, Gassendi and Boyle, in the seventeenth century, take hands with the Atomism of the ancients, while Leonardo da Vinci and Luis Vives, undoubtedly men of the freshest type of the new movement, are already passed far beyond the traditions of antiquity, and attempt to found a science of experience in complete independence of Aristotle and the whole of antiquity.

Similarly, it is very difficult to mark off sharply the beginnings of the refiorescence of antiquity. We spoke above of the middle of the fifteenth century, because it was at that time that Italian philology attained its complete development, and that Humanism entered upon its struggle against Scholasticism. But this movement had its prelude a full century earlier in the era of Petrarca and Boccaccio, and we cannot deny that the new spirit which then showed itself in Italy may be traced at least as far back as the age of the Emperor Frederick the Second, whose importance we have ascertained in the first chapter of this section. In this connection, however, the transformation of Scholasticism through the knowledge of Aristotle and the spread of Arabian literature, may also be regarded as one of the first and most important facts in the great process of regeneration. Philosophy, which forms the conclusion of the whole movement, and impresses its seal upon the completion of the great revolution, appears also at the beginning of the movement.

We have already seen, in the two last chapters, how, in the last centuries of the middle ages, under the influence of Arabian philosophy and Byzantine logic, there appeared now unbridled freethinking, and now painful struggle for liberty of thought. A special form of this abortive effort after liberty of thought is the doctrine of twofold truth, philosophical and theological, which may exist side by side in spite of their entire inconsistency. It is obvious that this doctrine is the true original of what has recently been called by a very ill-chosen but now firmly-rooted expression,'book-keeping by double entry.' - Prantl, Gesch. d. Logik, iii. S. science, took place in great part as r, remarks that it cannot be often early as the thirteenth century, and enough pointed ont "that the so-chiefly through the knowledge then called revival of antiquity, as regards made possible of Aristotle and of pliilosophy, mathematic and natural Arabian literature.

The chief seat of this doctrine in the thirteenth century was the University of Paris, where, even before the middle of the century, in fact, there appeared the curiously sounding doctrine, "that there have been many truths from eternity till now which were not God himself." A teacher at Paris, Jean de Brescain, excused himself in the year 1247 for his 'errors,' by observing that he had maintained the doctrines found heretical by the bishop as not' theologically' but only ' philosophically' true. In spite of the bishop's absolute prohibition of all such subterfuges, the audacity of these 'merely philosophical' assertions appears to have gone on increasing. For in the years 1270 and 1276, there is another long series of such propositions condemned, the whole of which are of obviously Averroistic origin. The resurrection, the creation of the world in time, the changeableness of the individual soul, were denied in the name of philosophy, while it was at the same time admitted that all these doctrines are true 'according to the Catholic faith. ' Their real attitude, however, by this freely admitted theological truth, appears by the circumstance that doctrines of the following kind appear among the condemned doctrines: "Nothing more can be known, because of the science of theology." "The Christian religion prevents us from learning anything more. " "The only wise men in the world are the philosophers." "The teachings of the theologians are based upon fables." « The facts will be found exhaus-contained in Maywald, Die Lehre von tively given in Renan's Averrods der Zweifachen Wahrheit, ein Ver ,'Paris, 1852), ii. 2, 3. A summary such der Trennnng von Theologie statement of all that specially relates unci Philosophic im Mittelalter (Ber to the doctrine of twofold truth is lin, 1871).

It is true that we do not know the originators of these propositions. They may possibly in great part never havo been maintained in books, at least, not with this openness, but maintained only in lectures and disputations. But the way in which the bishops attack the evil shows plainly enough that the spirit which produced such doctrines was widely spread and venturesome. The modestly sounding statement that all this is only 'philosophically true/ taken in connection with doctrines that exalt philosophy far above theology, and find the latter a hindrance to science, is obviously nothing more than a shield against persecution, and a means of keeping open a retreat in case of a trial. It is clear, moreover, that there was at that time a party which did not occasionally only, when interpreting Aristotle, advance these propositions, but also put them forth deliberately in opposition to the orthodox Dominicans. The same spirit appeared also in England and Italy, where, in the thirteenth century, almost simultaneously with these events in Paris, exactly similar principles crop up and are condemned by the bishops.

In Italy, at this time, Averroism was quietly taking deep root at the High School of Padua. It was this university that gave the intellectual tone to the whole northeast of Italy, and it was itself in turn under the influence of the statesmen and merchants of Venice, who were freethinking men of the world, with an inclination to practical Materialism. Here Averroism held its ground, although, to be sure, in company with the worshipping of Aristotle and all the barbarism of the Scholastics, until the seventeenth century; less controverted than at any other university, and on that account also seldomer mentioned. Like a 'strong fortress of barbarism,' Padua struggled against the Humanists, who, especially in Italy, almost all inclined to Plato, whose beautiful forms of language and conceptions charmed them, while they took care, with a few exceptions, not to lose themselves in the mystical side of Platonism. As against the Humanists, so the Scholastics of Padua, rationalistic indeed, but fettered by their traditions, struggled as long as they could against the physicists. Cremonini, the last of this school, taught at the University of Padua contemporaneously with Galilei: while the latter taught the Elements of Euclid for a trifling remuneration, Cremonini received a salary of 2000 gulden for his lectures on the scientific writings of Aristotle. It is said that when Galilei discovered the satellites of Jupiter, Cremonini would from that time never again look through a telescope, because the thing was contrary to Aristotle. But Cremonini was a freethinker, whose views as to the soul, although not strictly Averroistic, were certainly anything but ecclesiastical; and he maintained his right to teach anything that was in Aristotle with a firmness that deserves our recognition. Maywald, Zweif. Wahrh., S. II.; done. Les universites de Padoue et Kenan, Averroes, p. 219. do Bologne n'en font rcellemcut Maywald, S. 13; Renan, p. 208, qu'une, au moin-spourl'enseignement where may be found also, after Him-philosophique et medical. C'etuient reau, Philos. Soho-last., some remarks les memos professeurs qui, presque on the connection of English Aver-tous les ans, emigraient de Tune a roism with the Franciscan party. l'autre pour obtenir unc augmenta Benan, Averrois, p. 258: "Le tion de salaire. Pudoue d'un autre mouvement intellectual du nord-est cute, n'est que le quartior latin de de l'ltalie, Bologne, Ferrare, Venise, Venise; tout ce qui s'enseignait *it* so rattache tout entier a celui de Pa-Padoue, s' imprimait i Venise."

One man in this series of scholastic freethinkers deserves to be specially mentioned here: Petrus Pomponatius, the author of a book which appeared in 1516 on the immortality of the soul. The question of immortality was at that time so popular in Italy, that the students of a newly-appointed professor, whose tendency they wanted to learn, called to him in his first lecture to discuss the 80uL7 And it does not appear that the orthodox doctrine was the favourite one; for Pomponatius, who, from beneath the shield of the doctrine of twofold truth, delivered per

« Rcuan, Averroes, pp. 257, 326 folL Eenan, Averroes, p. 283.

Laps the boldest and acutest attacks upon immortality which were then known, was a very favourite teacher.

He was certainly not an Averroist; nay, he was the head of a school which engaged in a bitter war with the Averroists, and which quoted the commentator Alexander of Aphrodisias as the authority for its doctrines. But the apple of discord in this controversy was in reality only the doctrine of the soul and of immortality, and the 'Alexandrists' stood on all main points in the full current of Averroistic modes of thought. With regard, however, to the question of immortality, the 'Alexandrists' went more thoroughly to work; they rejected monopsychism, and declared the soul simply," according to Aristotle," to be not immortal—the rights of the Catholic faith being at the same time reserved as already explained.

Pomponatius, in his book on immortality, adopts a very respectful attitude towards the Church. He zealously approves the confutation of Averroism by Saint Thomas. But all the more bold are the ideas conveyed in his own criticism of the question of immortality. The treatment is on the whole strictly Scholastic—the bad Latin inseparable from Scholasticism not excluded. But in the last section of the work, where Pomponatius discusses "eight great difficulties" in the doctrine of immortality, he is by no means content with verbal expositions and quotations from Aristotle. Here all the scepticism of the age finds expression, even to the extent of very distinct approbation of the theory of 'the three impostors.' Cap. xiii. and xiv. In the last editions are unknown to me. The cap. (xv.) is expressed his submission passages quoted in my first edition to the judgment of the Church, were taken from M. Carriere, Die

There are *no* natural proofs of im-Philos. Weltanschauung der Rcfor mortality, and it rests therefore solely ma-tionszeit, Stuttg. u. Tub., 1847.
upon revelation. The strongest pas-They are, indeed, in essential points sages are in pp. 101 until near the end faithful, but are freer than is neces in the edition of Bardili (Tubingen, sary, and the some-what pathetic and 79'). PP- foU. in an edition elevated tone is foreign to the origi w.thout any place, 1534. The. ear-lier nal.
Pomponatius here considers the mortality of the soul as philosophically proved. The eight difficulties of the doctrine are the commonest general arguments for immortality; and these arguments Pomponatius refutes no more on the Scholastic method, but by sound common sense and by moral considerations. Among these difficulties the fourth runs thus: Since all religions ("onmes leges") maintain immortality, then if there is really no such thing, the whole world is deluded. To this, however, the answer is: That almost every one is deluded by religion must be admitted; but there is no particular mis-

fortune in that. For as there are three laws—those of Moses, Christ, and Mohammed,— they are either all three false, and then the whole world is deluded—or two at least are false, and then the majority are deluded. We must know, however, that according to Plato and Aristotle, the legislator (" politicus ") is a physician of the soul, and as the legislator is more concerned to make men virtuous than to make them enlightened, he must adapt himself to their different natures. The less noble require rewards and punishments. But some cannot be kept in check by these, and it is for them that immortality has been invented. As the physician says what is not true,—as the nurse allures the child to many things of which it cannot as yet understand the true reason: so acts the founder of a religion, and is completely justified in so acting, his final end being regarded as a purely political one.

We must not forget that this view was very widely held among the upper classes in Italy, and especially among practical statesmen. Thus Macchiavelli speaks in his Discourses on Livy: 49 "The princes of a republic or a kingdom must maintain the pillars of the religion they hold. If this is done, it will be an easy tiiing for them to keep their state religious, and therefore in prosperity and unity. And everything that favours their interests, even although they hold it to be false, they must favour and assist, and must do so all the more, the more prudent and politic they are. And as this conduct of the wise has been observed, the belief in miracles has arisen, which are exalted by religion, although they are equally false, because the prudent magnify them, no matter what their origin may have been, and then the respect paid to them by these men secures them universal belief." Thus Leo X. may have very well said within himself, when preparing to sit in judgment on Pomponatius's book: "The man is quite right, if only it would make no scandal!" Comp. Macchiavelli, Eriirter. iiherg. von Dr. Grutzmacker, Berlin, iiber d. Erste Decade des T. Livius, 1S71, S. 41.

To the third objection, that if our souls were mortal there could be no just ruler of the world, Pomponatius replies: "The true reward of virtue is virtue itself, which makes man happy; for human nature can have nothing higher than virtue, since it alone makes man secure and free from all disturbances. In the virtuous man all is in harmony; he has nothing to fear or hope, and remains unmoved in fortune or misfortune. To the vicious man.vice itself is punishment. As Aristotle shows in the seventh book of the Ethics, to the vicious man everything is spoiled. He trusts nobody; he has no rest, waking or sleeping; and leads, in tortures of soul and body, such a miserable life, that no wise man, however poor and weak he may be, would choose the life of a tyrant or a vicious aristocrat."

Spiritual apparitions are explained by Pomponatius to be the delusions of the excited fancy or the deceptions of priests. The 'possessed' are sick (Object. 5 and 6). At the same time, he admits a residuum of these appearances, and refers them to the influence of good and evil spirits, or to astrological causes. Belief in astrology was indissolubly bound up with the Averroistic rationalism.

In conclusion, Pomponatius protests with great energy against those persons (Object. 8) who maintain that vicious and guilty men commonly deny the immortality of the soul, while good and upright men believe it. On the contrary, he rays, it is quite obvious that many vicious persons believe in immortality, and at the same time allow themselves to be carried away by their pacsions, while many righteous and noble men have held the soul to be mortal. Among these he reckons Homer and Simonides, Hippokrates and Galen, Alexander of Aphrodisias and the great Arabian philosophers; finally, of our own countrymen (' ex nostratibus, ' here we see, even in the Scholastic, the spirit of the renascence!), Pliny and Seneca.

In a similar spirit Pomponatius wrote of the freedom of the will, and boldly set forth its inconsistencies. Here, in fact, he criticises the Christian idea of God as he acutely tracks out and exposes the contradiction between the doctrine of the omnipotence, omniscience, and goodness of God, and the responsibility of man. In a special treatise, moreover, Pomponatius attacked the belief in miracles, where it is indeed true that we must also take astrological influences, as natural and actual facte, as part of our bargain. Thus it is genuinely Arabian, for example, when he refers the gift of prophecy to the influence of the stars and to a mysterious communion with unknown spirits. On the other hand, the efficacy of relics depends upon the imagination of the credulous, and would be just as great if the relics were the bones of a dog.

There has been some controversy whether, in regard to these views of Pomponatius, his submission to the Catholic faith was more than a mere form. Such questions are, it is very true, in many similar cases extremely difficult to decide, since we are in no way justified in applying to them the standard of our own time. The immense respect for the Church—increased by so many a stake and autoda-fe—was quite sufficient to shed a holy awe about the creed, even in the minds of the boldest thinkers—an awe which veiled in impenetrable cloud the border-line between word and fact. But in what direction Pomponatius

M llaywald, Lehre von d. Zwcif. Waurh., S. 45 ff.

made the tongue of the balance incline in this contest between philosophical and theological truth, he has sufficiently indicated for us when he declares the philosophers alone to be the gods of the earth, and as far removed from all other men, of whatever condition, as real men are from painted men!

This equivocal character of the relation between faith and knowledge is in many ways a characteristic and constant feature of the period of transition to the modern freedom of thought. Nor could even the Eeformation discard it; and we find it, from Pomponatius and Cardan down to Gassendi and Hobbes, in the most various gradations, from timidly-concealed doubt to conscious irony. In connection with it appears the tendency to an equivocal defence of Christianity, or of individual doctrines, which loves to turn the darker side outwards; and there are instances as well of obvious intention to produce an unfavourable conviction, as in Vanini, as also cases such as that of Mersenne's "Commentary on Genesis," where it is hard to say what is the precise object.

Any one who finds the essential element of Materialism in its opposition to the belief of the Church, might reckon Pomponatius and his numerous more or less bold successors among the Materialists. If, on the contrary, we seek the beginnings of a positive Materialistic interpretation of nature, we shall fail to find any rudiment of such an interpretation even amongst the most enlightened Scholastics. A single, and an as yet quite unique, instance that may be thus reckoned appeared, indeed, as early as the fourteenth century. In the year 1348, at Paris, Nicolaus de Autricuria was compelled to make recantation of several doctrines, and amongst others, this doctrine, that *in the processes of nature there is nothing to be found but the motion of the combination and separation of atoms.* Here, then, is a formal Atomist in the very heart Prantl, Gesch. d. Logiic im Abendl., iv. S. 2 folL VOL. L *V* of the dominion of the Aristotelian theory of nature. But the same hold spirit ventured also upon a general declaration that we should put Aristotle, and Averroes with him, on one side, and apply ourselves directly to things themselves. Thus Atomism and Empiricism here go hand in hand together!

In reality, the authority of Aristotle had first to be broken before men could attain to direct intercourse with things themselves. While, however, Nicolaus de Autricuria, in complete isolation, so far as we yet know, was making a fruitless effort in this direction, there began about the same time in Italy the prelude to the great struggle between Humanists and Scholastics in Petrarca's violent assaults.

The decisive struggle fell in the fifteenth century, and although, on the whole, the relations to Materialism are somewhat distant — since the great Italian Humanists were for the most part Platonists—it is nevertheless interesting to observe that one of the earliest champions of Humanism, Laurentius Valla, first made himself extensively known by a " Dialogue on Pleasure," which may be regarded as the first attempt at a vindication of Epikureanism.52 It is true that in the issue the representative in the dialogue of Christian ethic carries off the victory over the Epikurean as over the Stoic; Vut the Epikurean is treated with a visible liking, which is of great weight in view of the general horror of Epikureanism which was still prevalent. In his attempts to reform logic, Valla was not always fair to the subtleties of Scholasticism, and his own treatment tinges logic very strongly with rhetorical elements. Yet the undertaking was of great historical importance, as the first attempt at a serious criticism which not only attacked the corruptions of Scholasticism, but did not shrink even before the authority of Aristotle himself. Valla is in other provinces also one of the first leaders of awakening criticism. His appearance is in Comp. Lorenzo Valla, ein Vortrag von J. Vahlen. Berlin, 1870, S. 6 foil. every respect a sign of the end of the unconditional dominion of tradition and infallible authorities.

In Germany, the Humanist movement, powerfully as it had begun, was early and completely absorbed by the theological movement. The very circumstance that here the opposition made the most decided and open break with the hierarchy, perhaps brought with it that the scientific department was partly neglected, partly treated in a more conservative spirit than elsewhere. It was only after the lapse of centuries that the attainment of liberty of thought atoned for this sacrifice.

It was Philip Melanchthon who presented the most decided example for the reform of philosophy on the old foundation of Aristotle. He gave out openly that he intended to introduce into philosophy, by going back to the genuine writings of Aristotle, a reform like that intended for theology by Luther in going back to the Bible. But this reform of Melanchthon's did not, on the whole, result for the good of Germany. It was, on the one hand, not radical enough; for Melanchthon himself, with all his subtlety of thought, was thoroughly hampered by the fetters of theology, and even of astrology. On the other hand, the immense weight of the reformer and the influence of his academical activity brought about in Germany a return In Scholasticism, which lasted until long after Descartes, &.ud formed the chief hindrance to philosophy in Germany.

It is worth observing, however, that Melanchthon introduced regular lectures upon psychology Avith his own textbook. His views often border closely enough upon Materialism, but are everywhere restrained within narrow limits by the doctrine of the Church, without any attempt at deeper reconciliation. The soul was explained by Melanchthon, after the false reading ej/ SeXeeta for *tvreXeX* uninterrupted; a reading upon which chiefly rested the assumption that Aristotle believed in the immortality of the soul Amerbach, the professor at Witteoberg, who wrote a strictly Aristotelian Psychology, was so embroiled with the reformer over this reading, that he left Wittenberg in consequence, and became a Catholic again.

A third treatise on psychology appeared about the same time from the hand of the Spaniard Luis Vives.

Vives must be regarded as the most important philosophical reformer of this period, and as a forerunner of Descartes and of Bacon. His whole life was an uninterrupted and successful struggle against Scholasticism. With regard to Aristotle, his view was that the genuine disciples of his spirit should go beyond him, and interrogate nature herself, as the ancients had done. Not out of blind traditions nor subtle hypotheses is nature to be known, but through direct investigation by the method of experiment. In spite of this unusual clearness as to the true foundations of inquiry, Vives seldom appeals in his Psychology to the facts of life in order to communicate the observations of himself and others. The chapter on the immortality of the soul is written in a thoroughly rhetorical style, and founds what is offered as an irrefutable argument on the slenderest proofs—in what has continued down to our own day to be a favourite fashion. And yet Vives was one of the clearest heads of his century, and his psychology, especially in the doctrine of the emotions, abounds in subtle observations and happy appreciations of character.

The honest naturalist of Zurich, Konrad Gessner, also wrote a Psychology about this time, which is interesting in its contents and treatment. After an extremely concise, almost tabular, statement of all possible views as to the nature of the soul, follows abruptly a detailed doctrine of the senses. Here Gessner feels himself at home, and lingers complacently in physiological expositions, which are in part of a very thorough character. It produces a very curious impression, on the other hand, if wo cast a glance at the same time over the fearful chaos of theories and opinions on the soul in the first part of the work. "Some hold," as Gessner tells us, with imperturbable calm, "the soul to be nothing; some hold it to be a substance. " 53

On all sides, then, we see the shaking of the old Aristotelian tradition, the unsettling of opinions, and the exciting of doubts, which probably only exhibit themselves very partially in literature. But very soon psychology, which was treated in such an extraordinary number of works from the end of the sixteenth century, again becomes systematised, and the fermentation of the period of transition makes room for a dogmatic Scholasticism, whose chief object it is to reconcile itself with theology.

But while theology still held full dominion over the sphere of mind, and violent controversies drowned the voice of calm judgment, rigid inquiry was quietly laying in the province of external nature an impregnable basis for an entirely revolutionised theory of the universe.

In the year 1543 appeared, with a dedication to the Pope, the book on the "Orbits of the Heavenly Bodies," by Nicolaus Copernicus of Thorn. Within the last days of his life the grey-headed inquirer received the first copy of his book, and then in contentment departed from the world.4

What now, after the lapse of three centuries, every school child must learn, that the earth revolves upon its own axis and round the sun, was then a great, and, despite a few forerunners, a new truth, diametrically opposed to the general consciousness. It was, however, a truth which contradicted Aristotle, and with which the Church had not yet reconciled herself. What to some extent sheltered the doctrine of Copernicus against the scorn of the conservative masses, against the Scholastic and ecclesiastical fanaticism, was the rigidly scientific form and the superfluity of proof of the work, on which the author had laboured, in the quiet leisure of his prebendal stall at Frauenburg, with admirable patience for three-and-thirty years. There is something really great in the thought that a man who is seized in the period of fiery creativeness by a world-stirring idea, with full consciousness of its range, should retire in order to devote the whole of his future life to the calm working out of this idea. And this explains the enthusiasm of his few earliest disciples, as well as the discomposure of the pedants and the reserve of the Church.

All the psychological treatises of articles "Seelenlehre " and " Vives" the Reformation period here men-in. the Encl. des ges. Erzieh.-und tioned appeared printed together in a Unterrichtswesens. single volume through Jacob Gessner ' Comp. Humboldt's Kosmos, ii. at Zurich in 1503; the three first S. 344 (E. T. ed. Otte, ii. 684, uad named also at Basel. Compare the note), and Anm. 22, S. 497 foil.

How critical the undertaking appeared in this aspect is shown by the circumstance that Professor Osiander, who carried the book through the press, in the customary preface added by him represented the whole doctrine of Copernicus as a hypothesis. Copernicus himself had no share in this concealment. Kepler, himself animated by haughty freedom of thought, calls him a man of free spirit; and, in fact, only such a man could have completed the gigantic task. Humboldt's Kosmos, ii. S. 345 rect contradiction with his dedication (E. T. ii. 686). "An erroneous to Pope Paul III. " The author of opinion unfortunately prevails, even the preface, according to Gassendi. in the present day, that Copernicus, was Andreas Osiander; not indeed, from timidity and from Apprehension as Humboldt says, "a mathematician of priestly persecution, advanced his then living at Nuremberg," but the views regarding the planetary move-well-known Lutheran theologian, ment of tho earth, and the position The astronomical revision of the of the sun in tho centre of tho plane-proofs was undoubtedly done by tary system, as mere *h apolheus,* which Johannes Schoner, professor of mafulfilled the object of submitting the thematics and astronomy in Nuromorbits of the heavenly bodies more berg. To Schoner and Osiander the cwnveniently to calculation, 'but charge of the printing was assigned which need not necessarily be either by Bhaticus, professor at Wittentrne, or even probable.' These sin-berg, and a pupil of Copernicus, begular words do certainly occur in the cause he considered Nuremberg to be Anonymous preface attached to the a "more suitable" place of publicawork of Copernicus, aud inscribed, tion than Wittenberg (Humboldt's *D. hypothctibus hajus operis;* but Kosmos, Anm. 24 to passage above they are quito contrary to the opinions quoted, ii. S. 498, E. T. at p. 686). expressed by Coperuicas, and in di-These proceedings were, in all proha

"The earth moves" became speedily the formula by which belief in science and in the infallibility of the reason was distinguished from blind adherence to tradition. And when, after a struggle of centuries, the victory in this matter had definitively to be yielded to science, this threw a weight into the scale in its favour, as though it had first given movement by a miracle to the hitherto motionless earth.

bility, very largely influenced by consideration for Melanchthon; for he devoted himself with predilection to astronomy and astrology, and was one of the keenest opponents of the Cupenician system.

At Bome there was at that time greater freedom, and the order of the Jesuits must first be founded in order to render possible the burning of Giordano Bruno and the trial of Galilei. With regard to this change, Ad. Franclc observes, in his notice of Martin's Galilee (Moralistes et Philosophes, Paris, 1872, p. 143): "Chose Strange! le double mouvement de la terre avait deja cte enseigne, au xv« siccle, par Nicolas de Cus, et cette proposition ne l'avait pas empeche de devenir cardinal. En 1533, un Allemand, du nom de Widmannstadt, avait soutenu la meme doctrine a Bome, en presence du Pape Clement VII., et le souverain pontife, entemoignage de sa satisfaction, lui fit present d'un beau mannscrit grec. En 1543 un autre pape, Paul III., occeptait la dedicace de l'ouvrage ou Copernie développait son systeme. Pourquoi done Galilee, soixante et dix ans plus tard, rencontrait-il tant de resistance, soulcvait-il tant de coleres?" The contrast is very happily put, but the solution is very unhappy if Franck thinks that the difference consists in this, that Galilei does not content himself with pure mathematical abstractions, but (with a disparaging reflection upon the speculations of Kepler!) called to his assistance actual observation and experience. As a matter of fact, whatever may have been the differences of their character and talents, Copernicus, Kepler, and Galilei worked in precisely the same spirit of scientific reform, of progress, and the breaking down of narrowing prejudices, without any regard to the limit separating the learned world and the common people. We will, therefore, not omit to quote the following passage — one which does its author honour—from Humboldt's Kosmos, ii. S. 346, E. T. it 687: "The founder of our present system of the universe was almost more distinguished, if possible, by the intrepidity and confidence with which he expressed his opinions, than for the knowledge to which they owed their origin. He deserves to a high degree the fine eulogium passed upon him by Kepler, who, in the introduction to the Budolphine Tables, calls him 'the man of free soul;' 'vir f uit maximo ingenio et quod in hoo exercitio (combating prejudices) magni momenti est, annuo liber. ' When Copernicus is describing, in his dedication to the Pope, the origin of his work, he does not scruple to term the opinion generally expressed amongst theologians of the immobility and central position of the earth an 'absurd acroam.i,' and to attack the stupidity of those who adhere to so erroneous a doctrine. 'If ever,' he writes, 'any empty-headed babblers ((1x010X6701), ignorant of all mathematical science, should take upon themselves to pronounce judgment on his work, through an intentional distortion of any passage in the holy Scriptures (propter aliquem locum Scripturae male ad suum propositum detortum), he should despise so presumptuous an attack!'"

One of the earliest and most decided adherents of the new system of the world, the Italian Giordano Bruno, is a thorough philosopher; and although his system as a whole must be described as pantheistic, it is, nevertheless, in so many ways related to Materialism, that we must not omit its consideration.

While Copernicus clung to Pythagorean traditions — the Index Congregation later described his whole doctrine as simply a *doctrina Pythagorica*—Bruno took Lucretius as his model. He very happily selected the ancient Epikurean doctrine of the infinity of worlds, and taught, combining it with the Copernican system, that all fixed stars are suns, which extend in infinite number throughout space, and have in turn their invisible satellites, which are related to them just as the earth is to the sun or the moon to the earth; a theory which, as against the old assumption of limited space, is of almost as much importance as the doctrine of the revolution of the earth.

"The infinity of forms under which matter appears," taught Bruno, "it does not receive from another and something external, but produces them from itself, and engenders them from its bosom. Matter is not that *prope nihil* which some philosophers have wished to make it, and as to which they have so much contradicted each other; not that naked, mere empty capacity, without efficiency, completeness, and fact. Even though it has no form of its own, it is not at least deprived of it, as ice is of heat, or as the depths are of light, but it is like the travailing mother as she expels her offspring from her bosom. Even Aristotle and his successors make the forms proceed from the inward potency of matter, rather than be produced in it after a kind of external fashion: but instead of finding this active potency in the inward fashioning of the form, they have recognised it for the most part only in the developed reality, seeing that the complete sensible appearance of a thing is not the principal ground of its existence, but only a consequence and effect of it. Nature produces its objects not by substraction and addition, like human art, but only by separation and unfolding. Thus taught the wisest men among the Greeks, and Moses, in describing the origin of things, introduces the universal efficient Being thus speaking: "Let the earth bring forth the living creature; let the waters bring forth the moving creature that hath life;" as though he said, Let matter bring them forth. For according to Moses the material principle of things is water, and therefore he says that the actively formative reason, which he calls 'spirit,' moved upon the face of the waters, and the creation was brought about through its imparting to them strength to bring forth. And so they are all of opinion that things arise, not by composition, but by separation and development, and therefore matter is not without forms—nay, it contains them all, and since it unfolds what it carries concealed within itself, it is in truth all nature and the mother of all living things." 8 I may take this opportunity of adding a supplementary remark to what has been said of Copernicus and Aristarchos of Samos on pp. 117, 118. That Copernicus was acquainted with the view of the ancient astronomer, is (according to Humboldt, Kosmos, ii. S. 349 ff., E. T. ii. 691) not improbable; he refers, however, expressly to two passages of Cicero (Acad. Qu. iv. 30) and Plutarch (De Placitis Philos., iii. 13), which first set him thinking as to the possible revolution of the earth. In Cicero the opinion of Hiketas of Syracuse is referred to; and in Plutarch, that of the Pythagoreans Ekphantos and Uerakkides. That he was first in cited to inquiry by the ideas of Greek antiquity is rendered quite certain, therefore, by Copernicus's own statements; but at the same time he nowhere refers to Aristarchos in particular. Comp. Humboldt, foe, *cU.,* and Lichtenberg, Nicolaus Copernicus, in fifth vol. of Vermischte Schriften (Neue Original-Ausgabe, Gottingen, 1844), S. 193 ff.

Bruno is not only very fond of quoting Lucretius, but he also sedulously imitates him in his didactic poem "De UniversoetMundis." His 'Polemic against the Aristotelian Cosmology' is discussed by Hugo Wernekke (Leipziger Dissert., printed Dresden, 1871). This passage i» taken from iloritz 426, 427. In this thoughtful work Carriere, Die philos. Weltansch. der Bruno is treated with special liking, lleformationszeitt in ihren Bez. zur Comp. , besides, Bartholmess,

O'egenwart, Stuttg. u. Tub. 1847, 8. Jordano Bruno, Paris, 1846, 2 vol.

If we compare this definition, which is declared by Carriere to be one of the most important facts in the history of philosophy, with that of Aristotle, we find this great and decisive difference: that Bruno conceived matter not as the *potential* but as the *actual* and *active.* Aristotle also taught that form and matter in things are one; but as he defined matter as mere potentiality of becoming all that form may make of it, real substantiality belonged to the latter only. These definitions were reversed by Bruno. He makes matter the true essence of things, and' makes it bring forth all forms out of itself. This principle is Materialistic, and we should therefore be fully justified in claiming Bruno entirely for Materialism, but that his development of his system assumes a Pantheistic turn on certain decisive points.

Even Pantheism, it is true, is in itself only a modification of some other Monistic system. The Materialist who defines God as the sum of all animated matter becomes at once a Pantheist without giving up his Materialistic views. But the natural consequence of directing the spirit to God and to divine things is usually this, that the starting-point is forgotten; that our treatment of the subject more and more tends to conceive the soul of the universe not as itself necessarily implicated in matter, but as at least in thought the prime creative principle. In this wise even Bruno developed his theology. He made such a compromise with the Bible, that he taught that, as the Bible was intended for the people, it was obliged to adapt itself even to their notions of natural history, since otherwise it would never have found any acceptance. Bruno was poetical in his way of expressing himself; the greater number of his works are poetical in form, written partly in Latin, partly in Italian. His profound spirit was ever ready to lose itself in a mystic darkness of contemplation; but, again, with equal boldness and recklessness, he ventured also to express his opinions with absolute clearness.

Carriere, We'tansch. der Rofor-is found also in Galilei again in his mationszeit, S. 384. This distinction, letter-totheGrand-Duchesa Christine: one already employed by the Arabian "De sacrae Scripturae testimoniis philosophers, between the ethical in conclusionibus mere naturalibus, purpose of the Bible and its way of quae sensata experientia et neces speaking in accordance with the views sariis demonstrationibus evinci poa of the time at which it was written, sunt temere non usurpandis."

Bruno had originally entered the order of the Dominicans, in order to find leisure for his studies; but having become suspected of heresy, he was obliged to flee, and from that time forward his life was unsettled, and marked by a long chain of persecutions and hostilities. He stayed in turn at Geneva, at Paris, in England and in Germany, at last to venture on the fatal step of returning to his native land. In the year 1592, at Venice, he fell into the hands of the Inquisition.

After many years' confinement, he was condemned at Rome, still unbowed and firm in his convictions. After being degraded and excommunicated, he was handed over to the secular authorities, with the request that they would " punish him as mercifully as possible, and without shedding of blood;" the well-known formula which meant that he was to be burnt. When his sentence was announced to him, he said: "I suspect you pronounce this sentence with more fear than 1 receive it." O-i the 17th February 1600, he was burnt in the Campofiore at Rome. His doctrines have undoubtedly exercised a great influence upon the succeeding developments of philosophy, although he fell into the background after the appearance of Descartes and Bacon, and, like so many great men of the Transition period, became forgotten

It was reserved for the first half of tho seventeenth century to reap in the sphere of philosophy the ripe fruits of the great emancipation which the Eenascence had secured in turn for the most various departments of man's intellectual life. In the first decades of the century Bacon made his appearance, towards its middle came Descartes; his contemporaries were Gassendi and Hobbe3, whom we must regard as the true revivers of a Materialistic philosophy. But besides this, the two more famous ' restorers of philosophy,' as they are usually styled, Descartes as well as Bacon, stand in a close and remarkable relationship to Materialism.

With regard to Bacon in particular, it would be almost more difficult in an exhaustive inquiry to prove sharply and clearly in what he differs from Materialism, than to show what he has in common with it.

Among all philosophical systems, Bacon places that of Demokritos highest. He asserts in his praise that his school had penetrated deeper than any other into the nature of things. The study of matter in its manifold transformations carries us farther than Abstraction. Without the assumption of atoms nature cannot be well explained. Whether final causes operate in nature cannot be definitely decided; at all events, the inquirer must confine himself to efficient causes only.

It is very common to carry back to Bacon and Descartes two opposing lines of philosophy, one of which stretches from Descartes through Spinoza, Leibniz, Kant, and Fichte to Schelling and Hegel; while the other runs from Bacon through Hobbes and Locke to the French Materialists of the eighteenth century; indirectly therefore, we must trace upon this latter line the Materialism of our own days.

And it is, in fact, merely accidental that the name of Materialism appeared first only in the eighteenth century; we have the thing in all essential respects already in Bacon, and we are only restrained from designating Bacon as strictly the restorer of the Materiabstic philosophy by the circumstance that he fixed his attention almost exclusively upon method, and that he expresses himself upon the most important points with equivocal reserve. The vain and superstitious absence of science in Bacon In this respect, the crashing Bacon von Verulam und iHe Methode judgment of Liebig (Ueber Francis tier Naturforschung, Miinchen, 1863) agrees in itself with the Materialistic philosophy—not indeed better, but also not worse, than with most other systems. Only, as to the extensive use which Bacon makes of ' spirits' (spiritus) in his natural philosophy, we may offer a few observations.

Bacon leans here upon tradition, but with a self-sufficiency in his treatment which did little honour to the 'restorer of the sciences.' 'Spirits' of all kinds play a great part in the cosmology and physiology of the NeoPlatonic-Scholastic philosophy; especially, too, among the Arabians, where the spirits of the stars govern the world by means of mystical sympathies and antipathies with the spirits that inhabit earthly things. The doctrine of 'spiritus' took scientific shape chiefly in psychology and physiology, in which its effects may be traced even to the present (for example, in the notion of the slumbering, waking, or excited 'animal spirits'). On this head Galen's theory of the psychical and animal 'spiritus' in connection with the doctrine of the four humours and the temperaments was very early in the Middle Ages fused with the Aristotelian psychology. According to this doctrine, which may be found at full length even in Melanchthon's Psychology, the four fundamental humours are prepared in the liver (second organic process after the first has taken place in the stomach); out of the noblest humour, the blood, the ' spiritus vitalis' is prepared by a new process in the heart; and this is finally (the fourth and last process) in the cavities of the brain refined into the ' spiritus animalis.' cannot be softened hy any reply (see the literature in Ceberweg, Grundriss, iii. S. 39, 3 Aufi., E.T. = Hist. of Phil. ii. 35-6); the facta are too forcible. The moat frivolous dilettanteism in his own scientific experiments, the degradation of science to hypocritical courtliness, ignorance or misapprehension of the great scientific achievements of a Copernicus, a Kepler, a Galilei, who had not waited for the 'Instauratio Magna, malignant hostility and depreciation of real inquirers in his immediate neighbourhood, such as Gilbert and Harvey—these are points enough to display Bacon's scientific character in as unfavourable a light as his political and personal character, so that the view of Macaulay (Critical and Historical Essays, 'Lord Bacon') already properly controverted by Kuno Fischer (Baco von Verulam, Leipzig, 1856, S. 5 II.), has lost all support.

Less simple is the judgment upon Bacon's method. Here Liebig has certainly emptied bath and babe together, although his critical remarks on the theory of induction (comp. also "Induction und Deduction," Miinchen, 1865) contain extremely valuable contributions to a complete theory of scientific method. And yet it is worthy of attention that thoughtful and learned writers on method like W. Herschel (Introd. to the Study of Natural Philosophy, 1832) and Stuart Mill, still regard Bacon's theory of induction as the first although inadequate foundation of their own theory. It is quite right that we have recently begun to recall the forerunners of Bacon in Methodology, such as Leonardo da Vinci, Luis Vives, and especially Galilei; and yet here again we must beware of such exaggerations as that, for instance, in Ad. Franck, Moral

This theory probably owed the deep hold which it obtained chiefly to the fact that it seemed to superficial thought a sufficient bridging over of the gulf between the sensible and the supersensible, a need which was felt as well by the Neo-Platonists as by the Christian theologians. Thus, for example, we find still in Melanchthon that the material and gradually refined 'spiritus' is the immediate bearer of influences, which in theory should be purely spiritual, but which, in fact, are represented by this learned theologian in very material fashion. Thus the divine spirit mingles with these vital and animal spirits of man; but if a devil has his abode in the heart, he blows upon the spirits and brings them into confusion.

To really logical thought the gulf is, of course, equally istes et Philosophes, Prris, 1872, p. works, we also take into account the 154: "La method» de Galilee, anter-authority of his exalted rank, and ieure a celle de Bacon et de Des-the fact that he, with a happy ap-precartes, leur est superieure a toutes ciation, gave its proper watehword to deux." Moreover, we must the age, we shall be doing nothing to not overlook the simple fact that, depreciate hU historical importBacon's great reputation did not anoe.

proceed from a later historical mis-Comp. the following passage at apprehension, but that it has come the end of the physiological part (p. down through a constant tradition 590 of the Zurich edition): " Galenus from his contemporaries down to our-inquit de animahominis: nos spiritus selves. This justifies us in asserting aut animam esse, aut immediatum the extent and the intensity of his instrumentum animae. Quod certe *influence,* and this influence, despite verum est, et luce sua superant solis all the weaknesses of his doctrines, et omnium stellarum lucem. Et yet essentially resulted in advantage quod mirabilius est, his ipsis spiriti to scientific progress and the import-bus in hominibus piis *miscetur* ipsa ance of the natural sciences. If, then, divinus spiritus, et cllicit magis ful in addition to his powerful style and gentes divina luco, ut agnitio Dei the kindling flushes of light in Bacon's sit illustrior et assensio firmior, et great between the supersensible and the finest particle of the finest matter, or the whole globe. The spirits of the modern 'spiritualists' of England and America, are therefore quite right when they shake their believers roughly by the coat-sleeve, or when they career around a room with heavy furniture.

But by the side of this modest, and in form, at least, rigidly scientific doctrine of the vital spirits in the animal organism, there stands the fantastic doctrine of the astrologers and alchemists, which resolves the essence of all things into the workings of such spirits, and thus destroys all distinction between the sensible and the supersensible. We may indeed maintain that the ' spirits' of this theory of nature are absolutely material, and identical with what we nowadays call forces; but even leaving out of sight that in this very notion of force there still perhaps lurks a remnant of this same want of clearness, what shall we think of a kind of matter that acts upon other material things, not by pressure and collision, but by *sympathy?* We have only to add to this, that the idea of nature held by the astrologers and alchemists in its more fantastic forms attributed even to inanimate things a kind of *consciousness,* and we shall no longer find it a very great step to Paracelsus, who conceived the 'spiritus' anthropomorphically, and peopled all the details of the world, both great and small, with innumerable demons, from whom all life and all activity proceed.

And now as to Bacon. To all appearance, indeed, he took up a tolerably decided opposition to the alchemistical theory of nature. He repeatedly treats the spirits as matter and material forces, so that we might believe that the Materialism of Bacon is nowhere to be more clearly seen than in his doctrine of the 'spiritus.' If we look, however, a little closer, we find that he not only adopts into his theory all kinds of superstitious assumptions from the wisdom of the Kahbalists, but that even his Materialistic rendering of magic into 'natural' phenomena is extremely threadbare, and often enough is an entire failure. Thus, for instance, Bacon does not hesitate to attribute to bodies a sort of power of conception, to make the magnet "perceive" the neighbourhood of the iron, and to exalt the "sympathy" and " antipathy" of the " spiritus" into a cause of natural phenomena; and accordingly the "evil eye," the sympathetic curing of warts, and so on, fit admirably into this kind of natural science. It is also quite in harmony with it when Bacon, in his favourite theory of heat, quietly ranks the astrological'heat' of a metal, a star, and so on, on a line with the physical heat.

motus eint ardentiores erga Deum. cia, et manifestos furores cfficinnt, et

K contra, ubi diaboli occupant impellunt corda et alia membra ad corda, *Suo afflatu* turbant spiritus in crudelissimos motus." Comp. Corpus corde et in cerebro, impediunt uui-Keformatorum, xiii. 88 sqq.

It is indeed true that the alchemistico-theosophic theory of nature derived from the Kabbala had won so deep a hold in England, and especially among the aristocratic class, that Bacon in all these matters is laying down nothing original, but is simply moving among the ideas of his environment; and we may in fact assume that Bacon, in his boundless servility, adopted, merely out of complaisance to the court, many more of such views than he could answer for to himself. On the other hand, again, we may observe that the assumption of soul running through all, and even through inorganic nature, as it was taught particularly by Paracelsus, stands in a very peculiar correlation with Materialism. It is the opposite extreme, which not only comes into contact with Materialism, but, in fact, frequently proceeds from it, since in the last result the production of spirit must be attributed to matter as such,— though through infinitely numerous gradations. The fantastical and personifying ornamentation of this doctrine of the universal diffusion of soul in matter, such as we find it in Paracelsus, belongs to the pointless absurdities of the age, and from this Bacon managed to keep himself toler "Comp. the extracts collected by Schaller, Gesch. der Naturphilosophie, Leipzig, 1841, S. 77-80.

ably free. His 'spiritus' have no hands or feet. And it is remarkable what a colossal misapplication the ' Eestorer of the natural sciences' could make of his spirits in the explanation of nature without being exposed by his more knowing contemporaries. But so is it with our history: we may take it up where we will, we shall find similar phenomena. As to the much-debated question of the relation of Materialism to morality, we may unhesitatingly assume that Bacon, if his character had been purer and firmer, would, by the peculiarity of his thinking, have undoubtedly been led to strictly Materialistic principles. We find not fearless consistency, but scientific halfness and hesitation here again, in connection with moral degeneracy.

As to Descartes, the progenitor of the opposite line of philosophical succession, who established the dualism between mind and material world, and took the famous 'Cogito ergo sum' as his starting-point, it might at first appear that, as opposed to the Materialistic philosophy, he only reacted upon it in point of its consequence and clearness. But how then shall we explain the fact that the worst of the French Materialists, De la Mettrie, wished to be a thoroughgoing Cartesian, and not without having good reasons for so wishing? Here again, then, we find a more direct connection, which we shall later have to explain.

With regard to the principles of investigation, Bacon and Descartes occupy primarily a negative attitude against all previous philosophy, and especially against the Aristotelian. Both begin by doubting of everything; but Bacon, in order that he may then be led to the discovery of truth by the hand of external experience; Descartes, to elaborate it by deductive reasoning out of that self-consciousness which was all that had remained to him amidst his doubts.

Here there can be no doubt that Materialism lies only upon Bacon's side, that the Cartesian system, if consis VOL. I. Q tently carried out from his fundamental principles, must have led to an Idealism in which the whole external world appears as mere phenomenon and only the ego has any real existence. Materialism is empirical, and rarely employs the deductive method, and then only when a sufficient stock of materials has been acquired inductively out of which we may then attain to new truths by a free use of the syllogism. Descartes began with abstraction and deduction, and that was not only not Materialistic, but also not practical: it necessarily led him to those obvious fallacies in which, among all great philosophers, perhaps, no one abounds so much as Descartes. But, for once, the deductive method came to the front, and in connection with it that purest form of all deduction, in which, too, as well as in philosophy, Descartes holds an honourable place— mathematics. Bacon could not endure mathematics; the pride of the mathematicians—or perhaps, more truly, their rigorousness—displeased him, and he required that this science should be only a handmaid, but should not demean herself as mistress of physics.

Thus then proceeded principally from Descartes that mathematical side of natural philosophy which applied to all the phenomena of nature the standard of number and of geometrical figure. It deserves attention that even in the beginning of the eighteenth century the Materialists —before this name had become general—were not seldom described as 'mechanici,' that is, as people who started with a mechanical view of nature. This mechanical view of nature had really, however, been originated by Descartes, and had been developed by Spinoza, and not less Leibniz, although the last-named philosopher was very far from numbering himself amongst the adherents of this movement.

In the Mcmoires pour l'Histoire referred to, although without men des Sciences et des Beaux Arts, Tre-tion of his name, who holds the most voux et Paris, 1713, p. 922, a certain probable view to be, that he himself 'Malcbranchist' living in Paris is is the only existing being.

Although, then, in the most essential points, Materialism starts from Bacon, it was nevertheless Descartes who finally impressed upon this whole way of thinking that stamp of *mechanism* which appeared most strikingly in De la Mettrie's "L'Homme Machine." It was really due to Descartes that all the functions as well of intellectual as of physical life were finally regarded as the products of mechanical changes.

To the possibility of a natural science at all, Descartes had helped himself by the somewhat hasty conclusion, that although otherwise we must indeed have doubted the reality of things outside us, we may nevertheless conclude that they are really existing, because otherwise God must be a deceiver in having given us the idea of the external world.

This *salto mortale* accordingly lands Descartes at once in the midst of nature, in a sphere where he laboured with much greater success than in metaphysics. As to the general basis of his theory of external nature, Descartes was not an adherent of rigorous Atomism: he denied the conceivableness of the atoms. Even if there are smallest particles which cannot possibly be any further divided, yet God must be able to divide them again, for their divisibility is still constantly conceivable. But in spite of this denial of atoms, he was yet very far from striking into the path of Aristotelianism. His doctrine of the absolute fulness of space has not only an entirely different basis in its notion of matter, but it must even in the physical theory take a shape which is nearly allied to Atomism. There he substitutes for the atoms small round corpuscles, which remain in fact quite as unchanged as the atoms, and are only divisible in thought, that is, potentially; in place of the empty space which the ancient Atomists adopted, he had extremely fine splinters, which have been formed in the interstices when the corpuscles were originally rounded. By the side of this view we may seriously a3k whether the metaphysical theory of the absolute fulness of space is not a mere makeshift, in order, on the one hand, not to swerve too far from the orthodox idea, and yet, on the other hand, to have all the advantages for a picturable explanation of natural phenomena which are possessed by Atomism? Descartes, moreover, expressly explained the movement of the particles as well as those of bodies out of mere conduction, according to the laws of mechanical impact. He named, indeed, the universal cause of all movement, God; but all bodies, according to him, are subject to a particular motion, and every natural phenomenon consists, without distinction of the organic or inorganic, merely of the conduction of the motion of one body to another; and thus all mystical explanations of nature were set aside at once, and that by the same kind of principle which was followed by the Atomists also.

In reference to the human soul, the point around which all controversies turned in the eighteenth century, Bacon was at bottom again a Materialist. He assumed, it is true, the *anima rationalis,* but only on religious grounds; intelligible he did not consider it. But the *anima sensitiva,* which alone he thought capable of a scientific treatment, Bacon regarded in the sense of the ancients as a fine kind of matter. Bacon, in fact, did not at all recognise the conceivableness of an immaterial substance, and his whole mode of thought was inconsistent with the view of the soul as the *form* of the body in the Aristotelian sense.

Although this was just the point on which Descartes seemed to stand most sharply opposed to Materialism, it is nevertheless in this very sphere that the Materialists borrowed from him the principles leading to the most important consequences.

Descartes, in his corpuscular theory, made no essential distinction between organic and inorganic nature. Plants were machines; and as to animals, he suggested, even though it was only under the form of an hypothesis, that he regarded them also as in fact mere machines.

Now the age of Descartes happened to occupy itself very busily with animal psychology. In France especially one of the best-read and most influential of authors, the ingenious sceptic Montaigne,4 had rendered popular the paradoxical proposition that the animals display as much, and often more, reason than men. But what Montaigne had playfully suggested, in the shape of an apology for Eaymund of Sabunde, was made by Hieronymus Eorarius the subject of a special treatise, published by Gabriel Naudaus in 1648, and bearing the title, "Quod animalia bruta saepe ratione utantur melius homine."

This proposition appeared to be a direct contradiction to that of Descartes, but there was, nevertheless, a synthesis of the two found possible in this position—that the animals are machines, and yet think. The step from the animal to man was then but a short one; and, moreover, here also Descartes had so prepared the way, that he may fairly be regarded as the immediate forerunner of outspoken Materialism. In his treatise " Passiones Animae," he calls attention to the important fact that the dead body is not only dead because the soul is wanting to it, but because the bodily machine itself is partially destroyed. If we reflect that the entire sum of the idea of the soul possessed by primitive peoples is due to the comparison of the living and the dead body, and that the ignorance of the physiological phenomena in the dying body is one of the strongest supports of the theory of a 'visionary soul' —that is, of that *more subtle man* who is supposed by the popular psychology to be present as the motive force in the inside of the man—we shall immediately recognise in this single point an important contribution to the carrying out of anthropological Materialism. And not less important is the unambiguous recognition of Harvey's great discovery of the circulate' *vf* the blood. With this the whole Aristotelo-Galeniah physiology fell to the ground; and although Descartes still held to the 'vital spirits,' they are at least in him entirely free from that mystical antithesis between matter and spirit, and from, the incomprehensible relations of' sympathy' and 'antipathy' to half-sensible half-supersensible 'spirits' of all kinds. With Descartes the vital spirits are genuine, materially-conceived matter, more logically imagined than Epikuros's soul-atoms, with their added element of caprice. They move themselves, and effect movement, just as in Demokritos, exclusively according to mathematical and physical laws. A mechanism of pressure and collision, which Descartes follows out with great ingenuity through all the separate steps, forms an uninterrupted chain of effects produced by external things through the senses upon the brain, and from the brain back again outwards through nerves and muscular filaments.

Montaigne is at the same time of animala as are most generally deone of the most dangerous opponents nied to them as being products of the of Scholasticism and the founder of 'higher faculties of the soul.' With French scepticism. The leading their virtues the vices of men are set Frenchmen of the seventeenth cen-in sharp contrast. We can therefore tury were almost all under his iuflu-understand that the manuscript, alence, friend and foe alike; nay, we though written by a priest who was find that he exercised an important a friend both of Pope and Emperor, influence even upon the opponents of had to wait so long for publication, bis gay and somewhat frivolous phi-The publisher, Naudaus, was losophy, as, for instance, upon Pascal a friend of Gassendi's, who also, iniand the men of Port Royal. like Descartes, has a very high esti The work of Hieronymus Bora-mate of the capacities of the animals, rius waited a full hundred years for Passiones Animae, Art. v.: "Er its publication, and it is therefore in roneum esse credere animam dare its origin *earlier* than the "Essais" motum et calorem corpori;" and Art. of Montaigne. It is distinguished by vi.: "Quaenam differentia sit inter a grim and serious tone, and the assi-corpus vivons et cadaver." duous emphasising of just such traits

In this state of things we may seriously ask whether De la Mettrie was not in truth quite justified when he traced his own Materialism to Descartes, and maintained that the wily philosopher, purely for the sake of the parsons, had patched on to his theory a soul, which was in reality quite superfluous. If we do not go quite so far as this, it is chiefly the unmistakable importance of the *idealistic* side of Descartes's philosophy that keeps us from doing so. Doubtful as is the way iu which he deduces the 'Cogito ergo sum,' and crying as are the logical tricks and contradictions by means of which the otherwise clear-thinking man seeks to construct the world from inside, yet the thought that the whole sum of phenomena must be conceived as the *representation* of an immaterial subject possesses an importance which cannot have escaped its own originator. What Descartes lacks is at bottom exactly what Kant ac' ved—the establishing of a tenable connection between a mafertaWy-conceived nature and an idealistic metaphysic, which regards this whole nature as a mere sum of phenomena in an ego which is as to its substance unknown to us. It is, however, psychologically quite possible that Descartes conceived the two sides of knowledge which appear harmoniously combined in Kantianism each by itself quite clearly, however they may seem, taken thus separately, to contradict each other; and that he clung to them the more obstinately as he saw himself compelled to hold them together by an artificial cement of hazardous propositions.

On the universal denial with agreement, comp. also Buckle, "Hiswhich Harvey's great discovery was tory of Civilisation in England," ii. met, and the importance of Descartes' 80, ed. 1871.

For the rest, Descartes himself did not originally consider very important the whole metaphysical theory with which his name is now chiefly connected, while he attributed the greatest value to his scientific and mathematical inquiries, and to his mechanical theory of all natural phenomena.68 When, however, his new proofs fer the irnmateriality of the soul and for the existence of God met with great approbation in an age disquieted by scepticism, Descartes was glad enough to pass for a great metaphysician, and paid increasing attention to this portion of his doctrine. Whether his original system of the Kosmos may have stood somewhat nearer to Materialism than his later theory, we cannot say; for it is well known that out of fear of the clergy he called back his already completely finished work, and subjected it to a thorough revision. Certain it is that he, against his better convictions, withdrew from it his theory of the revolution of the earth. This appears clearly enough from combien elles different des principcs a passage in his Essay on Method, vol. dont on s'est servi jusques a present, i. p. 191 foil, of the edition of Victor j'ai cru que je ne pouvois les tenir Cousin, Paris, 1824: ".. . bien cachees sans pecher grandement que mes speculations me plussent eontre la loi qui nous oblige a profort, j'ai cru que les autres en avoi-curer autant qu'il est en nous le bien ent aussi qui leur plaisoient pent-general de tous les hommes; car elles itre davantage. Mais, sitot que j'ai m'ont fait voir qu'il est possible de en acquis *quelqua notion glniraUs* parvenir a des oonnoissanoes qui soient *touchant la physique,* et que com-fort utiles a la vie; et qu'au lieu de mencant a les 6prouver en diverges cette philosophic speculative qu'on difficultes particulieres, j'ai remarque enseigne dans les ecoles, on en peut jusques ou elles peuvent conduiie, et trouver una pratique, par laquelle, connoisant la force et les actions du feu, de l'eau, de l'air, des astres, des cieux, et de tons les autres corps qui nous environnent, aussi distincteinent que nous connoissons les divers metiers de nos artisans," etc. Compare Note 17 to the following section. As to Descartes's personal character, very different opinions have made themselves heard. The point in dispute is whether his ambition to be considered a great discoverer, and his jealousy of other prominent mathematicians and physicists, did not sometimes carry him beyond the limits of what is honourable. Comp. Whewell, History of the Inductive Sciences, ii. 379, where he is said to have used without acknowledgment Snell's discovery of the law of refraction; and the severe remarks, on the other side, of Buckle, Hist. Civ. in Engl., ii. 77 foil., who, however, in several respects rates Descartes too high. With this may be compared his controversy with the great mathematician Format; his perverse and disparaging judgments as to Galilei's doctrine of motion; his attempt to appropriate, on the strength of a remarkable but by no means sufficiently clear expression, the authorship of Pascal's great discovery of the rarification of the atmosphere upon mountains, and so on. As to all these things, the last word appears to us not yet to have been spoken; and as to his denial of his own view from fear of the clergy, that rests upon quite a different footing. When, however. Buckle, after Lerminier (comp. Hist. of Civ. in Engl., ii. 82), compares Descartes with Luther, we must remind ourselves of the great contrast between the reckless boldness of the German reformer and the cautious evasion of the enemy which Descartes introduced into the struggle between freethinking and suppression. That Descartes modelled his system, against his better knowledge, after the doctrine of the Church, and apparently as far as possible after Aristotle, is a fact of which there can be no doubt in view of the following passages from his correspondence:—

To Mersenne, July 1633 (CEuvres, ed. Cousin, vi. 239): Descartes has heard with surprise of the condemnation of a book of Galilei's; conjectures that this is because of his theory of the earth's movement, and confesses that the same objection will apply to his own work:—" Et il est tellement lie avec toutes les parties de mon Traité que je ne Ten saurois detacher, sans rendre le reste tout defectueux. Mais comme je ne voudrois pour rien du monde qu'il sortlt de moi un discours ou il se trouv &t le moindre mot qui fut des approuvé de l'église, aussi aimé-je mieux le supprimer que de le faire paroitre estropié. " To the same, January 10, 1634 (vi. 242 foil.): "Vous savez sans doute que Galilée a éte repris depuis peu par les inquisiteurs de la foi, et que son opinion touchant le mouvement de la terre a éte condamné comme hérétique; or je vous dirai, que toutes les choses, que j'expliquoia en mon traite, entre lesquelles étoit aussi cette opinion du mouvement de la terre, dépendoient tellement les unes des autres, que c'est assez de savoir qu'il en ait une qui soit fausse pour connoltre que toutes les raisons dont je me servais n'ont point de force; et quoique je pensasse qu'elles fussent appuyées sur des démonstrations tris certaines et très évidentes, je ne voudrois toutefois pour rien du monde les soutenir contre l'autorite de l'église. Je sais bien qu'on pour roit dire que tout ce que les inquisiteurs de Kome ont décidé n'est pas incontinent article de foi pour cela, et qu'il faut premièrement que le concile y ait passé; mais je ne suis pointu amoureux de mes pensées que de me vouloir servir de telles exceptions, pour avoir moyen de les maintenir; et le désir que j'ai de vivre au repos et de continuer la vie que j'ai commencée en prenant pour ma devise ' bene vixit qui bene latuit,' fait que je suis plus aise d'etre délivré de la crainte que j'avois d'acquérir plus de connoissances que ie ne désire, par le moyen de mon écrit, que je ne suis fâché d'avoir perdu le temps et la peine que j'ai employée a le composer.' Towards the end of the same letter he says, on the contrary (p. 246): "Je ne perds pas tout-à-fait espérance qu'il n'en arrive ainsi que des antipodes, qui avoient éte quasi eu même sorte condamnés autrefois, et ainsi que mon Monde ne puisse voir le jour aveo le temps, auquel cas j'aurois besoin moimême de me servir de mes raisons." This latter expression especially is as clear as can be desired. Descartes could not make up his mind to dare to use his own understanding, and so he determined to propound a new theory, which enabled him to secure his object of avoiding an open conflict with the Church.

THIRD SECTION. SEVENTEENTH CENTURY MATERIALISM. *THIRD SECTION.* SEVEN-

TEENTH CENTURY MATERIALISM. CHAPTER I. GASSENDI.

When we attribute to Gassendi in particular the revival of an elaborate Materialistic philosophy, the position we assign him needs some words of vindication. We lay especial stress upon this, that Gassendi drew again into the light, and adapted to the circumstances of the time, the fullest of the Materialistic systems of antiquity, that of Epikuros. But this it is upon which those have relied who reject Gassendi from the period of an independent philosophy which was inaugurated by Bacon and Descartes, and regard him as a mere continuer of the obsolete period of the reproduction of old classical systems.1 Gassendi is indeed, as was scarcely knew more of the contents of the fire made sufficiently clear in the first edi-burnt books from oral communication of the History of Materialism, tion than has been preserved to us a *forerunner* of Descartes, and in-in the table of contents. Later, of dependent of Bacon of Verulam. course, when Descartes, through fear Descartes, who was usually not over of the Church, invented a world prone to the recognition of others, re-which rested upon essentially diffcrgards Gassendi as an authority in ent principles from those of Gassendi, scientific matters (comp. the follow-he changed his tone also in reference ing places in his letters: Oeuvres, to Gassendi; especially as he had beed. Cousin, vi. 72, 83, 97, 121); come a great man through his atand we may with the utmost probatempt to find a compromise between bility assume that he was also ac-science and ecclesiastical doctrine, quainted with the "Exercitationes And upon a stricter examinaParadoxicae," 1624, and even that he tion of the relations between Gassendi and Descartes, the right of the to the denial of God! It is former to be considered the first re-incomprehensible how Schaller, in presentative of a theory of the world his Gesch. d. Naturphil., Leipzig, which has lasted down to our own 1841, could set Mobbes before Gasdays only becomes more clear, for sendi. It is true enough that in Descartes also, the more narrowly we point of years the former is the older, regard him, enters into a more dis-but then he was as unusually late in tinct relation to the extension and his development as Gassendi was unpropagation of Materialistic modes of usually early, and during their interthought. Voltaire, indeed, said in course in Paris, Hobbes was distinctly his "Elements of the Newtonian the learner, to say nothing of GasPhilosophy" (Ocuvrcs oompl. , 1784, sendi's literary productions pubt. xxxi. c. i.), that he had known many lished so long before. who had been led on by Cartesianism

This, however, is to overlook the essential difference that existed between the Epikurean and every other ancient system in relation to the times in which Gassendi lived. Whilst the prevailing Aristotelian philosophy, displeasing as it was to the fathers of the Church, had in the course of the middle ages almost fused itself with Christianity, Epikuros remained the emblem of utmost heathenism, and also of absolute contradiction to Aristotle. If we add to this the impermeable masses of traditional calumnies with which Epikuros was overwhelmed, the groundlessness of which a discerning scholar here and there had pointed out, without, however, striking a decisive blow, the rehabilitation of Epikuros, together with the revival of his philosophy, must appear a fact which, regarded merely in its negative aspect as the completed opposition to Aristotle, may be placed by the side of the most independent enterprises of that time. Nor does this consideration exhaust the full significance of Gassendi's achievement.

It was not by accident, nor out of mere love of opposition, that Gassendi lighted upon Epikuros and his philosophy. He was a student of nature, a physicist indeed, and an empiric. Bacon had already held up Demokritos, and not Aristotle, as the greatest of the ancient philosophers. Gassendi, whose thorough philological and historical training equipped him with a knowledge of all the Bystems of antiquity, embraced with a sure glance exactly what was best suited to modern times, and to the empirical tendency of his age. Atomism, by *his* means drawn again from antiquity, attained a lasting importance, however much it was gradually modified as it passed through the hands of later inquirers.

It might, indeed, appear hazardous to make the Provost of Digne, the orthodox Catholic priest Gassendi, the propagator of modern Materialism; but Materialism and Atheism are not identical, even if they are related conceptions. Epikuros himself sacrificed to the gods. The men of science of this time had acquired through long practice a wonderful skill in keeping upon a formal footing of friendliness with theology. Descartes, for example, introduced his theory of the development of the world from small particles with the observation, that of course God had created the world at one time, but that it was very interesting to see how the world might have developed itself, although we know that it had really not done so. But when he is once launched upon the scientific theory, then this development hypothesis alone is visible; it best harmonises with all the facts, and fails in no single point. And thus the divine creation becomes a meaningless formula of acknowledgment. So fares it likewise with motion, in which God is the prime cause—which, however, troubles the inquirer no further. The principle of the maintenance of force through constant transmission of mechanical impact, with its very untheological contents, yet receives a theological form. In the same way, then, the Provost Gassendi goes to work. Mersenne, another theologian, given to the study of science, and at the same time a good Hebraist, had published a Commentary on Genesis, in which all the objections of Atheists and Naturalists were answered, but in such fashion that many shook their heads; and at least the greatest industry was applied to the collection rather than the refutation of these objections. Mersenne occupied a middle position between Descartes and Gassendi, and was a friend of both men, as he was of the the English Hobbes. This last was a decided partisan of the King and of the Episcopal High Church, and is at the same time regarded as the head and father of the Atheists.

Naumann, in his Grundr. d. chemical phenomena out of physical Thenno-chemie, Braunschweig, 1869, changes. It is also not correct to say;i work of great scientific merit, ob-(toe. *cit.,8.* 10,11) that before Dalton serves unjustly, S. 11: "The chemi-none had tested the correctness and' cal theory of atoms has, however, applicability of Atomism by reference nothing, or next to nothing, in com-to the facts. This had been done mon with the atomistic doctrine pre-immediately after Gassendi, by Boyle viously propounded by Lucretius and for chemistry, and by Newton for Dcmokritos." The historical conti-physics; and although it may not unity, which we shall prove in the have been done as the science of toaequcl, indicates a community right day would have it done, yet we must from the beginning of the develop-not forget that even Dalton's theory merit, in spite of all the differences is now a discarded standpoint. to be found in the final product. Naumann is quite right in saying Both views, moreover, have this also (with Fechner, Atomlehre, 185c,, S. in common—which Fechner points 3), that in order to controvert modern out as the most important feature of Atomism, it is necessary first to know Atomism—that they both suppose what it is. But we may also remark, *discrete* molecules; and although this that in order to controvert the conmay not perhaps bo so all-important nection of ancient with modern to the chemist as it is to the physicist. Atomism, it is necessary first to know still it remains an essential point: the *historical* no less than 'the scienand yet the more essential one is tific' facts. concerned, as is Naumann, to explain

It is interesting, too, that Gassendi does not draw the theory of his ambiguous conduct from the Jesuits, as he well might have done; but bases it on the example of Epikuros. In his Life of Epikuros is a long discussion, the point of which lies in the principle, that mentally Epikuros might think as he would, but in his outward demeanour he was subject to the laws of his country. Hobbes stated the doctrine still more sharply: the state has unconditional power over worship; the individual must resign his judgment, but not mentally, for our thoughts are not subject to command, and therefore we cannot compel any one to believe.3 De Vita et Moribus Epicuri, iv. 4: Religionis patriae interfuit caerimo"Dico solum, si Epicurus quibusdam iiiis, quas mente tamen improbaret. videri posse, illi quandam excusationis speciem obbendi. Intererat enim, quia jus civile et trauquillitas publica illud ex ipso exigebat: Improbabat, quia nihil cogit animum Sapientis, ut vulgaria sapiat. Intus, erat sui juris, extra legibus obstrictus aocietatis hominum. Ita per salvebat eodem tempore quod et aliis debebat, et sibi.... Pars haeo tum erat Sapientiae, ut philosophl sentirent cum paucis, loquerentur vero, agerentque cum multis." Here the last clause especially seems to be more applicable to Gassendi's time than to Epikuros, who enjoyed great liberty of teaching and speaking, and availed himself of it. Hobbes (Leviathan, c. xxxii.) maintains that obedience to the state religion involves also the duty of not contradicting its doctrines. This course, indeed, he followed according to the letter, but at the same time was restrained by no scruples from withdrawing the VOL. I.

But the rehabilitation of Epikuros, and the exposition of his doctrine, required great caution in Gassendi. We see clearly from the preface to his book on the life and morals of Epikuros, that it seemed a bolder thing to follow Epikuros than to set forth a new cosmogony. Nevertheless the justification of his cause he wisely does not seek deeply, but puts together superficially, though with a great expenditure of dialectic skill—a proceeding which has always succeeded better with the Church than a serious and independent attempt to reconcile its doctrines with strange or hostile ingredients.

Is Epikuros a heathen?—so too was Aristotle. If Epikuros attacks superstition and religion, he was right, for he knew not the true religion. Does he teach that the gods neither reward nor punish, and does he honour them for their perfection?—we have only the thought of childish instead of servile reverence, and therefore a purer and more Christian conception. The errors of Epikuros must be carefully corrected; which is done, however, in that Cartesian spirit which we have just observed in the doctrines of the creation and of motion. The frankest eagerness is shown to vindicate for Epikuros among all ancient philosophers the greatest purity of morals. In this way, then, are we justified in regarding Gassendi as the true regenerator of. Materialism, and the more so when we consider how great was the actual influence he exercised upon succeeding generations.

ground from under all religion—for those who are clever enough to draw conclusions. The "Leviathan" appeared in 1651; the first edition of the treatise "De Vita et Moribus Epicuri" in 1647; yet here no weight can be laid on the priority of the thought; it lay entirely in the time and in the general questions (where there was no reference to mathematics and natural science). Hobbes had undoubtedly been independent long before he came to know Gassendi. Observe the unusually solemn tone in which Gassendi, towards the conclusion of the preface to the "De Vita et Moribus Epicuri," reserves the doctrine of the Church: "In Roligione Majores, hoc est Ecclesiam Catholicam, Apostolicam et Romanam sequor, cuius hactenus decretn defendi ac porro defendant, nee me ab ilia ullius unquam docti aut indocti separabit oratio."

Pierre Gassendi, the son of poor peasants, was born in 1592, near Digne in Provence. He became a student, and was at sixteen years of age a teacher of Rhetoric, and three years later Professor of Philosophy at Aix. He had already written a book which clearly shows his leanings— the "Exercitationes Paradoxicae ad versus Aristoteleos," a work full of youthful zeal, one of the sharpest and most contemptuous attacks upon the Aristotelian philosophy. This was later, in the years 1624 and 1645, printed in part, but five books at the advice of his friends were burnt. Advanced by the learned senator Peirescius, Gassendi was soon afterwards made a canon and then provost at Digne.

This rapid career led him through various departments. As Professor of Rhetoric he had to give philological instruction, and it is not improbable that his preference for Epikuros grew up in this period from his study of Lucretius, who in philological circles had long been highly prized. When Gassendi in 1628 undertook a journey to the Netherlands, the philologist Eryceus Puteanus, of Louvain, gave him a copy of a gem with a portrait of Epikuros, which was very highly reverenced by himself. Do Vita et Moribus Epicuri, con-sio oculos, sic ora ferebat. Intuere elusion of the preface To Luiller): imaginem dignam istis lineis. istis

"Habcs ipse jam penes te duplicem manibus, et porro oculis omni illius effigiem, alteram ex gemma ex-um.' Alteram exprcssam ex statua.
pressam, quam dum Lovanio facerem Romae ad ingressum interioris Palatii iter, communicavit mecum vir ille Ludovisianorum hortorum exstante, eximius Eryceus Puteanus, quamque quam ad me misit Naudacus nostet etiam in suis epistolis cum hoc eulo-(the publisher of the essay of Hier gie evulgavit: 'Intuere, mi amice, onymus Rorarius mentioned in the ct in lincis istis spirantem adhuc previous section) usus opera Henrici mentem magni viri. Epicurus est; HoneniiineademfamiliaCardinalitia pictoris. Tu hue iiiserito utram rules, sua Aristoteleos, Hagae Comitnm.

The "Exercitationes Paradoxicae" must, in fact, have been a work of uncommon boldness and great acuteness, and we have every reason to suppose that it did not remain without influence upon the learned world of France, for the friends who advised the burning of the five lost books must have been acquainted with their contents. It is also intelligible that Gassendi would take counsel of men who were near his own standpoint, and were capable of understanding and appreciating the contents of his work from other aspects than the consideration of its dangerousness. So may in those times many a fire have quietly smouldered unsuspected, the flames of which were to break out later in quite other directions. Happily at least a brief statement of the contents of the lost books has been preserved to us. From this we see that in the fourth book not only the Copernican theory was advanced, but also the doctrine of the eternity of the world, which had been drawn from Lucretius by Giordano Bruno. As the same book contained an assault upon the Aristotelian elements, we may very easily conjecture that Atomism was here taught in opposition to Aristotle. This is the more probable because the seventh book, according to this table of contents, contained a formal recommendation of the Epikurean theory of Morals.

Gassendi was, moreover, one of those happy natures who can everywhere allow themselves a little more than other people. The precocious development of his mind had not with him, as with Pascal, led to an early satiety of knowledge and a melancholy existence. Light-hearted and amiable, he everywhere won himself friends, and, with all the modesty of his demeanour, he allowed himself gladly, amongst those he could trust, to give the reins to ku inexhaustible humour. In his anecdotes the traditional medicine came very badly off, and he has suffered bitterly enough from her retaliation. It is notable that amongst the authors who had influenced him in his early youth, and freed him from Aristotle, he mentions in the first line, not the witty scoffer Montaigne, but the pious sceptic Charron and the serious Luis Vives, who always unites a strong moral judgment with his logical acumen.
quando ct non male altera, ut video, 1656, Piaef.: "Uno verbo docot refert alteram, et memiui utramque (b. vii.) Epicuri de voluptate senten congruere cum alia in amplissimo tiam: osteudendo videlicet, qua ra eimeliarcho Viri nobilis Casparis tione summum bonum in voluptate

Monconiflii Lierguii, propractoris constitutum ait, et quemadmodum

Lugdunensis, asservata." laus virtutum actionumque human Exercitatiunes Paradoxicae adver-arum ex hoc principio depeudeat."

Like Descartes, so Gassendi, too, must renounce, in setting forth his philosophy, "the use of his own intellect," only it did not occur to him to push the process of accommodation to the doctrines of the Church further than was anywhere necessary. Whilst Descartes made a virtue of necessity, and veiled the Materialism of his natural philosophy in the broad mantle of an idealism dazzling by its novelty, Gassendi remained essentially a Materialist, and viewed the devices of him who had formerly shared his views with unconcealed dissatisfaction. In Descartes the mathematician has the upper hand; in him, the physicist: while the other, like Plato and Pythagoras in antiquity allowed himself to be seduced by the example of mathematics to overpass with his conclusions the field of all possible experience, *he* clung to empiricism, and except so far as ecclesiastical dogma seemed unconditionally to demand it, never forsook the borders of a speculation which ever framed its very boldest theories on the analogy of experience. Descartes soared aloft to a system which violently severs thought and sensuous intuition, and by this very means makes its way to the most hazardous assertions; Gassendi maintained with unshaken steadfastness the unity of thought and sensuous intuition.

In the year 1643 he published his " Disquisitiones Anticartesianae," a work justly distinguished as a model ot controversy, as delicate and polite as it is thorough and witty. If Descartes began by doubting of everything, even of what was given in sense; Gassendi showed that it is plainly impossible to realise an abstraction from all that was given in sense—that therefore the ' Cogito ergo sura' was anything rather than the highest first truth from which all others were deduced.

In fact, that Cartesian doubt which is taken up some fine morning (" semel in vita") in order to free the soul. from all the prejudices imbibed since childhood, is a mere frivolous playing with empty ideas. In a concrete psychical act thought can never be separated from sense elements; but in mere formulae (as, *e.g.*, we reckon with *J* — 1, without being able to represent this magnitude to ourselves), we may amuse ourselves by rejecting in the same way the doubting subject, and even the act of doubt. We gain nothing by this, but we also lose nothing except—the time devoted to speculations of this kind.

Gassendi's most famous objection, that existence may just as well be inferred from any other action as from thinking/ is so obvious, indeed, that it has often been repeated independently of Gassendi, and as often said to be superficial and unintelligible. Biichner declares that the argument is the same as if we were to say, " The dog barks, therefore he is." Buckle, on the contrary, declares such criticism to be short-sighted, since it is not a logical but a psychological process that is in question.

But, as against this well-meant defence, we must bear in mind the fact, as clear as sunshine, that it is Descartes, in fact, who confuses the logical and psychological processes, and that when we clearly discriminate them the whole argument collapses.

To begin with, this *formal* correctness of the objection is quite indisputably established in the words of the "Principia" (i. 7), " Eepugnat enim, ut putemus id quod cogitat, eo ipso tempore, quo cogitat, nihil esse." Here the purely logical argument is employed by himself, and / The example, 'I walk, therefore his rejoinder,—in other respects quits I am,' originates not with Gassendi, agreeing with this objection, but with Descartes, who uses it in s Buckle, Hist, of Civilis, ii. 87 n.
justifies Gassendi's second objection. But if it is proposed to substitute the psychological method, then the first of Gassendi's objections asserts itself: This psychological process does not, and can not exist; it is a pure fiction.

The justification adopted by Descartes himself appears to go furthest, which relies upon the logical deduction, and makes the distinction that in one case the premiss 'I think' is certain, whilst, on the other hand, in ' I go to walk, and therefore I am,' the premiss upon which it rests is doubtful, and therefore the conclusion is impossible. But this also is idle sophistry; for if I really go to walk, I can assuredly consider my walking as the mere phenomenal side of an act entirely different in itself, and I can do the same in precisely the same way with my thinking as a psychological phenomenon; I cannot, however, without absolute untruth, annul the *idea* that I go to walk, any more than I can the idea of my thinking, especially if in *cogitare* one includes, with Cartesius, also *vclle, imaginare,* and even *sentire.*

And, least of all, can the inference to a subject of thinking be justified, as Lichtenberg has shown in the excellent remark: "Shall we say ' it thinks' as we say 'it lightens': to say ' cogito' is too much if we are to translate it' I think.'" It is practically necessary to assume, to postulate the *19* The credit for the priority of this question, which, in the simplest war, remark appears to be due to Kant, demonstrates so clearly the surrepti who says in the Krit. d. r. Vern. tious nature of the Subject.

Elementarl., ii. 2, 2, 1 Hauptst. We may mention, by the way, that (Paralogismen d. r. Vern.), E. T., p. the attempt to prove the existence of 239: "By this I, or He, or It which the soul from the very fact of rfouoc, thinks, nothing more is represented in very striking agreement with the than a transcendental subject of 'Cogito ergo sum,' was first intro thought = *x,* which is cognised only duced by the Father Augustine, who by means of the thoughts that are thus argues in the 10th Book 'De its predicates, and of which, apart Triuitate: "Si quis dubitat, vivit from these, we cannot form the least si dubitat, unde dubitet meminit; conception." At the same time, this si dubitat, dubitare se intelligit." does not detract from the great merits This passage is quoted in the once of Lichtenberg's statement *vt* the widely spread "Margarita Philci»phica" (i486, 1503 and often) at the had used this argument in order to

In 1646, Gassendi became Eegius Professor of Mathematics at Paris, where his lecture-room was crowded by listeners of all ages, including well-known men of letters. He had only with difficulty resolved to quit his Southern home, and being soon attacked by a lung complaint, he returned to Digne, where he remained till 1653. In this period falls the greater part of his literary activity and zeal in behalf of the philosophy of Epikuros, and simultaneously the positive extension of his own doctrines. In the same period Gassendi produced, besides several astronomical works, a series of valuable biographies, of which those of Copernicus and of Tycho Brahe are especially noteworthy. Gassendi is, of all the most prominent representatives of Materialism, the only one gifted with a historic sense, and that he has in an eminent degree. Even in his " Syntagma Philosophicum," he treats every subject at first historically, from all possible points of view.

Of cosmical systems, he declares the Ptolemaic, the Copernican, and the Tychonic to be the most important. Of these, he entirely rejects the Ptolemaic, declares the Copernican to be the simplest and the one most thoroughly representing the facts; but one must adopt that of Tycho, because the Bible obviously attributes motion to the sun. It affords us an insight into the time, that the once so cautious Gassendi, who on all other points kept peace between his Materialism and the Church, could not even reject the Copernican system without drawing upon himself, by his laudatory expressions, the reproach of a heretical view of cosmology. Yet the hatred of the supporters of the old cosmology becomes in some measure intelligible when we see how Gassendi contrived to undermine its foundations without open assault. A favourite argument of the opponents of Copernicus was, that if the earth revolved, it would be impossible for a cannon-ball fired straight up into the air to fall back upon the cannon. Gassendi thereupon, as he relates himself, had an experiment made: on a ship travelling at great speed a stone was thrown straight up into the air. It fell back, following the motion of the ship, upon the same part of the deck from which it had been thrown. A stone was dropped from the top of the mast, and it fell exactly at its foot. These experiments, to us so ordinary, were then, when men were only beginning, by the aid of Galilei, to understand the laws of motion, of great significance, and the main argument of those who denied the motion of the earth was by their assistance hopelessly overthrown.

beginning of the roth hook, "De show that that ego which thinks

Auima." Descartes, who had his is *an immaterial substance.* Des attention culled to its agreement cartes therefore quite rightly em with his principle, seems not to phasises as his special property pre have known it; he admits that cisely that element which is most

Augustine had, in fact, proposed to obviously surreptitious. Comp.

prove the certainty of our existence Oeuvres, t. viii., ed. Cousin, p. 421. in this way; he himself, however,

The world Gassendi regarded as one ordered whole, and the only question is as to the nature of the order, especially if the world possesses a soul or not. If by the worldsoul one means God, and it is only meant that God by his being and presence maintains, governs, and so in a sense constitutes the soul of all things, this may always be possible.

All are agreed also that heat is diffused throughout the universe; *this heat might also be called the soul of the world;* and yet to attribute to the world, in the strict sense, a vegetative, feeling, or thinking soul contradicts the reality of things. For the world neither produces another world, as the plants and Tanimals, nor grows or nourishes itself by food and drink; still less has it sight, hearing, and other functions of things possessing souls.

Place and time are viewed by Gassendi as existing quite independently, neither substance nor accident. At the point where all corporeal things cease space still extends without limit, and time sped before the creation of the world as regularly as now. By the material principle or *materia prima* is meant that matter which cannot be further dissolved. So man is composed of head, heart, belly, and so on. These are formed out of chyle and blood; these again from food, and food from the so-called elements; but these also are again composed of atoms, which are therefore the material principle or *materia prima.* Matter is consequently in itself as yet without form. But there is also no form without a material'body, and this is the durable substratum, while forms change themselves and go. Matter is therefore itself indestructible, and it is incapable of being produced, and no body can arise out of nothing, although this does not go to deny the creation of matter by God. The atoms are in point of substance identical, but vary in figure.

In the treatise "De Motu Im-letter of Galilei's on the reconcilin presso a Motore Translato," which, as tion of the Holy Scriptures with the it was pretended, was printed against doctrine of the earth's revolution, at the author's wish, togethei with a Lyons, 1649.

The further exposition of atoms, void, the denial of infinite divisibility, the motion of the atoms, and so on, closely follows Epikuros. We need only remark, that Gassendi identifies the weight or gravity of the atoms with their inherent capability of self-determined motion. For the rest, this motion also has been from the beginning bestowed by God upon the atoms.

God, who made the earth and sea bring forth plants and animals, created a finite number of atoms, so as to form the seeds of all things. Thereupon commenced that alternation of generation and dissolution which exists now, and will continue to exist.

'The first cause of everything is God/ but the whole inquiry is concerned only with the secondary causes, which immediately produce each single change. Their principle, however, must necessarily be corporeal. In artistic productions, the moving principle is indeed independent of the material; but in nature the active cause works inwardly, and is only the most active and mobile part of the material. In the case of visible bodies, one is always moved by the other: the self-moving principles are the atoms.

The falling of bodies Gassendi explains to be due to the attraction of the earth; but this attraction cannot be an 'actio in distans.' Unless something from the earth reached the stone and overpowered it, it would not trouble itself about the earth; just as the magnet must in some real if invisible manner lay hold upon the iron in order to draw it to itself. That this is not to be conceived crudely, as done by the throwing out of harpoons or hooks, is shown by a remarkable picture employed by Gassendi to explain this attraction, of a boy attracted by an apple, a figure of which has reached him through the senses. It is worth remarking here that Newton, who in this matter trod in Gassendi's steps, by no means thought of his law of gravitation as an immediate operation exerted at a distance. With regard to this, it seems to me very doubtful whether the account in Ueherweg, Hist. Phil., iii. 15foil., E. T. ii. 14, is correct—an account resting perhnps partly on a misunderstanding of the account in the first edition of the " History of Materialism," but partly also on an actual error in that account. Ueherweg says of Gassendi: "Gassendi's Atomism is less a doctrine of dead nature than is that of Epikuros. Gassendi ascribed to the atoms force, and even sensation, just as a boy is moved by the image of an apple to turn aside from his way and approach the apple-tree. So the stone thrown into the air is moved by the in0uence of the earth, reaching to it to pass out of the direct line and to approach the earth. " Erroneous above all appears to have been the transference of sensation to the atoms, as was assumed in the first edition of the " History of Materialism," S. 125, while, upon revision, I am not in a position to find a voucher for this. The error seems to have arisen in this way—that Gassendi, in fact, with regard to the difficult question how the *sentient* can proceed from the *nonsentient,* does in a very remarkable respect go far beyond Lucretius. I am indeed sorry that I can here only quote Bernier, Abrégc de la i'hilos.

de Gassendi, vi. 48 foil., as while revising I have no complete edition of Gassendi at my service, and the press cannot be longer delayed. There it runs: "En second lieu (among the reasons which Lucretius has not adduced, but, according to Gassendi, might have adduced) que toute sorte de semence estantaniméo, et que non seulement les animaux qui uaissent de Taccouplement, mais ceuit mesme qui s'engendrent de la pourriture estant forinez de petites molecules seminales qui out este assemblées et formees ou des le commencement du monde ou depuia, *on ne petit pas absotuinent dire, que les choses sensibhs st fasscnt tie choses intensities,* mais plut6st qu'elles se font de choses qui bien qu'elles ne sentent pas effectivement, sont neanmoins, *ou contiennent en effet les jirincipes du sentiment,* de mesme que les principes du feu sont contenus, et caches dans les veine- des cailloux, ou dans quelque autre matiere grasse." Gassendi therefore assumes here at least the possibility that organic germs, with the disposition towards sensation, exist right from the beginning of creation. These germs, however, despite their originality (naturally quite inconsistent with the cosmogony of Epikuros) are not atoms, but *combinations of atoms,* although of the simplest oha-of the Philosophy of Newton (Oeuvres racter. A misunderstanding is compl., 1784, t. xxxi. p. 37): "Newpossible as to the application of the ton suivait les ancienncs opinions de image of the boy who sees an apple to Dcmocrite, d'Epicure et d'unc foule a purely spiritual influence. This re-de philosophes rectifies par uotre fers primarily only to a complex pro-célebre Gassendi. Newton a ditplucess. of attraction, which, however, sicurs fois a quelques f rancois qui takes place in a purely physical way. vivent encore, qu'il regardait Gassendi It remains, indeed, questionable whecomme un esprit tres juste et trts ther Gassendi has here carried out sage, et qu'il ferait gloire d'etre entieMaterialism as consistently as Des-rement de son avis dans toutes les cartes in the "Passiones Animae," choscs dont on vient de parler." where everything is resolved into Bernier, Abrege de la Phil, de flow and impact of particles. Gassendi, Lyon, 1684, vi. 32-34. Voltaire reports in his Elements

The evolution and dissolution of things is nothing but the union and separation of atoms. When a piece of wood is burnt, the flame, smell, and ashes, and so on, have already existed in their atoms, only in other combinations. All change is only movement in the constituents of a thing, and hence the simple substance cannot change, but only continue its movements in space.

The weak side of Atomism, the impossibility of explaining sensible qualities and sensation out of atoms and space *(cf.* above, p. 18 foil., and 143 foil.), appears to have been quite appreciated by Gassendi, for he discusses this problem at great length, and not only endeavours to put the explanations offered by Lucretius in the best light, but also to strengthem them by new arguments. At the same time he admits that there is something left unexplained—only he maintains that this is the same with all other systems. This is, however, not quite correct, since the form of the combination, upon which the influence here depends, is with the Aristotelians something essential; but in the case of Atomism it is nothing.

Gassendi stands widely apart from Lucretius in accepting an immortal and incorporeal spirit; and yet this spirit, like Gassendi's God, stands so entirely out of relation to his system, that we can very conveniently leave it out of sight. Nor is Gassendi led to adopt it for the sake of this question of unity; he does so because religion demands itJust because his system only recognises a material soul composed of atoms, the qualities of immortality and immateriality must be supplied by the spirit. The manner in which this is established strikingly reminds us of Averroism. Diseases of the mind, for example, are diseasesof the brain; they do not affect the immortal reason, only this cannot find expression because its instrument is destroyed. But whether it is in this instrument that the individual consciousness, the ego, is seated, which is, in fact, itself disturbed by the disease, and does not look upon it as a spectator *ab extra*—this point Gassendi takes good care not to examine too closely. Besides, quite apart from the constraint of orthodoxy, he might well feel little inclination to follow the windings of this problem, because they would lead him away from the sphere of experience.

The theory of the external world, so admirably supported by Atomism, Gassendi had very much more at heart than psychology, in which he made shift with a minimum amount of original speculation, and that only for the completion of his system, while Descartes, independently of his metaphysical doctrine of the ego, attempted in this sphere also to make an independent contribution.

At the University of Paris, where the Aristotelian philosophy still held sway over the older teachers, the views of Descartes and of Gassendi gained increasing hold on the younger blood, and there arose two new schools—those of the Cartesians and the Gassendists, one of which in the name of reason, the other in the name of experience, were eager to inflict a final blew upon Scholasticism. This conflict was the more remarkable because just at that time, under the influence of reactionary tendencies, the philosophy of Aristotle had received a fresh impulse. The theologian Launoy, otherwise a thoroughly learned and comparatively a freethinking man, exclaims in astonishment, as he mentions the views of his contemporary, Gassendi, "If Ramus, Litaudus, Villonius, and Clavius had so taught, what would have been done to them!" 4

Gassendi did not fall a victim to theology, because he was destined to fall a victim to medicine. Being treated for a fever in the fashion of the time, he had been reduced to extreme debility. He long, but vainly, sought restoration in his Southern home. On returning to Paris, he was again attacked by fever, and thirteen fresh blood-lettings ended his life. He died the 24th of October 1655, in his sixty-third year. The reformation of physics and natural philosophy, usually ascribed to Descartes, was at least as much the work of Gassendi. Frequently, in consequence of the fame which Descartes owed to his metaphysic, those very things have been credited to Descartes which ought properly to be assigned to Gassendi: it was also a result of the peculiar mixture of difference and agreement, of hostility and alliance, between the two systems, that the influences resulting from them became completely interfused. Thus Hobbes, the Materialist and friend of Gassendi, was a supporter of Descartes's corpuscular theory, whilst Newton conceived the atoms after the fashion of Gassendi It was reserved for later discoveries to reconcile the two theories, and to permit of the co-existence of atoms and molecules, after each conception had received its natural development. So much, however, is at least certain, that the Atomism of our own day has, step by step, been developed from the theories of Gassendi and Descartes, and so its roots reach back to Leukippos and Demokritos.

Joannis Lannoii de Varia Arieto-o. xviii. p. 328 of the edition I have telis in Academia Purisieusi Fortuisa, used, that of Wittenberg, 1720. CHAPTER II.

TnOMAS HOBBES OF MALMESBUKY.

Amongst the most remarkable characters that meet us in the history of Materialism must unquestionably be numbered the Englishman, Thomas Hobbes of Malmesbury. His father was a simple country clergyman of modest education, but possessed of sufficient ability to read the necessary homilies to his flock.

When, in the year 15 38, the haughty Armada of Philip of Spain was threatening the English coasts, and the people were in a state of anxiety and excitement, the wife of this clergyman, in her alarm, gave premature birth to a boy, who, in spite of his delicacy as an infant, was destined to live to his ninety-second year. This babe was Thomas Hobbes.

Hobbes was to attain not merely his celebrity, but also bis later tendency and his favourite occupations, only very late in life, and by very indirect methods.

For when, in Ids fourteenth year, he repaired to the University of Oxford, he was, according to the spirit of the studies then prevailing there, initiated into logic and physic based upon the principles of Aristotle? For five full years he endeavoured with great zeal to master these subtleties, and in logic especially made great progress. No doubt it had some influence upon his future development that he now devoted himself to the Nominalistic School—that is, to the school which is in principle so closely related to Materialism; and although Hobbes later entirely dropped these studies, nevertheless he remained a Nominalist.

A

Indeed, we may assert that he gave to this school the boldest development that history exhibits, by combining with the doctrine of the merely conventional value of universal concepts the doctrine of their relativity, very nearly in the sense of the Greek Sophists.

When in his twentieth year, he entered the service of Ijord Cavendish, afterwards Duke of Devonshire. This position decided the whole external course of his life, and seems, moreover, to have exercised a permanent influence upon his views and principles.

He undertook the duties of companion or tutor to the con of Lord Cavendish, who was about his own age, and whose son again he was to educate in his later years; so that he stood in intimate relations with three generations of this distinguished house. His life was, therefore, that of a private tutor in the circles of the highest English nobility.

This situation introduced him to the world, and gave him that lasting practical turn which commonly marked the English philosophers of that period; he was emancipated from the narrow circle of Scholastic wisdom and clerical prejudices in which he had grown up; in his frequent journeyings he became acquainted with France and Italy, and in Paris especially he found leisure and opportunity to hold intercourse with the most famous men of the age. At the same time, however, these very circumstances early taught him subordination and inclination to the Koyalist and High Church party, in opposition to the efforts of the English democracy and the dissenting sects. His Latin and Greek he soon began to forget in his new position, and by way of compensation speedily picked up on his first travels with the young lord some knowledge of Erench and Italian. As he everywhere perceived that the Scholastic logic was an object of contempt with all sensible men, he let it completely drop, and began instead to apply himself again zealously to his Greek and Latin, but more en their literary side. Eut even in these studies he was helped by his practical sense, which had already turned in the direction of politics.

As then the storms which preceded the outbreak of the English Eevolution began to stir, he translated in the year 1628 Thukydides into English, with the express object of frightening his countrymen by an exhibition of the follies of democracy, as they were pictured in the fortunes of the Athenians. The superstition was at that time widely spread, which even in our own days is not entirely extinguished, that history is directly useful as a teacher; that examples drawn from it may be readily applied, and that in the most altered circumstances. The party that Hobbes embraced was already obviously enough the legitimist and conservative, although his own personal way of thinking, and the famous theory that was derived from it, was fundamentally and directly opposed to all conservatism.

It was in the year 1629, when travelling through France with another young nobleman, that Hobbes began to study the Elements of Euklid, for which he soon conceived a strong liking. He was then already forty-one years old, and was now for the first time turning his attention to mathematics, in which he soon attained to the summit of the science as it then was, and which led him to his systematic mechanical Materialism.

Two years later, and upon a fresh tour through France and Italy, he began at Paris the study of the natural sciences, and he soon made the chief object of his investigations a problem which, in the very putting of it, clearly indicates his

Materialism, and the answer to which furnishes the watchword to the Materialistic controversies of the coming century. This problem is as follows:— In the first edition it was here their policy. It is simpler to point further remarked that this theory out that the principles of the " Levia would have better suited with the than " may in fact be still better har

Napoleonic policy of our days. This monised with the despotism of Crom expression might be liable to misconwell than with the pretensions of struction, since the Bonaparte family the Stuarts to their hereditary divine seek to adopt a certain legitimism in right.

What kind of motion can it be that produces the sensation and imagination of living beings?

During these studies, which lasted for many years, he was in daily communication with the Minim Friar Mersenne, with whom, moreover, after his return to England in 1637, he opened a correspondence.

As soon, however, as, in 1640, the Long Parliament began its session, he, who had so eagerly declared himself against the popular side, had every reason to withdraw himself; and he betook himself accordingly to Paris, where he was now in constant intercourse with Gassendi, as well as with Mersenne, and not without appropriating much from his views. His stay in Paris lasted through a long series of years. Amongst the refugee Englishmen then gathered in great numbers at Paris, he occupied a much respected position, and was selected to give instruction in mathematics to the future Charles II. Meanwhile he had composed his chief political treatises, the "De Cive" and the " Leviathan," in which, and in the " Leviathan" with special outspokenness, he propounded the doctrine of a downright and paradoxical, but by no means a legitimist Absolutism. This very treatise, in which, moreover, the clergy had discovered many heresies, destroyed for a time his popularity at court. He fell into disgrace, and as he had at the same time violently attacked the Papacy, he was obliged to quit Paris, and avail himself of the muchabused freedom of Englishmen.

After the restoration of the King, he reconciled himself with the court, and lived in an honourable retirement of devotion to his studies. As late as his eighty-eighth year he published a translation of Homer; and in his ninetyfirst year a Cyclometry.

As Hobbes once lay ill at St. Germain of a violent fever, Mersenne was sent to him to take care that the famous man should not die outside the Eomish Church. After Mersenne had announced the power of the Church to remit sins, Hobbes begged that he would rather tell him when

Vol. 1. s he had last seen Gassendi, and so the conversation immediately turned upon other subjects. The attentions of an English bishop, however, he accepted, on condition that he should confine himself to the written prayers prescribed by the Church.

Hobbes's views upon natural philosophy are partly scattered through his political writings, but partly laid down in the two works "De Homine" and "De Corpore." Thoroughly characteristic of his way of thinking is his introduction to philosophy:—

"Philosophy seems to me to be amongst men now in the same manner as corn and wine are said to have been in the world in ancient time. For from the beginning there were vines and ears of corn growing here and there in the fields, but no care was taken for the planting and sowing of them. Men lived therefore upon acorns; or, if any were so bold as to venture upon the eating of these unknown and doubtful fruits, they did it with danger of their health... . And from hence it comes to pass that those who content themselves with daily experience, which may be likened to feeding upon acorns, and either reject or not much regard philosophy, are commonly esteemed, and are indeed, men of sounder judgment than those who, from opinions, though not vulgar, yet full of uncertainty, are carelessly received, do nothing but dispute and wrangle, like men that are not well in their wits."

Hobbes points out how difficult it is to expel from men's minds a fallacy which has taken root, and which has been strengthened by the authority of plausible authors; and the more difficult because true, that is, exact philosophy scorns not only the " paint and false colours of language, but even the very ornaments and graces of the same," and because the first grounds of all philosophy are "poor, and in appearance deformed."

After this introduction follows *a definition of philosophy,* Vol. i. pp. 1, 2, ed. Moleaworth, Elements of Philosophy: The First Section, Concerning Body.

which might equally well he called a negation of philosophy, in the ordinary sense of the word:

It is the knowledge of effects or of appearances, acquired from the knowledge we have first of their causes, and conversely of possible causes from their known effects, by means of true ratiocination. All reasoning, however, is computation; and accordingly ratiocination may be resolved into addition and subtraction.16

Not only does this definition transform the whole of philosophy into natural science, and completely set aside the transcendental principle, but the Materialistic tendency is still plainer in the explanation of the *object* of philosophy. It consists in this, that we *foresee effects,* and so are able to apply them to the purposes of life. It is well known that the notion of philosophy here expressed has taken such deep root in England, that it is impossible to render the sense of the word "philosophy" by the corresponding German word, and the true " natural philosopher" is nothing but the experimenting physicist. Hobbes appears here as the logical successor of Bacon; and as the philosophy of these men has certainly exercised a considerable influence in furthering the material progress of England, so, conversely, it was itself a product of that inborn national spirit then already hastening to its mighty development—the spirit of a sober and practical people striving after power and wealth The definition was still further the words "eonceptis" and "quae abridged in the first edition, in order esse possunt" are by no means superto show as olearly as possible the fluous. They denote, in definite optransition of philosophy into natural position to the Baconian induction, science. It runs in the original: the nature of the hypothetical-deduc"Philosophia est effectuum seu phae-tive method, which begins with a nomenon ex eonceptis eorum causis theory, and tries and corrects it by seu generationibus, et rursus genera-reference to experience. Compare tionum, quae esse possunt, ex cogni-what is said further on in the text as tis effectibus per rectam ratiocina-to the relation of Hobbes to Bacon tionem acquisita cognitio." If we and Descartes. The passages quoted wish to observe more closely the are in the treatise De Corpore, i. r, *method* which is also suggested in this Opera Latina, ed. Molesworth, i. definition, we must remember that 2, 3.

In spite of these so obvious relations, it is impossible not to recognise also the influence of Descartes in this definition; and here we must, of course, keep clearly in our minds the Descartes of the "Essay upon Method," without troubling ourselves with the traditional notions of Cartesianism. In this maiden work, in which Descartes ranks his *physical* theories far above his metaphysical ones in point of importance, he boasts of the former that they open the way, "in room of the speculative philosophy usually taught in the schools, to discover a practical, by means of which, knowing the force and action of fire, water, air, the stars, the heavens, and all the other bodies that surround us, as distinctly as we know the various crafts of our artisans, we might also apply them in the same way to all the uses to which they are adapted, and thus render ourselves the lords and possessors of nature." We might indeed remark, that all this had already been more forcibly said by Bacon, with whose doctrine Hobbes had been thoroughly acquainted from his early youth; but this agreement extends only to the general tendency, while Descartes' method in one very essential point differs from the Baconian.

Bacon begins with induction, and expects by his mounting from the particular to the universal to be able to force his way to the *real* causes of phenomena. When these have been attained, there follows deduction, partly for the filling in of details, partly, however, for the practical application of the truths discovered.
Compare note 66 in the previous of self-observation!) from this tensection, dency, he entirely mistakes the na Kuno Fischer and v. Kirch-ture of the deductive process, which mann, in translating this passage may in the one sphere be regulated (Rene Descartes' Hauptschriften, S. by experience, but not in the other. 57; and Phil. Bibl., Rene Descartes' Descartes himself was still quite clear rhil. Werke, i. S. 70 ff.), refer quite enough on this point in the year 1637, rightly to the relationship between and accordingly claimed an objective Descartes and Bacon. Yet when the validity for his physical theories, but latter *(loc. cit.* Anm. 35) tries to claim not for his transcendental specu-laDescartes as an *empiricist,* and to de-1 ions. duce the 'Cogito crj,-o sum ' (as result
Descartes, on the contrary, proceeds, in fact, synthetically, and yet not in the sense of Plato and Aristotle, with pretensions to an absolute certainty of his principles (this modification was reserved for the reactionary development of his metaphysic!), but with the distinct consciousness that the real demonstrative power lies in experience. He proposes the theory tentatively, explains the phenomena by means of it, and so tests the theory by experience. This method, which may be designated as the hypotheticodeductive method (although, if classified according to the *nervusprobandi,* it belongs to induction, and must be treated under inductive logic), stands nearer to the actual procedure of scientific inquiries than the Baconian, although neither of them adequately represents the true nature of scientific inquiry. Hobbes, however, has here no doubt consciously sided with Descartes against Bacon, whilst later Newton again (of course more in theory than in actual practice!) reverted to Bacon.

Hobbes deserves high praise for this, that he recognised frankly and unreservedly the great achievement of modern science. While Bacon and Descartes were still refusing it, Hobbes gave to Copernicus the place of honour that was his due, just as, in short, in nearly all controverted points, with perhaps the single exception of the doctrine of vacuum, into the denial of which he allowed himself to be seduced by Descartes, he declared distinctly and decidedly for the rational and correct view. In this respect—as well as for the determination of his tendency—the dedication to his treatise "De Corpore" is of great interest. There it is said that the doctrine of the earth's diurnal revolution was the invention of the ancients, but that both it and astronomy, that is, celestial physics, springing up together with it, were, by succeeding philosophers, *strangled with the snares of words.* And therefore the beginning of astronomy, except observations, is not to be derived from farther time than from Nicolaus Copernicus, who, in the age next preceding the present, revived the opinion of Pythagoras, Aristarchos, and Philolaos. After this, Galilei had first opened the gate of natural philosophy (physics), and lastly, the science of man's body had been founded by Harvey through his doctrines of the circulation of the blood and the generation of animals. Before this there had been nothing but every man's experiments by himself, and the natural histories that were no certainer than civil histories. But then all the physical sciences had been extraordinarily advanced by Kepler, Gassendi, and Mersenne, while Hobbes vindicates for himself (referring to his book " De Give") the foundation of ' Civil Philosophy.' Especially decisive is the follow-Logici Circulum vocant, incidere; ing passage of the "Dissertatio de nam cum experientia maximum effecMethodo" (near the end): "Rationes tuum istorum partem ccrtissimam enim mihi videntur in iis (that is, in esse arguat, *cautae a quibus illos elicio,* the 'hypotheses' of Dioptrics, and so *rum tarn iis probandis quam explication)* tali serie connexae, ut sicut ulti-*dis inserviunt, contraque ipsae ab illis* mac demonstrantur a primis, quae *probantur.*" illarum causae sunt, ita reciproce ' To the Earl of Devonshire, Lon primae ab ultimis, quae insarum sunt don, 23d April 1655, Opera Latiua, effecta, probentur. Nee est quod ed. Molesworth, vol. i. p. vii. quis putet, me hie in vitium, quod

In old Greece, he goes on, there walked a certain phantasm, for superficial gravity a little like philosophy, though full within of fraud and filth. With Christianity had been mingled first some harmless sentences of Plato, but afterwards many foolish and false ones out of Aristotle; and so, instead of the faith, there entered a thing called theology, which, halting on one foot (because she rests partly on the Holy Scripture, but partly on the Aristotelian philosophy), is like the Empusa, and has raised an infinite number of controversies and wars. This Empusa cannot be better exorcised than by the establishing of a State religion instead of the opinions of private men, at the same time basing religion upon Holy Scripture, but philosophy upon *natural reason.*

These ideas are very boldly carried out, especially in the "Leviathan," and we are surprised now by perverse paradoxes, and now by the natural directness and keenness of his judgment. With regard to his opposition to Aristotle, there is a specially notable passage in the fortysixth chapter, where he indicates the confusion of name and thing as the root of the evil. Hobbes undoubtedly hits the nail upon the head when he considers the hypostasising of the copula Est as the original source of innumerable absurdities. Aristotle has made 'being' into a thing, just as though there were in the universe an actual object which could be designated by the term 'being!' We may imagine to ourselves what would have been Hobbes's judgment upon Hegel!

His attack upon theology, which is treated as mischiefmaking abomination, is only apparently a defence of belief in the letter. It is, in truth, much rather allied with a concealed aversion to religion. But Hobbes has a quite uncommon hatred of theology, in so far as she is connected with the claims of ecclesiastical supremacy. This he absolutely rejects. The kingdom of Christ is not of this world, and therefore the spiritual authority has no claim to any sort of obedience. Accordingly, Hobbes attacks with especial animosity the doctrine of papal infallibility. Generally speaking, also, it is a necessary consequence of his definition of the notion of philosophy that any idea of a speculative theology is quite impossible. The knowledge of God is in no way a part of science, because as soon as it is no longer possible to add or to subtract, the province of reflection ceases. It is true, indeed, that the connection between cause and effect leads us to the assumption of a last cause of all motion, a first moving principle; but the further definition of its nature remains somewhat quite unthinkable, and contradictory in thought, so that the actual recognition and completion of the idea of God must remain as the function of religious faith. The doctrine of papal infalli-supremacy of the Pope over all the bility js controverted by Hobbes in princes of the earth. The whole ar the "Leviathan," c. xlii., ed. Moles-gument shows that Hobbes recog worth, iii. 554, foil. This polemic niscd the full force of the dangers forms one portion of the elaborate Ik-contained in these pretensions — futation of Cardinal Bellarmine's book dangers which are only in our own in favour of the Jesuit doctrine of the days becoming visible to everybody.
The blindness and thoughtlessness of faith has been in no system so expressly stated as in this, although/ Bacon, and even Gassendi, occupy in many respects a ve lar position. And accordingly Schaller very exc says of the attitude of Hobbes to religion: "How psychologically possible is also a mystery, so that it necessary to have faith in the possibility of such a failih.' But the true point of support upon which this theoAv of faith rests is found in Hobbes's political system.

Hobbes, as is well known, is regardedasthe found the absolutist theory of government, which"Si from the necessity of escaping the war of all aga: by means of a supreme will. He assumes that man thoughts are naturally for the preservation of his interests, even though peaceably disposed, yet can without hurting the interests of others, since hJ struggles to preserve his own. Hobbes denies the totelian principle that man, like the bee, the a beaver, is, from the very constitution of his nature, tical animal. It is not through political instinc through fear and reason, that man enters into unioi his fellows, with the object of preserving their coi Schaller, Gereh d. Naturphil., Leipzig, 1841, S. 82. But we need not seek any clearer explanation of this point in Schaller; very able, and in the main certainly correct, is the judgment of Kuno Fischer as to the position of morality and religion in Hobbes (Baco von Verulam, S. 393 ff., E. T. Oxenford, p. 420 foil.); yet in the too onesided reference of this whole tendency to Bacon, while Descartes is conceived as the exact antithesis, there is a defect, which is due to the Hegelian method of classification, which makes everything very clear, but not unfrequently does violence to the often very complicated threads. A necessary conseql this is that Kuno Fischer, wl rule estimates such phenomel delicate tact, has failed to ro; the worldly frivolity which, cartes, underlies his reverent! jection to the judgment of the'. Entirely hypocritical HobbeJ gious sentiments can hardlj been; at least, he was oerta honourable partisan of the Cbj his country in opposition tof licism; and it was probably J this sense that men like *Xl* and Descartes—and in a lessi *i* even Gassendi—were lealouj lies.
security. With peculiar consistency, moreover, Hobbes denies even any absolute difference between good and evil, virtue and vice. The individual man, therefore, cannot succeed in giving any established validity to these notions either: he allows himself, in fact, to be guided by his interests; and so long as the higher will of the State does not exist, this can as little be made a subject of reproach to him as to the beast of prey that destroys the weaker animals.

Although these principles are strictly in harmony with each other and with the whole system, Hobbes might at the same time, without any inconsistency, have admitted as probable at least the existence of a political impulse, and even of a natural gravitation to the adoption of such customs as guarantee the happiest possible condition of all men. The denial of the freedom of the will, which is a matter of course in Hobbes's system, by no means implies an egoistic ethic as its necessary result. It is simply that, with an unnatural extension of the idea, even the effort to make one's surroundings happy, in so far as this gratifies a natural impulse, is called egoistic. Hobbes. however, knows nothing of this unnatural extension of the idea: the egoism of his State-founders is a pure, complete, and unsophisticated egoism, in the sense in which this notion indicates just the opposition of personal interests to foreign and to joint interests. Hobbes, who undervalued the euristic value of feeling, in rejecting the natural instinct to political life, and to the intellectual apprehension and appropriation of the general interests, missed the one path which could have conducted him even from his Materialistic standpoint to higher ethicopolitical principles. In rejecting the Aristotelian *£uov Ttoxtttkov,* he enters upon the path which, co-operating with the rest of his fundamental doctrines, must necessarily lead him into paradoxical consequences. It is just because of this unshrinking consistency that Hobbes, even when he goes wrong, is still so extraordinarily instructive; and we can, in fact, scared)' name a second author who has been so unanimously abused by the disciples of all schools, while at the same time he stimulated them all to greater clearness and precision.

The first founders of the State, as later in Eousseau, so in Hobbes also, make a compact; and in this respect his theory is thoroughly revolutionary—knowing nothing of an original divine arrangement of ranks, of hereditary divine right to the crown, and conservative fancies of that kind. Hobbes holds the monarchy to be the best form of government, although he thinks that, of all his principles, this has been least satisfactorily demonstrated. Even the hereditariness of monarchy is a mere arrangement of utility; but that the monarchy, where it exists, must be absolute, follows simply from the demand that the governance of the State, even when it is intrusted to a society or an assembly, must possess absolute force.

For his egoistical rabble of human beings has not the slightest inclination by nature to maintain any form of constitution or to observe any laws: fear alone can compel it to this. In order, therefore, that the multitude may at least continue united, and the war of all against all may be avoided as the greatest possible evil, the egoism of the rulers must have the force to assert itself absolutely, so as to keep in check the unbridled, and, in its totality, the very much more harmful egoism of all its subjects.

The government, besides, cannot be kept in check; if it violates the constitution, then the citizens, to offer a successful resistance, must *trust one another,* and that is what the egoistic creatures cannot do; but each individual is weaker than the government. Why then need it stand upon ceremony?

The formula out of which grows multitude becomes a unity which we the unity of the State runs thus:— call a State. "Atque haec est gene

"Ego huic homini. vel huic coetui, ratio,nagni illius Leviathan, vel ut auctoritatem et jus meum regendi dignius loquar, mortalis Dei."—Le meipsum concedo, ea conditione, ut viathan, c. xvii., iii. 131, ed. Moles tu quoque tuam auctoritatem et jus worth. As to the *natural* tuum tui regendi.in eundem trans-*equality 0!* all men (in opposition to fevas. " As each individual speaks Aristotle, who speaks of born masters thus to every other, the atomistic and slaves), comp. ibid. c. xv.,p. 118.

That every revolution that is strong enough is also justified, as soon as it succeeds, in establishing any new form of authority, is a necessary consequence of this system: tyrants need not comfort themselves with the proverb,'Might comes before right,' since, in fact, might and right are absolutely identical. Hobbes does not care to linger among these consequences of his system, and rather loves to paint the advantages of an absolute hereditary monarchy; but all this does not modify the theory. The name "Leviathan" is only too significant of this monster of a State, which is guided by no higher considerations, which, like a god upon earth, ordains law and judgment, right and possession, at its own will, and even arbitrarily determines the ideas of *good* and *evil,"®* and in return assures to all those who bow the knee before it and do it sacrifice, protection for their lives and property.

To the absolute authority of the State, moreover, belongs the right of prescribing to its subjects their religion and their whole way of thinking. Exactly like Epikuros and Lucretius, so Hobbes also derives religion from terror and superstition; but while they for this very reason declare that to rise above the limits of religion is the highest and noblest duty of the philosopher, Hobbes knows how to turn this common material to account for the purposes of his State. His real view of religion is so trenchantly expressed in a single sentence, that we cannot but be surprised at the unnecessary breath that has often been spent upon the theology of Hobbes. He lays down the following definition: *"Fear oj power invisible, feigned by the mind or imagined from tales publicly allowed,* Religion: *not allowed,* Superstition." When Hobbes, then, in the same book, with the utmost calmness mentions as simple facts the building of the tower of Babel, or the miracles worked by Moses in Egypt, 25 we must nevertheless recall with astonishment his definition of religion. The man who compared the miracles to 'pills' which we must swallow down without chewing can, in fact, only not have held those miraculous stories for superstitions, because in England the authority of the Bible is established by the supreme political power. When, therefore, Hobbes is speaking upon religious subjects, we must constantly distinguish these three cases. *Either* Hobbes speaks directly from his own system, and then he views religion as only one form of superstition; *or* he is referring incidentally to some particular points, when he only practically applies a principle of his system—then he views the doctrines of religion as simple facts, with which, however, science has nothing more to do; Hobbes is then sacrificing to Leviathan.

So long as the State does not out of mere self-will nnd vanity, are interfere, everything, according to held inviolable *(loc. ciL,* c. vii. p. 52).

Hobbes, is good for any particular That any private person should make man that is the object of his desire himself the judge of good and evil, and (Leviathan, 0. vi. iii. 42, ed. Molesw.). hold it a sin to do anything against

Conscience is nothing but a man's his conscience, is reckoned among the secret consciousness of his deeds and worst offences against civic obedience words, and this expression is often (0. *X7x.* p. 232). misapplied to private opinions, which, Leviathan, o. vi. p. 45: "Metus tus ad turrem Babel, quo tempore potentiarum invisibilium, rive fictae Deus omnem hominem sermonis sui, illae sint, sive ab historiis acceptae propter rcbellionem, oblivione pershit publiee, *religio* est; si publice cussit." Ibid., c. xxxvii. p. 315: *acccpt&e nOn sint superstitio," Hohbes* "Potestatem ergo illi dedit Deus indeed goes on to add: "Quandoautem convertendi virgam, quam in mami potentiae illae re vera tales sunt, quales habebat. in serpentem, et num seraccepimus, *vera religio;"* but this is pentem in virgam," *kc.* only an apparent saving clause. For Hobbes is speaking from this as the State alone decides which is to standpoint, for example, in treating be the accepted religion, and as it of the *origin* of religion. This is remust not be contradicted for political ferred absolutely to some natural reasons, obviously the notion of " vera characteristic or other of man (comp. religio" is a merely relative one—and Lev., c. xii. *ad* tint.), among others, we may be the more content that it to the inclination to hasty conclusions, should be so, since in a scientific sense and so on. And so we have this sumthere is nothing to be said as to re-mary (p. 89, Eng. Works, iii. 98): ligion in general. "In these four things—opinion of Comp. Kuno Fischer, Baco von ghosts, ignorance of second causes,

Verulam, S. 404, E. T. 430. Levia-devotion towards what men fear, and than, c. xxxii. iii. 266. taking of things casual for prognostics -8 Comp. Leviathan, c. iv. iii. 22: —consisteth the natural seed *(semen*

"Copia haec omnis... interiit peui-*naturale)* of religion."

The worst contradictions are thus, at least in form, explained away, and we have only the *third* case left— where Hobbes is offering to Leviathan, as it were *de lege ferenda,* respectful suggestions for the purification of religion and for the abolishing of the worst superstitions. Here we must indeed recognise that Hobbes does all that is in his power to lessen the gulf between faith and knowledge. He distinguishes the essential and the non-essential elements of religion; he tries to explain away obvious contradictions between Scripture and faith—as, for example, the doctrine of the revolution of the earth—by distinguishing between the mode of expression and the moral purpose of Scripture; he explains ' possession' as a disease; maintains that miracles have ceased since the founding of Christianity, and even allows us to see that the very miracles are not miracles to everybody. If we add to this the remarkable rudiments of a historico-critical treatment of the Bible, we easily see that the whole armoury of Eationalism is already to be found in Hobbes, and only needs to have its range of application extended.

Next, as to his theory of *external nature,* we must first observe that Hobbes absolutely identifies the idea of body with that of substance; so that when Bacon carries on a controversy against the immaterial substance of Aristotle, Hobbes has already got beyond him, and without hesitation distinguishes between the 'body' and the 'accidens.' Hobbes declared everything to be body that, independently of our thought, occupies a portion of space, and coincides withltT As opposed to this, the accident is not a really objective thing, like body, but it is the way in which the body is conceived. This distinction is really sharper than that of Aristotle, and, like all Hobbes's definitions, betrays the mathematically-trained mind. In other respects Hobbes adheres to the explanation that the accident is in the subject, in such a way that it cannot be regarded as any part of it, but that it may be away, and yet the body does not cease to be. The only constant accidents which cannot be wanting without the body's thereby ceasing to exist are extension, and figure. All_others, such as rest motion, colour, hardness, and so on, may vary, while the body itself remains, and they are, therefore, not corporeal, but simply jnodes-in which we coaceixe the __bpdy.

Comp. amongst others, the fol-ipsa miracula non omnibus miracnla lowing passages of the "Leviathan," sunt."

Op. Lat. iii. 64, foil. 207: "Miracnla Comp. for instance "Leviathan," en mi, ex quo tempore nobis Chris-c. xxxii. 276: "Libri testamenti novi tianis positae sunt leges divinae, cess-ab altiore tempore derivari non pos averunt." "Miracula narrantibus sunt, quamabeo, quo rectores ecclesi credere non obligamur." "Etiam arum collcgcrant," and what follows.

y: /Motion Hobbes defines as the 'continual relinquishing of / one place and acquiring of another,' where it is obviously overlooked that the idea of motion is already contained in the 'relinquishing' and 'acquiring of a place. As compared with Gassendi and Bacon, there appears not unfrequently in Hobbes's definitions a return to Aristotelianism, if not in principle, at least in the mode of expression—a fact which is to be explained by the course of his intellectual development.

In the definition of matter, this inclination towards Aristotle is particularly evident. Hobbes declares that „,-v matter is neither one of the bodies nor a special body dis tinct from all others, and it follows, therefore, that *itjjn* fact nothing else than a mere name. Here the Aristotelian conception is obviously taken as the foundation, but it is improved upon in a way thoroughly corresponding to the improvements in the notion of 'accident.' Hobbes, who sees that possibility or chance cannot be in things, but only in our conception of things, quite rightly corrects the main defect of the Aristotelian system, by substituting fo the accident as an accidental element in the *object* the accidental *subjective* conception. Instead of matter as a substance, that *can become* anything, and *is* nothing definite, comes in the same way the statement that rrmtter is the body conceived generally, that is, an absJtractiojLoLfS thinking subject. The permanent element, which persists through all changes, is for Hobhes not matter, but the 'body,' which only changes its accidentia, that is, is now conceived by us in one way and now in another. But at the bottom of this changing conception there lies something permanent, namely, the motion of the parts of the body. And therefore when an object changes its colour, becomes hard or soft, breaks into particles, or combines with new particles, the original quantity of the corporeal thing persists; we *name,* however, the object of our perception differently in accordance with the new impressions that it makes upon our senses. Whether we suppose a new body to be the object of our perception, or only attribute new qualities to the old body, depends merely upon the language in which we express our conceptions, and so indirectly from our own will, since words are but counters. And thus, too, the distinction between body (substance) and accident is a merely relative one, dependent upon our conceptions. The real body, which, by the continual movement" of its parts, excites the corresponding movements in our organ of sensation, is subject to no other change whatever than the mere motion of its parts.

It is worth remarking here that Hobbes, by means of his doctrine of the relativity of all concepts, as well as his theory of sensation, does in fact outrun Materialism much as Protagoras outran Demokritos. That Hobbes was not an Atomist we have already seen; but looking also at the whole connection of his ideas as to the nature of things, he could not possibly have been an Atomist. As he applies it to all other concepts, so he applies the category of relativity to the idea of 'great' and 'small' in particular. The distance of many of the fixed stars from the earth is so great, he says, that, as compared with it, the whole distance of the earth from the sun appears as a mere *point;* so also is it with the particles which to us appear small. There is in this direction also an infinity; and what the human physicist regards as the *smallest* particle, because he needs to assume it for his theories, is in its turn a world with innumerable gradations from the greatest to the smallest.30

In his theory of *sensation,* we have already in germ the sensationalism of Locke. Hobbes supposes that the movements of corporeal things communicate themselves to our senses by transmission through the medium of the air, and from thence are continued to the brain, and from the brain finally to the heart. To every movement corresponds an answering movement, in the organism, as in external nature. From this principle of reaction Hobbes derives sensation; but itis not the immediate reaction of the external organ that constitutes sensation, but only the movement that starts from the heart, and then returns from the external organ by way of the brain, so that an appreciable time always elapses between the impression and the sensation. By means of this regressiveness of the movement De Corpora, iv. 27 (i. 362-364, ed. Molesw.). Here also occurs (p. 364) a very noteworthy passage in respect of method: "Agnoscunt mortales magna esse quacdam, etsi finita, ut qaae vident ita esse; agnoscunt item infinitum esse posse magnitndinem eorum quae non vident: *medium* vero esse inter *infinitum* et eorum quae vident cogitantve *maximum,* non statim nee nisi multa eruditione persuadentur." When, indeed, the theoretical question of divisibility, and of the relativity of greatness and smallness, no longer comes into view, Hobbes has no objection to make to describing the "corpuscula" as " atomi," as, for instance, in bis theory of gravitation, De Corpore, iv. 30 (p. 415).
A more particular inquiry into the doctrine of 'conatus' as the form of motion here referred to is beyond our present object. For a fuller exposition see in Baumann, Die Lehren von Raum, Zeit und Mathem., i. S. 321 ff. The special fault found with the theory at S. 327, that the sensation is only produced by the conatus returning from the heart, seems to me to be not wholly justified; for even although, according to Hobbes's theory, a reaction against the impact of the object takes place instantaneously in the part first acted upon, yet this by no means hinders the propagation of the motion under ever new actions and reactions towards the inward parts, where the motion can become regressive. Let us suppose, for example, for simplicity's sake, a series of elastic balls placed in a straight line, A, 11, c,. .. n, and let us suppose that A impinges directly upon B, the impulse being then propagated through C and so on to N; let x strike at right angles against a fixed wall, then the motion will return right through the whole series, without being hindered by the circumstance that sometime before B has also reacted against A, thus limiting its movement. It must, however, of course, be allowed to the originator of the hypothesis to identify with the sensation not the first (limiting) reaction of B against A, but the returning impact from B to A, a view which, there can be no doubt, suits the facts incomparably better. Comp. the remarks in § 4 (i. p. 319 sq., ed. Molesw.) on the effect of an interruption of the communication. of sensation, which is an 'endeavour' (conatus) towards the objects, is explained the transposition outwards of the images of sense.32 The sensation is identical with the image of sense (phantasma), and this again is identical yy with the motion of the ' conatus' towards the objects; not merely *occasioned* by it. And thus Hobbes by a bold phrase hews asunder the Gordian knot of the question how the sensation as a subjective condition is related to the movement; but the matter is thereby made none the clearer.

The subject of the sensation is the man as a whole; the object is the thing which is felt: the images, however, or the-jsense-qualities, by means of which we perceive the thing, are not the thing itself, but a motion originating within us. And thus there does not proceed from shining bodies any light, or from sounding bodies any noise, but only certain forms of motion from each. Light and sound! are sensations, and first arise as such within us as reactionary motion proceeding from the heart. From this results the sensationalistic consequence that all so-called sense-qualities, as such, belong not to things, but originate only in ourselves. Coupled with this, however, is the Materialistic principle that even human sensation is *K"'* nothing but the motion of corporeal particles, occasioned by the external motion of things. Hobbes never thought of abandoning this Materialistic principle in favour of a consistent Sensationalism, because, like Demokritos in antiquity, he started from the mathematical and physical consideration of external things. Therefore his system remains an essentially Materialistic system, in spite of the germs of Sensationalism which it bears within it.

With regard to his view of the universe, Ilobbes Con's De Corpore, iv. xxv. 2 (i. p. existit phantasma; quod propter co318): "Ut cum conatus ille ad intima natum versus externa semper videtur ultiiuus actus sit eorum qui Sunt in tanquam illiquid situm extra organctu sensionis, tum demum ex ea num." reactione aliquandiu durante ipsum VOL. I. T fines himself exclusively to the phenomena which are knowable, and can be explained by the law of causality. Everything of which we can know nothing he resigns to theologians. A remarkable paradox is contained in the doctrine of the corporeality of God, which is, of course, since it contradicts an Article of the Anglican Church, not exactly asserted, but only suggested as a very possible inference. If one could have overheard a confidential conversation between Gassendi and Hobbes, one might perhaps have caught a dispute on the question whether the all-animating heat or the all-embracing ether must be regarded as the Deity.

Compare as to this especially the Appendix to the "Leviathan," c. i., where it is insisted that everything possessed of real independent existence is body. Then it is suggested that even all spirits, such as the air, are corporeal, although it may be with infinite gradations of fineness. Finally, it is pointed out that such expressions as "incorporeal substance" or "immaterial substance," are nowhere found in Holy Scripture. It is true that the first of the Thirtynine Articles teaches that God is without "body" or "parts," and, therefore, this will not be expressly denied; but the twentieth Article says that the Church may require nothing to be believed that is not founded upon Holy Writ (iii. 537 ff.). The result of this obvious contradiction, then, is, that Hobbes insists, at every opportunity, upon the incomprehensibility of God, attributes to Him only negative predicates, and so on; while, by the citation of authorities such as Tertullian (iii. 561), by frequent discussions of Biblical expressions, and especially by the cunning employment of premisses whose final conclusion is left to be drawn by the reader, he tries everywhere to excite the feeling iuat the idea of God would be very intelligible if we conceived Hiui either as a body or as a phantasm, that is, nothing; and that the whole incomprchensibleness is due to this, that we have ever been bidden to speak of God as'' incorporeal." Comp. , *inter alia.* Opera, iii. 87, 260 sq., 282 (here, in particular, the words are very clear: "Cum natura Dei incomprehensibilis sit, et nomina ei attribuenda sint, *non tain ad naturam eius, quam ad honorem, quern, illi exhibere debemut congruentia."* The quintessence of Hobbes's whole theology is probably, however, most clearly expressed in a passage in the "De Homine," iii. 15, Op. ii. 347 sq., where it is bluntly said that *God rule! only through nature,* and that His will is only announced through the State. Wo must not indeed conclude from this that Hobbes identified God with the *rum* of nature—pantheistically. He seems rather to have conceived as God a *part* of the universe—controlling, universally spread, uniform, and by its motion determining mechanically the motion of the whole. As the history of the world is an outflow of natural laws, so the power of tho State is, as the actually effective might, an outflow of the divine will.

CHAPTER III. THE LATER WORKINGS OF MATERIALISM IN ENGLAND.

There is almost a full century of interval between the modern development of Materialistic systems, and between that reckless authorship of a De la Mettrie, who dwelt with special pleasure on just those aspects of Materialism which must be repugnant to the Christian world. It is true, indeed, that even Gassendi and Hobbes had not entirely avoided the ethical consequences of their systems; but both had contrived a means of making their peace with the Church—Gassendi by his superficiality, Hobbes by an arbitrary and unnatural inference. If there is, in this respect, a fundamental distinction between the Materialists of the seventeenth and those of the eighteenth century, yet the chasm between them, apart from purely ecclesiastical dogma, is by far the broadest in the sphere of ethic. Whilst De la Mettrie, quite in the manner of the philosophical dilettanti of ancient Eome, with a frivolous complacency made desire the principle of life, and by his low conception still tainted the memory of Epikuros after thousands of years, Gassendi had in every way brought forward the more serious and deeper aspect of the Epikurean ethic. Hobbes, though only after curious subterfuges, ended by adopting the current semi-Christian, semi-bourgeois morality, which he regarded indeed as narrow, but as justifiably narrow. Both lived very simply and honestly, according to the ordinary ideas of their time.

In spite of this great distinction, the Materialism of the seventeenth century, with all its affinities even to the 'Systeme de la Nature,' forms one connected chain, while the present, although again between De la Mettrie and Vogt or Moleschott there is just such an interval of a century, must be regarded as something entirely independent. The philosophy of Kant, and still more the great scientific achievements of the last few decades, demand this special estimate as distinctly from the standpoint of theoretical science, while, on the other hand, a glance at the material conditions and the social circumstances must lead us to embrace in an inner unity the whole period down to the French Revolution.

If we first direct our attention to the state and civil society, we shall perceive an analogy between those two earlier periods which markedly separates them from the present. Hobbes and Gassendi lived at the courts, or in the aristocratic society of England and France. De la Mettrie was protected by Frederic the Great. The Materialism of both the past centuries found its support in the worldly aristocracy, and the difference of its relation to the Church is partly a result of the different attitudes taken up by the secular aristocracy and the courts towards the Church. The Materialism of our own times has, on the contrary, a thoroughly popular tendency; it rests upon nothing but the right to express its convictions and the receptivity of a great public, to whom the results of science, variously combined with Materialistic doctrine, are made accessible in the most convenient shape; and therefore, to understand the ever-important transition from the Materialism of the seventeenth to that of the, eighteenth century, we must keep before us the relations of the higher classes of society, and the changes which were at this time taking place amongst them.

One most striking feature was the peculiar direction of all the efforts that appeared in the second half of the seventeenth century in England. After the restoration of the monarchy, there had there ensued a violent reaction against the eccentric and hypocritical austerity of the Puritanism which had dominated the Eevolutionary period.

Patronage of Catholicism went, at the court of Charles the Second, hand in hand with riotousness of living. The statesmen of that time were, according to Macaulay, perhaps the most corrupt portion of a corrupt society, and their frivolity and luxuriousness were only exceeded by the shamelessness with which, devoid of all political principles, they pursued politics as a plaything of their ambition.

The character of frivolity in religion and morals was the character of the courts. France, it is true, was in the van, and set the fashion, but France at this period was in the full bloom of her so-called 'classical literature,' and the brilliancy of her influence abroad, as well in literature as in politics, constituted the age of Louis the Fourteenth, and gave to the efforts of the nation as well as of the court a certain impetus and a worth which carried them far beyond the Materialistic tendency towards the useful. But in the meantime the growing centralisation, combined with the oppression and plundering of the people, prepared that great mental fermentation which was to result in the Eevolution. In France, as in England, Materialism took root; but in France only its negative elements were taken up, while in England men began to apply its principles in ever-increasing measure to the direction of the whole life of the people. And hence we may compare the Materialism of France with that of the Roman Empire; men adopted it in order to corrupt it, and to be corrupted by it. It was quite otherwise in England. Here also frivolity reigned among the upper classes. One might be credulous or not, because one had no principles either way, and was at bottom both, according as either favoured one's passions. But Charles the Second had learned from Hobbes, besides the doctrine of his own omnipotence, Macaulay, Hist. of Engl., i. c.ii. in the Morals of the Community," and Comp. especially the sections "Change "Profligacy of Politicians." something better also. He was a zealous physicist, and had a laboratory of his own; and the whole aristocracy followed his example. Even Buckingham took to chemistry, which was as yet, of course, not devoid of the mystic attraction of alchemy—the search for the philosopher's stone. Peers, prelates, and lawyers devoted their leisure hours to experiments in hydrostatics. Barometers were manufactured and optical instruments of the most varied uses. Elegant ladies of the aristocracy drove to the laboratories to have shown to them the experiments of electric and magnetic attraction. The aimless curiosity and idle dilettanteism of the great allied themselves with the serious and solid studies of specialists, and England entered upon a path of scientific progress which appears as the fulfilment of the prophecies of Bacon. There was aroused on every hand a genuine Materialistic spirit, which, far from being destructive in its tendency, rather led England at this very time to an unheard of development, to which in France the fragments of the renascent Epikureanism united themselves with increasing bigotry, in order to introduce that restless oscillation between extremes which characterises the period previous to Voltaire's appearance; and it was a necessary result that here the spirit of frivolity increased, while it formed in England a transitional phenomenon, appearing just while the spiritual principles of the Eevolution were passing into the Materialistic principles of the great mercantile epoch.

"The war between wit and Puritanism," writes Macaulay of this time, "soon became a war between wit and morality. Whatever the canting Roundhead had regarded with reverence was insulted; whatever he had proscribed was favoured. As he never opened his mouth except in Scriptural phrase, the new breed of wits and fine gentlemen never opened their mouths without the vilest oaths. In poetry, the licentious style of Dryden replaced that of Shakespeare, after the Puritanical hatred of secular poetry in general had suppressed all talent." 3 Maoanlay, Hist. of Engl., i. o. Literatuxgesch. d. 18 Jahrh. , L (3d iii., '"State of Science in England;" cii.), p. 17, calls the foundation of comp. also Buckle, Hist. of Civilisathe 'Regalia Societas Londini pro tion. ii. 363 ft., where particular men-soientia naturnli promovenda' (15th tion is made (p. 371) of the influence of July 1662) "die ruhmvollste That the foundation of the Royal Society, Rarls II.

" (the most glorious act of in whose activity centred the indue-Charles H.), whioh is, indeed, strictly tire spirit of the time. Hettner, speaking, not saying very much.

About this time the female parts on the stage, which had been previously played by youths, were first assigned to actresses: the demands on their license were ever greater and greater, and the theatre became a centre of immorality. But increasing luxuriousness went hand in hand with increasing productiveness, until soon the former was more than balanced by the latter. In the keen competition of the race after wealth, the complacency of the earlier period succumbed, with a portion of its vices, and the Materialism of pleasure was supplanted by the Materialism of political economy.? Commerce and industry rose to a height which earlier times had never conceived. The means of transit were improved, long-abandoned mines were reopened, all with the energy peculiar to epochs of material production, and which, wherever it is powerfully excited, reacts favourably upon energy and enterprise in other respects. At this time began those enormous towns of England, partly to spring up out of the ground, partly to develop in the gigantic proportions which, within less than two centuries, made England the wealthiest country in the world. Hist, of Engl., i. c. iii., "Immo-Comp. Hettner, Litg. d. 18 Jahrh., i.
rality of the Polite Literature of Eng-206 foil.; comp. also Karl Marx, Das land." Comp. further on this point, Kapital, i. 339, Anm. 57, on Mande

Hettner, Literaturg. des 18 Jahrh., ville as predecessor of Adam Smith, i. 107 foil. Rnd ibid., 377, Anm. 111, on the in

"Although the classical political fluence of Descartes and of the Eng economy of the English only later lish philosophers, particularly Locke, arose as a developed science, its roots upon political economy. On Locke, lie in this period. And the 'Mate-comp. further Note 74 below, rialism'of political economy appears Macaulay, Hist, of Engl., i. a. in full development so early as in iii. , "Growth of the Towns." Mandeville's Fuble of the Bees (1708).

In England the Materialistic philosophy burst into luxuriance. There is no question that the enormous forward movement of this country is quite as intimately connected with the acts of philosophers and men of science, from Bacon and Hobbes to Newton, as the French Revolution with the appearance of Voltaire. It may just as easily be overlooked, however, that the philosophy which had passed into life and practice had, in doing so, ceased its independent existence. The completion of Materialism in Hobbes admitted, in fact, of no further development of the doctrine.

Speculative philosophy retired, and left the field to practical tendencies. Epikuros had wished to help the individual, and that by means of his philosophy itself; Hobbes endeavoured to benefit the whole of society, but not directly through his philosophy, but rather through the results to be attained by it. With Epikuros the essential object is to set aside religion; Hobbes employs religion, and those citizens who favour the popular superstitions, naturally, must seem to him better citizens than those who reach the same result by the way of philosophy. The object of belief is for the masses better and more cheaply attained when belief is propagated simply from generation to generation, than if the individuals should only, through respect for authority and acquiescence in its necessity, succeed in regulating their religious ideas.

And, moreover, philosophy is a superfluity in the collective economy of the civic life as soon as the citizens can secure all its results without the philosophy, *i.e.,* as soon as they, as a rule, submit to the power of the State, only revolt when they have some prospect of success, and, in ordinary times, devote their whole strength and activity to the material improvement of their position, to the production of new benefits, and the perfection of existing arrangements. As philosophy is only of advantage in furthering this line of conduct, as the best and most profitable, it will be obviously a simple saving of labour if we succeed in persuading the people to this conduct without communicating the doctrines of the philosophy to every individual. Only for kings or their advisers, or for the heads of the aristocracy, will the philosophy be of value, since these must take care to keep the whole in its course. These stringent inferences from the doctrine of Hobbes look, in fact, as though they had been simply abstracted from the more recent intellectual history of England, so closely has the nation, on the whole, developed itself after the pattern prescribed by Hobbes. The higher aristocracy retains a personal freedom of thought, together with a sincere, or shall we say, what has become a sincere, respect for ecclesiastical institutions. Men of business regard all doubt of the verities of religion as 'unpractical;' for the arguments for or against their theological foundations they have no appreciation; and if they shudder at 'Germanism,' that is rather with reference to the security of the *present* life than with any reference to the expectation of a life *beyond* the grave. Women, children, and the sentimental are unreservedly devoted to religion. But in the lower classes of society, for whose maintenance in a state of subjection a life of refined sentiment does not seem requisite, there is again scarcely any remnant of religion, except the fear of God and the clergy. Speculative philosophy is thought superfluous, if not mischievous. The notion of a philosophy of nature has passed into that of physical science; and a modified selfishness, which has secured an excellent understanding with Christianity, is fully recognised by all classes of society as the only foundation of individual or public morality.

We are far indeed from referring to the influence of a Hobbes this wholly original, and, in its way, model development of modern England; nay, it is much rather the lively characteristic of the nature of this people in their process of development; it is the sum of all the historical and material circumstances, from which both are to be explained—the philosophy of Hobbes, and the subsequent turn taken by the national character. But at all events, we must regard Hobbes in a higher light when we see, as it were, prophetically figured in his doctrines the later phenomena of the English national life. Keality is often much more paradoxical than any philosophical system, and the actual behaviour of mankind contains more inconsistencies than a thinker could with all his efforts heap together; aud of this orthodox but Materialistic England affords us a striking example.

And again, in the sphere of natural science there arose at this time that peculiar combination, which even to this day causes so much surprise to the scholars of the Continent, of a thoroughly Materialistic philosophy with a great respect for the dogmas and customs of religious tradition. Two men there are in particular who represent this spirit in the generation after Hobbes—the chemist Eobert Boyle, and Sir Isaac Newton.

» Buckle, Hist. of Civil, in Engl., i. 390, suys of Hobbes: "The most dangerous opponent of the clergy in the seventeenth century was certainly Hobbes, the subtlest dialectician of his time; a writer, too, of singular clearness, and, among British metaphysicians, inferior only to Berkeley (?).... During his life, and for several years after his death, every man who ventured to think for himself was stigmatised as a Hobhist, or, as it was sometimes called, a Hobbian." These observations are not incorrect, although, unless we take the other side of the matter into account, they present an incorrect picture of Hobbes and his influence. This other side is described by Macaulay, Hist. of Engl., i. 86, pop. ed. (c. ii.)—" Change in the Morals of the Community:" "Thomas Hobbes had, in language more precise and luminous than has ever been employed by any other metaphysical writer, maintained that the will of the prince was the standard of right and wrong, and that every subject ought to be ready to profess Popery, Mahometanism, or Paganism at the royal command. Thousands who were incompetent to appreciate what was really valuable in his speculations eagerly welcomed a theory which, while it exalted the kingly office, relaxed the obligations of morality, and degraded religion into a mere affair of state. Hobbism soon became an almost essential part of the character of the fine gentleman." Further on, however, it *a* aaid very truly of this same sort of frivolous gentlemen, that by their means the English High Church came again to wealth and honour. Little as these elegant voluptuaries were inclined to regulate their life according to the precepts of the Church, they were soon just as ready "to fight knee-deep in blood" for her cathedrals and palaces, for every line of her formularies, and every thread of her vestments. In Macaulay's wellknown Essay on Bacon occurs the following noteworthy passage as to Hobbes: "... His quick eye soon discerned the superior abilities of Thomas Hobbes. It is not probable, however, that he fuUy appreciated the powers of his disciple, or foresaw the vast influence, both for good or for evil, which that most vigorous and acute of human intellects was destined to exercise on the two succeeding generations."

The modern world sees these two men separated by a great gulf. Boyle is now named only in the history of chemistry, and is, in his significance for the general intellectual life of modern times, almost forgotten; while the name of Newton shines as a star of the first magnitude. Their contemporaries did not see the matter quite in this light, and still less can the more accurate investigations of history be found to affirm this judgment. Newton will have to be less exclusively valued than is usually the case, while Boyle will be found entitled to a prominent place of honour in the history of the sciences. Yet Newton remains the greater man; and even though his explanation of the movements of the heavenly bodies by means of gravitation appears to be a ripe product of time, it was, nevertheless, not a mere chance that this was gathered by a man who united, in so rare a measure, mathematical talent, physical modes of thought, and the enduring capacity for labour. In his leaning to a clear physical and mechanical conception of the course of nature, Boyle entirely agreed with Newton; and Boyle was the older of the two, and must, in regard to the introduction into natural science of Materialistic foundations, be considered as one of the greatest of the pioneers. With him chemistry enters upon a new epoch.4 The breach with alchemy More correct is the judgment of mathematical talent with the quali

Buckle, Hist. Civil, in Engl., i. 367: ties of character described in the text.

"After the death of Bacon one of the Thus even Gmelin, Gesch. d. most distinguished Englishmen was Chemie, Gott., 1798, begins the certainly Boyle, who, if compared "Zweite Hauptepoohe," or *modern* -with his contemporaries, may be said history of chemistry, with "Boyle's to rank immediately below Newton, Zeitalter (1661-1690)." He rightly though, of course, very inferior to observes (ii. 35), that no man contri him as an original thinker." To the buted so largely "to destroy the au latter remark we can scarcely subthority which alchemy had usurped scribe, for Newton's greatness by no over so many minds and sciences"as means consisted in the originality of did Boyle. He is treated with Lis thinking, but in the union of rare greater fulness in Kopp, Gesch. d. and with Aristotelian notions was completed by Boyle. While these two great students of nature thus naturalised the philosophy of a Gassendi and a Hobbes in the positive sciences, and by their discoveries secured to it a definitive victory, they both, nevertheless, remained Deists in all sincerity, and without any Hobbian reservations. As they remain occupied with the phenomenal world, this was not to be achieved without great weaknesses and inconsistencies; but if they stand lower on this account as philosophers, their influence on the unfolding of the scientific method has thereby been all the healthier. As in so many other points, so in this, Boyle and Newton may be regarded as having set the fashion—that they initiate a rigid severance between the fertile field of experimental inquiry and all those problems which are transcendental, or at least, in the present condition of the sciences, are unapproachable. And hence both exhibit the liveliest interest for questions of method, but only a very slender interest for speculative questions. They are distinctly empiricists; and this must especially be firmly maintained of Newton, if any one is inclined, because of the great generality of his principle of gravitation and his mathematical endowments, to give undue prominence to the deductive side of his intellectual activity.

Robert Boyle (born in 1626) was a son of Viscount Cork, and availed himself of his considerable property in order to live wholly for science. Naturally grave and inclined to melancholy, the doubts as to the Christian faith which were probably excited by his scientific studies were regarded by him very seriously; and as he sought to combat them in his own case by Bible-reading and reflection, he felt also the necessity of making others also feel that a reconciliation was possible between faith and knowledge. With this aim he founded public lectures, to which those Essays, amongst others, owe their origin by which Clarke endeavoured to convince the world of the existence of God. Clarke, who had put together a natural religion out of Newton's cosmological notions, entered the lists against every view that would not fit this system, and wrote accordingly not only against Spinoza and Leibniz, but also against Hobbes and Locke, the fathers of English Materialism and Sensationalism. And yet the whole cosmology of the great physicists Boyle and Newton, in whose footsteps he trod, peculiarly interwoven as it was with religious elements, could not have arisen without that same Materialism from which these quite other consequences were drawn.

Chemie, i. 163 ff.: "We see in in the history of the doctrine of

Boyle the first chemist whose enaffinity, ii. 274 ff.—where, amongst deavonrs in chemistry were chiefly other things, it is said of Boyle, that directed by the one noble impure of he from the beginning conceived the the investigation of nature;" and problem of the elements in precisely then again frequently in the special the same sense in which it is now divisions of the History—especially being handled.

If we think of the religious and somewhat moody character of Boyle, we must only wonder the more at the straightforwardness of judgment with which he broke through the nets of alchemy. It cannot be denied, moreover, that his scientific theories here and there in chemistry, and especially medicine, still bear traces of the mysticism which at that time was generally dominant in the sphere of those sciences, though at the same time he became the most influential opponent of this mysticism. His 'Chemista Scepticus' (1661), whose very title contains a declaration of war with tradition, is with justice regarded as a turningpoint in the history of chemistry. In physics he made most important discoveries, some of which were later attributed to others; yet it must be admitted that his theories often lack the necessary clearness and completeness, so that he does much more in the way of disturbance and preparation than of final accomplishment.4 Buckle, Hist. Civil, in Engl.,i. statics, and the original discovery of 368, attributes specially to Boyle the the law (later called after Mariotte) first exact experiments into the rela-according to which the density of air tion between colour and heat, the varies as its pressure. With regard foundation of the science of hydro-to hydrostatics, however, Buckle himsclf only gives Boyle the first place among Englishmen, and io so doing indirectly admits the greater importance of Pasoal (comp., *loc. cit.*. Note 68, where indeed it may be further suggested that the importance of both these men is overrated. According to Diihring, Gesch. d. Princ. der Mechanik, S. 90 ff., Galilei was in this branch also the really originating mind; Pascal only makes an ingenious application of his principles; and as to Boyle, whom Diihring does not even name, in this branch also his chief service is to have clearly exhibited the new principles by experiment). As to the 'Law of Mariotte,' the absolute certainty of Boyle's asserted priority appears to me still somewhat doubtful. Boyle had obviously a great disinclination to hasty generalisations, and, moreover, as it appears, was not fully conscious of the importance of sharply formulated laws. In his principal work on this subject, the " Continuation of New Experiments touching the Spring and Weight of the Air nnd their Effects," Oxford, i &jo,, the dependence of pressure upon volume

What safely guided him in spite of all defects of his natural character was, above all, his sincere hatred of the phrase-building and pretended knowledge of Scholasticism, and his exclusive confidence in what he saw himself and could show to others as the result of his experiments. He was one of the first members of the 'Royal Society' founded by Charles II., and scarcely any member worked more zealously in the spirit of its foundation. In connection with his experiments he kept a regular *diary* and never omitted, on finding anything of unusual importance, to lay it before the eyes of his colleagues and other capable persons. This conduct alone would entitle him to a place in the history of modern sciences, which could not have attained their present eminence without adding to experiment the constant control of experiment as welL is quite clear; Boyle, in fact, gives methods for the accurate numerical determination of the pressure and quantity of the air remaining in the receiver; at the same time the result is nowhere distinctly drawn out. Thus we find, for instance, Exp. 1, § 6, p. 4 of the Latin edition of Geneva, 1694: ".... facta inter varios aeria in phiala oonstricti expansionis gradus, et respectivas succrescentes Mcrcurii in tubum elati altitudines comparatione, judicium aliquod ferri possit de vi aeria elastica, prout variis dilatationis gradibus infirmati, *ted obKrvatumibu tarn curiotis tuperndi."* Boyle must also be mentioned with praise for the stress which he was, perhaps, the first among the modern physicists to attach to the demand for well-considered and accuratelyprepared apparatus.

Comp. especially the essay Experimentorum Nov. Physico-Mech. Continuatio II. (A Continuation of New Experiments, London, 1680), where the days are everywhere given on which the experiments were performed.

This love of experiment, however, is very essentially supported by the Materialistic theory of the essence of natural bodies. In this connection his essay on the " Origin of Forms and Qualities " is of especial interest. He mentions here a long series of opponents of Aristotle, all of whose writings had been useful to him; but he had gained more from Gassendi's small, but extremely valuable compendium of the Philosophy of Epikuros than from all others. Boyle regrets that he had not earlier adopted his theories. The same laudation of the philosophy of Epikuros is found also in other essays of Boyle's, of course in connection with the most vehement protests against its atheistic consequences. We have seen that, in the case of Gassendi, there is some doubt as to the sincerity of this protest; in Boyle's case there can be none. He compares the universe with the ingenious clock of Strasburg Cathedral; 7 to him it is a mighty mechanism, working according to fixed laws; but for this very reason it would, like the clock at Strasburg, have an intelligent originator. Of the elements of Epikureanism, Boyle rejects most distinctly the Empedoklean doctrine of the rise of the purposeful from the unpurposeful. His cosmology, exactly like that of Newton, bases teleology upon the mechanism itself. Whether in this respect intercourse with his younger contemporary, Newton, who also thought much of Gassendi, worked upon Boyle, or whether conversely Newton rather borrowed from Boyle, we cannot certainly say; it is enough that the two men were so far agreed that they ascribed to God the first origination of motion among the atoms, and that even later they attributed to God certain modifying interferences with the course of nature, but that they sought the ordinary rules of everything that happens in nature in the mechanical laws of the motion of atoms.

Origin of Forms and Qualities, Comp. Exercitatio IV. de Utili according to the Corpuscular Philo-tate Phil. Naturalis, where this sub sophy, Oxford, 1664, and often; Latin, ject is treated at great length. "Some

Oxford, 1669, and Geneva, 1688. I Considerations touching the TJseful cite the latter edition. ness of Experimental Natural Philo *Loc* cit.Discursusad Lectorem: sophy," appeared first at Oxford,

'' Plus certe commodi e parvo illo sed 1663-64. In Latin under the title locupletissimo Gassendi syntagmate Exercitationes de Utilitate Phil. Nat., philosophiae Epicuri perceperam, Lindaviae, 1692,4". (Gmelin, Gesch. modo tempestivius illi me assue-d. Chem., ii. 101, mentions a Latin rissem. " edition, 'London, 1692, 40.')

The absolute indivisibility which gave the name to the atoms of Demokritos is entirely and readily given up by the moderns. This is due either to the consideration that God who made the atoms must surely be able to divide them, or it is a result of that relativity which was most consciously present in Hobbes: an absolutely smallest is no more admitted even in the elements of the physical world. Boyle troubles himself little on this point. He gives his view the name of 'philosophia corpuscularis,' but is very far, indeed, from adopting the serious modifications made in Atomism by Descartes. He considers matter impenetrable, and believes in the void space combated by Descartes. With regard to this question, he engaged in a somewhat bitter controversy with Hobbes, who explained vacuum to be only a rarer kind of atmosphere. To each smallest particle of matter Boyle ascribes its definite figure, size, and movement; where several of these unite, there must be further taken into account their position in space, and the order of their combination. And then from the varieties of these elements are explained, exactly as in Demokritos and Epikuros, the various impressions made by bodies on the sense organs. But everywhere Boyle declines to enter further into psychological questions: he busies himself only with the world as it was on the eve of the last day but one of creation; that is, so far as we must regard it merely as a system of corporeal things. The origin and the destruction of things is with Boyle, as with the ancient Atomists, only the combination and separation of atoms, and in the same light—with a reservation always for the case of miracles—he regards also the processes of organic life. The principle everywhere spread by Descartes, that in death the machine of the body is not merely abandoned by the actuating forces of the soul, but is in its inner particles destroyed, is extended by Boyle with physiological demonstrations, and he shows that numerous phenomena which have been ascribed to the activity of the soul are purely corporeal in their nature. With equal clearness he combats, as one of the leaders of the iatromechanic tendency, the then usual doctrine of drugs and poisons, to which the effects they have upon the human body —to produce perspiration, for instance, to render deaf, and so on—are attributed as a peculiar force and property; while these effects are really only the result of the contact of the general properties of those matters with the constitution of the organism. So to pounded glass was attributed a special "facultas deleteria," instead of keeping to the simple explanation that the small fragments of glass wound the intestines. In a series of briefer essays, Boyle, whose zeal in these questions of method almost equalled his industry in positive research, attempted to prove the mechanical nature of heat, of magnetism, and of electricity, of the interchanges of solid, fluid, or gaseous condition, and so on. Here, of course, he must very often be content, like Epikuros, though with much correcter views, with the supposition of mere possibilities; yet these hypotheses are everywhere sufficient for his immediate object—the banishment of latent qualities and substantial forms, and the introduction of the idea of a really picturable causality running through the whole province of nature.

Comp. the controversial work: nature even when at rest. Motion,

Examen Diulogi Physici Domini however, is the 'modus primarius' of

Hobbes de Natura Aeris, Geneva, matter, and its division into 'corpus 1695. cula' is, as with Descartes, a conse DeOri;jineQual.etForm.,Geneva, quence of the motion. Comp. in the j 688, p. 28 foil. Yet we must observe same work, p. 44 foil, that Boyle does not make motion an "i Comp. the Tractutus de Ipsa essential characteristic of matter, Natura (I can here again only quote which remains unchanged in its the Latin edition of Genera, 168S), an essay interesting also in a philo-ant cases, through the special inter sophical regard, sect. i. *ad fin.,* p. 8. position of the Creator.

So, for example, in the Tractatus » De Utilitate Phil. Exper., Exerc. de Ipsa Natura, p. 76, the regularity v. § 4, Lindaviae, 1692, p. 308: "Corof nature is praised, in which even pus enimhominisvivi non saltem conapparent disturbances, as, for ex-cipio tanquam membrorum et liquoample, the eclipse of the sun, the rum congeriem simplicem. sed taninundations of the Nile, and so on, quam machiuam, e partibus ccrtis must be regarded as foreseen conse-sibi adunitis con si stent em." De quences of the natural laws laid down Origine Formarum, p. 2: "Corpora once for all by the Creator. By the viventium curiosas hasce et elaboratas side of these the halting of the sun machinas;" and very frequently elsein the time of Joshua, and the pas-where. sage of the Israelites through the Red ' De Orig. Form., Gen., 1688,

Sea, will be regarded as exceptions, p. 81.

which may occur in rare and import- De Orig. Form., p. 8. VOL. I. C

Less many-sided but more intense was the influence of Newton in the establishment of a mechaniccd conception of the universe. More sober than Boyle in his theology, and, in fact, suspected by the orthodox of Socinianism, Newton only showed in advanced life, and with failing powers, that leaning to mystical speculations on the Eevelation of John, which forms so marked a contrast to his great scientific, achievements. His life, until the completion of all the important results of his inquiry, was the quiet existence of a scholar, with full leisure for the development of his wonderful mathematical powers, and the quiet completion of his magnificent and extensive undertakings; then suddenly rewarded for his services by a brilliant position, he continued to live for a long series of years without making any essential addition to the results of his scientific labours. As a boy, he is said to have been remarkable only for mechanical skill. Quiet and delicate, he neither made progress in the school, nor developed any capacity for the business of his father; yet when, in his eighteenth year (1660), he proceeded to Trinity College, Cambridge, he speedily astonished his tutor by the facility and independence with which he appropriated the doctrines of geometry. He belongs to the number of those special mathematical geniuses which the seventeenth century—as though a universal development of European humanity had pressed in that direction—produced in such surprising wealth. A nearer view of his achievements shows that almost everywhere mathematical work, marked alike by genius and application, is the active spirit that inspires everything. As early as 1664, Newton discovered his theory of fluxions, which he published twenty years later, when Leibniz was threatening to rob him of the honour of the discovery. Almost as long a time he carried with him the idea of gravitation; but while fluxions were immediately turned to brilliant account in his calculations, the proof of the unity between the falling motion of bodies and the attraction of the heavenly bodies still needed a mathematical process of which the premisses were for some time unattainable. The calmness, however, with which Newton so long kept both great discoveries to himself, that he might make quiet use of the one, and that the other might ripen, deserves our admiration, and strikingly reminds us of the similar patience and fortitude of his great predecessor Copernicus. But in this also can we discern a great trait of Newton's character, that even after he was quite satisfied as to his discovery of the connection between the law of falling bodies and the elliptic orbits of the planets, and had the full calculations before him, he did not make a separate announcement of it, but incorporated it in his great work the " Principia" (1687), which treated so comprehensively all the mathematical and physical questions connected with gravitation, that Newton could justly give it the proud title of "The Mathematical Principles of Natural Philosophy." Newton's "Annotationes in V.i-manuscripts is said to have brought ticinia Danielis, Habacuoi et Apoca-on an illness which acted deleteri lypseos," appeared at London in ously on his intellect. Comp. the 1713. biographical sketeh given bj Littrow Newton was in 1696 made Master in his translation of Whewell's His of the Royal Mint, with a salary of toryof the Inductive Sciences, Stuttg.,

£1500 sterling. As early as the 1840, ii. 163, note. But see Brewster, year 1693, the loss of a portion of his Memoirs of Newton, ii 139 foil. Tb.

Yet more important was another trait of a similar nature. We have already pointed out that Newton was very far indeed from perceiving in attraction, that 'fundamental force of all matter,' as the discoverer of which he is now so much praised. Yet it is true that he had made the theory of some such universal attractive force necessary, by laying completely aside his unripe and vague conjectures as to the material cause of attraction, and kept strictly to what he could prove—the mathematical causes of the phenomena, supposing that there was some principle of approximation operating inversely as the square of the distance, let its physical nature be what it may.

We here reach one of the most important turning-points in the whole history of Materialism; and in order to set it in its true light, we must interject a few remarks on the real service rendered by Newton.

We have in our own days so accustomed ourselves to the abstract notion of forces, or rather to a notion hovering in a mystic obscurity between abstraction and concrete comprehension, that we no longer find any difficulty in making one particle of matter act upon another without immediate contact. We may, indeed, imagine that in the proposition,' No force without matter,' we have uttered something very Materialistic, while all the time we calmly allow particles of matter to act upon each other through void space without any material link From such ideas the great mathematicians and physicists of the seventeenth century were far removed. They were all in so far still genuine Materialists in the sense of ancient Materialism, that they made immediate contact a condition of influence. The colb'sion of atoms or the attraction by hook-shaped particles, a mere modification of collision, were the type of all Mechanism and the whole movement of science tended towards Mechanism.

In two important points the mathematical formula of the laws had been reached before the physical explanation—the laws of Kepler, and the law of fall, discovered by Galilei; and thus these laws troubled the whole scientific world with the question of the cause—naturally the physical, the mechanical cause—the cause to be explained from the collision of small particles—of the movement of falling and the motion of the heavenly bodies. In particular, for a long time before and after Newton, the cause of gravitation was a favourite subject of theoretical physics. In this universal sphere of physical speculation, the thought of the essential identity of both forces naturally lay very near; there was indeed, in the axioms of the Atomism of that time, but one single fundamental force in all the phenomena of nature! But this force operated under very various circumstances and shapes, and even then men had begun to be content no more with the bare possibilities of the Epikurean physics. They demanded the construction, the demonstration, the mathematical formula. In the consequent working out of this demand lies Galilei's superiority to Descartes, that of Newton and Huyghens to Hobbes and Boyle, who still found satisfaction in long-spun explanations of how the thing might be possible. In consequence of this effort on the part of Newton, it now again happened, and for the third time, that the mathematical construction went ahead of the physical explanation, and on this occasion the circumstance was to attain a significance unsuspected by Newton himself.

And thus that great generalisation, celebrated by its connection with the story of the fall of the apple,57 was by no means the most important feature in Newton's discovery. Apart from the influence of the theory we have just mentioned, we have here again sufficient traces to show that the idea of an extension of gravity into space was not far away. Nay, the thought had already occurred to the ancients that the moon would fall to the earth it it were not kept suspended by the force of its revolution. Newton was acquainted with the composition of forces, and so it lay directly in his path to carry that idea further into the theory—that the moon does actually fall towards the earth. From this falling motion and a forward motion in the direction of the tangent results the orbit of the moon. Regarded as the personal achievement of a great scientific power, the thought here was less important in itself than the criticism brought to bear upon the thought. Newton, as is well known, laid his calculations aside, because the result gave no exact agreement with the motion of the moon. Without wholly giving up his main notions, Newton seems to have sought an explanation of the difference in the operation of some other influence to him unknown; but as he could not complete his demonstration without an exact knowledge of this disturbing force, the whole matter remained for a time in abeyance. Later, as all the world knows, Picard's measurement of the degree (1670), proved that the earth was greater than had hitherto been supposed, and the correction of this factor supplied the desired accuracy to Newton's calculations.

Comp. Whewell's Hist. of the as he sat alone in a garden, he reInduct. Sci., ii. 166 foil. From this fleeted upon gravity, and inferred it appears that so much may be taken that as gravity still operates at the from Newton's own communications, greatest distances from the centre of according to a tolerably credible tra-the earth of which we have any dition coming through Pemberton knowledge, it must therefore *infiu*an! Voltaire—that so early as the *ence the motion of the moon.* year 1666, in his twenty-fourth year, Comp. Diihring, Krit. Gesch. thesis, and we hare shown in the der allg. Principien der Mechanik, text how Atomism must have fin Berlin, 1873, p. 175. lb. p. itio foil., thered this synthesis. But Newton's are noteworthy expressions of Coper-merit lay in this, that he turned the nicus and Kepler. See moreover in universal thought into a mathema AVhewell, Hist. Induct. Sci., ii. 150, tioal problem, and, above all, that he the views of Borelli. It must also effected a brilliant solution of the be observed that Descaites in his problem.

Vortical Theory found also the me- In this respect Huyghens espe chanical cause of gravity; so that the oially had done very much by way of idea of the unity of both phenomena preparation, while the first begin was at that time commonly taught. nings of the correct theory are here

Diihring justly observes that the again to be traced to Galilei. Comp. true problem was to bring the vague Whewell, Hist. Induct. Soi., ii. 80 idea of an approximation or ' fall' of foil.; Diihring, p. 163 foil. 188. the heavenly bodies into agreement Whewell, Hist. Induct. Sci., ii. with Galilei's mathematically defi-168, with which, however, must be nite notion of tbe fall of terrestrial compared, as to the story of the be bodies. These foierunners constantly ginning of the calculation, Hettner, show how near was the actual syn-I. iterntaix. *i.* 18 Jahrh., i, *ta%*

Of great importance, not only for this demonstration, but also especially for its far-reaching consequences, was Newton's assumption that the gravitation of a planet is only the sum of the gravitation of all its individual portions. From this immediately flowed the inference that the terrestrial bodies gravitate towards each other; and further, that even the smallest particles of these masses attract each other. So arose the first foundation of molecular physics. But here the generalisation itself lay so near that it was within immediate reach of every supporter of the Atomistic or corpuscular theory. The effect of the whole could not be other than the sum of the effects of its constituent portions. If we suppose, however, that even Atomism must have made this doctrine impossible, because it bases everything upon the collision of the atoms while it is here a question of attraction, we only confound once more what, since Kant and, Voltaire, has been currently called the doctrine of Newton with Newton's real view of these things.

We must here recollect the modification of Atomism made by Hobbes. The 'relativity' of the conception of an atom bore its physical fruits in the more decided distinction between the ether and 'ponderable' matter. There can be bodies, according to Hobbes, which are so small as to be incognisable by our senses, and which in a certain relation may justly be termed 'atoms.' At the same time, others may be supposed to exist by the side of these, which, compared with them, are microscopically small, and by the side of these again others still smaller, and so on to infinity. Physics begin by using the first member of this chain, in order to resolve the original constituents of all bodies into heavy atoms; that is, atoms subject to gravitation; and then to assume other particles, infinitely finer atoms, without weight, and yet material, subject to the same laws of collision, of motion, and so on. In these was sought the cause of gravity, and no prominent physicist at that time thought of any other kind of cause than the mechanism of the motions resulting from impact.

Descartes, then, was hy no means alone in deducing, as he did, gravity from the collision of ethereal particles. 1 It has in our time become a custom to condemn severely his daring hypotheses as compared with the demonstrations of a Huyghens or a Newton. We do not remember that these men undoubtedly all most thoroughly agreed with Descartes, through whose school they had passed, in the unitary and mechanical, in short, the picturably mechanical conception of phenomena.

The now prevailing theory of *actio in distans* was regarded simply as absurd; and Newton was no exception. He repeatedly declares in the course of his great work that, for methodological reasons, he disregards the unknown physical causes of gravity, but does not doubt their existence. So he observes, for example, that he regards the centripetal forces as attractions, although, perhaps, if we will employ the language of physics, they might more accurately be called impulses *(impulsus).* Indeed, when the zeal of his followers went so far as to declare gravity to be a fundamental force of matter (by which all further mechanical explanation from the collision of imponderable particles was excluded), Newton felt himself obliged, in the year 1717, in the preface to the second edition of his "Optics," to protest expressly against this view. Princip. iv. the whole of the last paragraph:— Phil. Nat. Prino. Math., i. 1 1 *ad* "Adjicere jam liceret nonnulla de *init.* : a passage of quite the same spiritu quodnm subtilissimo corpora, tendency may be found towards the crassa pervadente et in iisdem latent?, conclusion of this section. (In the cuius vi et actionibus particulae coredition Amstelodami, 1714, pp. 147 porum ad minimas distantias se muand 172; orig. ed. 1687, pp. 162 and tuo attrahunt, et contiguae facta 191.) In the latter passage Newton cohaerent; et corpora electrica agunt calls the hypothetical matter, which, ad distantias majores, tam repellendo, by its impulsion, produces gravita-quam attrahendo corpuscula vicina; tion, 'spiritus. ' There are here, of et lux emittitur, reflectitur, refrincourse,verydifferentpossibilitiesmengitur, inlicctitur et corpora calefacit; tioned, amongst them the actual ten-et sensatio omnis excitatur, et memdency of bodies towards each other, bra animalium ad voluntatem movenand even the action of an incorporeal tur, vibrationibus scilicit huius spinmedium; but the special object of tus per solida nervorum capillamenta the passage is to show the uncondi-ab externis sensuum organis ad ceretional and universal validity of the brum et a cerebro in musculos propamathcmatical developments, be the gatis. Sed haec paucis exponi non physical cause *what it may.* Where possunt; neque adest sufficiens copia Newton's favourite idea lies betrays experimentorum, quibus leges actioitself clearly enough at the conclusion sum huius spiritus accurate deterof the whole work. We will here add miuari et monstrari debent."

Even before the appearance of this last declaration of Newton's, his great predecessor and contemporary, Huyghens, declared he could not believe that Newton regarded gravity as an essential property of matter. Huyghens, besides, in the first chapter of his Essay on Light, roundly declared that in the true philosophy the cause of all natural effects must be explained *'perrationes mechanicas.'* We see now how these views hang together, and can understand how even men like Leibniz and Johann Bernouilli were offended by the new principle; nay, that the latter did not desist from an attempt to see whether a mathematical construction could not be deduced from the principles of Descartes which should be also sufficient for the facts.

All these men are unwilling to separate mathematics from physics, and they were unable to comprehend the theory of Newton as a *physical* theory.

The same difficulty occurred here which had opposed the doctrine of Copernicus, and yet the cases were in a very essential point unlike. In each case a prejudice of the senses was to be overcome; but in the case of the earth's revolution, we could, at least in the last resort, bring the laws themselves to our aid, in order to be convinced that what we feel is only relative and not absolute motion. But in the other case it was a question of making one's own a physical conception, which contradicted, and still contradicts to-day, the picturable principle of all physics.65 Newton himself, as we have seen, shared this view, but he clearly separated the mathematical construction which he could supply from the physical which he could not find, and so he became, against his will, the founder of a new cosmical theory, containing obvious inconsistency in its first elements. His *'hypotheses non Jingo'* threw down the old foundation of theoretical Materialism, in the same instant in which it appeared predestined to celebrate its loftiest triumphs. Comp. TJeberweg, Hist. Phil., iii. achievements of Newton, and espe 3 Aufl. p. 102, E. T. ii. 89, 90. cially in mathematics. Compare Lit Whewell, Hist. Ind. Sci. , ii. 149. trow's interesting note in his transla

And yet men like Huyghens, Ber-tion (ii. S. 141, ff.). especially with nouilli, and Leibniz were then almost regard to the opposition with which the only men on the Continent who Newton's theory of gravitation was could estimate at their full value the at first received in England.

We have already pointed out that Newton's peculiar service is, above all, to be sought in his completion of the mathematical proof. The thought, indeed, that the laws of Kepler are to be explained by central force, which is inversely proportional to the square of the distance, had occurred simultaneously to several English mathematicians.'' Newton, however, was not only the first to reach the goal, but he accomplished the task with such masterly comprehensiveness and certainty, and shed in its accomplishment such a fulness of light over all parts of mechanics and physics, that the "Principia" would still be an admirable book, even though the main principle of the new doctrine had not so brilliantly established itself. His example appears to have so dazzled the English mathematicians and physicists, that they lost their independence, and for a long time left the lead in the mechanical sciences to the Germans and the French. We can, therefore, very well understand that the attempts to explain gravity from picturable physical principles constantly recur, as, for instance, in Lesage, for whose attempt at a solution (1764) see Ueberweg's Hist. Phil., iii., 3 Aufl., S. 102, E. T. ii. 89, 90. Recently a similar attempt has been made by IT. Schramm, Die Allg. Bewegung der Haterie als Grundursache aller Naturerscheinungen, Wien, 1872. It is au illustration of the force of habit, that such attempts are now-a-days very coldly received by specialists. They have once for all accepted the theory of *actio in distant,* pnd feel no further need to substitute anything for it. The remark of Hagenbach, Zielpunkte der Physik. Wissensch., S. 91, that similar attempts are still ever being made to explain attraction by what are supposed to be "simpler" principles, is a characteristic misunderstanding. It is a question, In such attempts, not of simplicity, but of picturableness as an element of intelligibility.

The expression 'hypotheses non fingo' is found at the conclusion of the work, a few lines before the passage quoted above (Note 62), together with the explanation: "Quidquid ex phaenomenis non deducitur, hypothesis vocanda est; et hypotheses sen metaphysicae, seu physic&e seu qualitatum occult&rum, seu mechanicae, in philosophia experimental! locum non habeut." The true method of experimental science Newton declares to be—that the principles ("propositiones") are gathered from phenomena and generalised by means of induction. In these far from correct statements, as well as in the four 'Rulea for the Investigation of Nature,' laid down at the beginning of the third book, there is expressed conscious opposition to Descartes, against whom Newton was very strongly prejudiced. Compare the story told by Voltaire in Whewell, Hist. Ind. Sci., ii. 148. Newton himself recognised that Christopher Wren and Hooke (of whom the latter indeed would claim the priority in the whole proof of gravitation) had discovered the rela-greater. Comp. Wnewell, Hist. In

From the triumph of this purely mathematical achievement there was curiously developed a new physics. Let us carefully observe that a purely mathematical connection between two phenomena, such as the full of bodies and the motion of the moon, could only lead to that great generalisation in so far as there was presupposed a common and everywhere operative material cause of the phenomena. The course of history has eliminated this unknown material cause, and has placed the mathematical law itself in the rank of physical causes. The collision of the atoms shifted into an idea of unity, which as such rules the world without any material mediation. What Newton held to be so great an absurdity that no philosophic thinker could light upon it, is prized by posterity as Newton's great discovery of the harmony of the universe! and, rightly understood, it is his discovery, for this harmony is one and the same, whether it is brought about by a subtle matter, penetrating everywhere and obeying the laws of collision, or whether the particles of matter regulate their movements in accordance with the mathematical law without any material intervention. If in this later case we wish to get rid of the absurdity, we must get rid of the idea that anything acts where it is not; that is, the whole conception of the mutual influence of the atoms falls away as an anthropomorphism, and even the conception of causality must assume an abstracter shape.

tion of the inverse square of the distance indepen-duct. Sci., ii. 156-158. tance independently of him. Halley, Comp. Snell, Newton und die who, in contrast to Hooke, was one of Median. Naturwissenschaft, Leipzig, the most unenvious of Newton's ad-1858, p. 65. mirers, had even conceived the happy So Newton expressed himself in thought that the attraction must a letter to Bentley of the year 1693. necessarily lessen in that proportion, Comp. Hagenbach, Zielpunkte der because the spherical surface over Physikal. Wissensch. Leipzig, 1871, which the radiating force spread itself p. 21. became in the same proportion ever

The English mathematician Cotes, who, in the preface to the second edition of the "Principia," which he edited in 1713, made gravity an essential property of all matter, accompanied this idea, which has since dominated science, with a philippic against the Materialists who make everything arise of necessity and not through the will of the Creator. He regards it as an especial merit of the Newtonian system that it makes everything arise out of the most unfettered purpose of God. The laws of nature, in the opinion of Cotes, exhibit many traces of the wisest purpose, but none of necessity.

Half a century had not passed away when Kant in his "Allgemeine Naturgeschichte u. Theorie des Himmels" (1755), combined with the popularisation of theNewtonian theory that bold extension of it which we now commonly designate the Kant-Laplace hypothesis. In the preface to this work, Kant admits that his theory bears a considerable likeness to those of Epikuros, Leukippos, and Demokritos.70 No one thought any longer of seeing in the universal attraction of material particles anything but a mechanical principle, and in our day the Materialists prefer to assign to the Newtonian cosmology of the universe the role that, until the eighteenth century, was always assigned to the Atomism of the ancients. It is the theory of the necessary origin of all things in virtue of a property that is inherent in all matter as such.

In their influence upon the general movement of thought, the religious tendency of Newton and Boyle soon and easily separated itself from the scientific significance of

»» Kant'» Wcrke, Hg. v. Hartenstein, Leipzig, 1867, i. a«6.

their achievements. Yet upon England itself it appears to have exercised some effect; indeed, this unique mixture of Materialism and religiosity may be regarded as a peculiar product of English soil. Similarly the conservative feature in their character may in some measure be connected with the time and the circumstances in which they lived and had their influence. Buckle has made the interesting remark, that the revolutionary period, and especially the great political and social storms of the first revolution in England, exercised a great and penetrating influence upon the sentiments of the literary class, chiefly through the shattering of authorities and the awakening of the sceptical spirit.? He considers also Boyle's scepticism in chemistry to be a fruit of the spirit of the age. Under Charles the Second especially the progress of the revolution, at least in one respect, went uninterruptedly forward—the spreading of the spirit of experimental inquiry. On the other hand, we must, of course, also remark, that the flower of Boyle's and Newton's inquiries falls in the comparatively quiet and reactionary period between the two revolutionary storms, and that they personally concerned themselves little with politics.? The political struggles exercised a very different influence on the life of the man who, after Bacon and Hobbes, must be regarded as the most prominent continuator of the philosophical movement in England, and whose influence on the Continent was more important than that of both his predecessors.

"Hist. of Civil, ii. 70 foil. As to «In Whewell, Hist. Induct. Set, the case of the conversion of Sir ii. 153 foil., there is a sketeh of the

Thomas Browne (foe. *cit.,* 72 foil), we disturbance exercised by the revolu may adduce the rumour mentioned tionary storms in the life and activity in Morhof's Polyhistor.that he wrote of the chief English mathematicians the "Eeligio Medici" in order to and scientific men. Several of these free himself from the suspicion of joined with Boyle in 1645 to form atheism. But if this instance was the ' Invisible College,' the first germ not so much in point as Buckle seems of the Royal Society founded later by to think, yet the general view which Charles the Second.

it is adduced to illustrate is undoubtedly correct.

John Locke (born in 1632), the head of the English Sensationalists, stands also in manifold relation to the history of Materialism. Standing in point of age between Boyle and Newton, his chief activity only appeared after Newton's had closed in its principal objects, and his literary activity was strongly and decisively influenced by the events which introduced and accompanied the second English revolution. In the case of Locke, as in that of Hobbes, his entrance into one of the first English families became the foundation of his later worldly position. Like Hobbes, he was initiated into philosophy at the University of Oxford, but the contempt of Scholastic training, which was only late established in the case of Hobbes, was with him already in the student period. Descartes, whose acquaintance he made at this time, exercised some influence on him, but he speedily turned to medicine, and so his first position was that of medical adviser in the house of Lord Ashley, afterwards Lord Shaftesbury. In his ideas of medicine, he agreed admirably with the celebrated physician Sydenham, who at that time was from England paving the way for a reform of the degenerate art of healing similar to that attempted later by Boerhave from the Netherlands; and thus early he proves himself to be a man of healthy common sense, equally averse from superstition and metaphysics. Locke was also an enthusiastic student of natural science. And so we find in Boyle's works a diary kept by Locke for many years of atmospheric observations with the barometer, thermometer, and hygrometer. But Lord Ashley turned his attention to political and religious questions, to which he then devoted an interest as lasting as it was intense.

"While Hobbes stood on the side of absolutism, Locke belonged to the liberal movement—nay, he was, and perhaps not unjustly, regarded as the father of modern constitutionalism. The axiom of the separation of the legislative and administrative power, which in the time of Locke was actually accomplished in England, he was the first to develop as a definite theory.73 "With his friend and protector Lord Shaftesbury, Locke, after occupying for a short time a post at the Board of Trade, was driven into the vortex of opposition. For years he lived on the Continent, partly in voluntary banishment, partly from the actual persecution of the Government. In this school was hardened his zeal for toleration and civil freedom. The offer of powerful friends who would have procured him pardon from the court, he declined with an appeal to his innocence, and it was only the Eevolution of 1688 that restored him to his fatherland.

At the very outset of his political activity, Locke worked out in 1669 a constitution for the State of Carolina in North America, which turned out badly, however, and has little agreement with his later and ripened Liberalism. The more important, however, on the other hand, were his Essays on the Coinage, which contained a too one-sided recognition of the interests of the national creditors; but in the discussion developed so many luminous observations, that he must be regarded as an important forerunner of English political economy. *1* Comp. Mohl, Gesch. u. Liter, der Staatswissench., i. 231 foil.
On the controversy between Locke and the finance minister Lowndes, comp. Karl Marx, Zur Kritik der Folit. Oekonomie, Berlin, 1859, 1 Heft, p. 53 foil. Lowndes, on occasion of recotnage of the bad and depreciated pieces, wished to make the shilling lighter than the earlier legal requirement. Locke insisted that the coinage should be in accordance with the legal standard, which had, however, long ceased to be observed in practice. The result followed that debts (and among them notably the national obligations) which had been contracted in light shillings bad to be repaid in heavy ones. Lowndes based his substantially more correct view upon bad arguments which were victori ously refuted by Locke, with a precise indication of the latter's relation to the different parties. Marx says: "John Locke, who represented the new 'bourgeoisie' in all its forms, the industrial interest against the working-class and the paupers, the commercial interest against the oldfashioned lending class, the monied aristocracy against the national debtors; and, in fact, in one of bis books proved the common sense of the *bourgtoit* to be the norm of human intelligence, took up the gauntlet also against Lowndes. Locke conquered, and money borrowed at ten or fourteen shillings the guinea was repaid in guineas of twenty shillings."
For the rest it is further asserted by Marx (well known to be the most learned living historian of political economy), that Locke's most valuable contribution to the theory of money See the account in the 'Epistle

We have here, then, yet another of those English philosophers who, in the midst of active life, and furnished with great knowledge of the world, devoted themselves to the solution of abstract questions. Locke projected his famous work, "Essay concerning Human Understanding," so early as 1670, but it was not till twenty years later that it was published in its complete form. Although the absence of the author from his native country may have had something to do with this, there is no doubt that Locke was constantly busied with the ideas once conceived, and that he sought to give more and more completeness to his work.

Just as it was a very ordinary circumstance—an aimless controversy between some friends—that led him to entertain the question of the origin and limits of human knowledge, so he employs everywhere in his investigations ordinary and yet forcible points of view. We have still in these days in Germany so called philosophers who, with a kind of metaphysical bungling, write huge treatises on the formation of ideas, with no pretension whatever, of course, to " exact observation by means of the inner sense," without also the thought ever occurring to them that there are nurseries—it may be in their own houses—in which we may observe at least the outward indications of the formation of concepts with our own eyes and ears. This sort of weed does not grow in England. Locke betakes himself in his polemic against innate ideas to children and idiots. All the uneducated have no suspicion of our abstract propositions, and can they nevertheless be innate? The objection that these ideas are actually in the mind, although it is not conscious of it, he characterises as irrational. Eor what we know is exactly that which is in the mind. Nor can we say that the general propositions are first known to consciousness when we begin to use our understanding. On the contrary, the knowledge of the particular is prior. Long before the child recognises the logical law of contradiction it knows that sweet is not bitter.
are but a beating out of what had to the Reader,'prefixed to the'Essay been already developed by Petty in concerning Human Understanding;" a treatise of the date of 1682. Comp. see for this also Hettner, Literature.

Marx, Das Kapitul, Kritik der Folit. d. 18 Juhrh., L S. 150.
Ockou., Hamburg, 1867, i. S. 60.

Locke shows that the converse is the true way in which the understanding is formed. We do not first have certain general propositions in our consciousness, which receive their special content later through our experience; but experience, sensible experience, is the first source of our knowledge. The senses first give us certain simple ideas, an expression which is very common in Locke, and means very much what the Herbartians call 'Vorstellungen.' Such simple ideas are sounds, colours, the sense of resistance to touch, the ideas of extension and of motion. If the senses have frequently given us such simple ideas, there results a combination of what is Like amongst them, and this is the way in which abstract ideas are formed. To sensation comes the internal sense of reflection, and these are "the only windows" by which the darkness of the uneducated understanding is illuminated. The ideas of substances, of changing properties, and of relations, are compound ideas. We know at bottom nothing of substances except their attributes, which are taken from simple sense-impressions, such as sounds, colours, and so on. Only through these attributes showing themselves frequently in a certain connection do we succeed in forming the compound idea of a substance which underlies the changing phenomena. Even feelings and emotions spring from the repetition and manifold combination of the simple sensations which the senses convey to us.

It was only then that the old Aristotelian, or presumably Aristotelian, propositions that the soul is originally a *tabula rasa,'* and that nothing can be in the mind which-was not previously in the senses, attained that importance

Vol. 1. x which we now commonly assign to them: in this sense they may be attributed to Locked

Whenever the human mind, which occupies a merely receptive attitude towards sense-impressions, and even the formation of complex ideas, proceeds to fix by means of words the abstract ideas it has acquired, and to connect these words arbitrarily with thoughts, it enters upon the path where there is no longer the certainty of natural experience. The further man gets from the sensible, the more liable is he to error; and it is nowhere so common as in language. So soon as the words are treated as adequate pictures of things, or are confounded with real picturable things, while they are really only arbitrary signs for certain ideas which must be used with great care, the field is opened to innumerable errors. Locke's criticism of the understanding turns into a criticism of language, which in its main idea is probably of higher value than any other portion of the system. In fact, the way was paved by Locke to the important distinction of the purely logical from the psychologico-historical element of speech; but, apart from the previous labours of the philologists, has as yet scarcely been demanded as essential. And yet by far the majority of the conclusions which are generally applied in the philosophical sciences are logical fallacies, because of the constant confusion of notion and word. And so the old Materialistic view of the merely conventional force of words turned with Locke into the effort to *make* words merely conventional, because only when thus limited have they a fixed sense. In the last book Locke examines the nature of truth and of our cognitive faculties. Truth is the correct combination of signs (words, *e.g.)* forming a judgment. Truth in mere words can be nothing but a chimera. The syllogism has little use, for our thought always mediately or immediately directs itself to particulars. "Eevelation" can give us no simple idea, and therefore cannot really extend our knowledge. Belief and thought are so related that the latter alone is decisive, so far as it goes; yet there are certain things which Locke finally admits transcend the reason, and are therefore objects of belief. Strength of conviction, however, is no sign of truth; even of revelation the reason must judge, and enthusiasm is no evidence of the divine origin of a doctrine.

The image of the " tabula, in qua liarities that constitute the nature nihil est *actu* scriptum " occurs in Ar-of human ideas. This point, the istotle. Do Anima, iii. c. 4. In Locke, subjective antecedent conditions of book ii. c. i. § 2, the mind is regarded ideation as foundation of our whole simply as "white paper," but with-phenomenal world, Locke did not out any reference to the Aristotelian sufficiently notice. With reantithesis of potentiality and actu-gard to the proposition, "Nihil est in ality. This antithesis is, however, intellectu, quod non fuerit in sensu" just in this case of great importance, (to which Leibniz, in his polemic since the Aristotelian 'potentiality' against Locke, made the addition of receiving all kinds of characters is "nisi ipse intellectus;" comp. Ueconceived as a real property of the berweg, Hist. Phil., iii. 3 Aufl. S. 127, tablet, not as mere conceivability or E. T. ii. 112), we should bear in mind absence of hindering circumstances, what Aristotle says, De Anima, iii. Aristotle therefore stands closer to c. vii. viii. Even Thomas Aquinaa 1 hose who, like Leibniz, and, in a taught that actual thinking in maa deeper sense, Kant, do not, indeed, is first brought about by the co-opera. mippose that these are complete ideas tion of the intellectus with a sensuous in the soul, but that the *conditions* phantasms. But potentially the arc present from which, upon contact mind already includes within itself with the external world, exactly that all that can be thought. This imporphenomenon will result which wo call tant point loses all its significance in *to have ideas,* and with those pecu-Locke.

Great influence was, moreover, exercised by Locke's "Letter on Toleration" (1685-92), "Thoughts on Education" (1693), the "Essay on Government" (1689), and the "Eeasonableness of Christianity" (1695); but only a portion of these writings belong to the history of Materialism. With certain glance Locke had discovered the point in which the hereditary medieval institutions were rotten— the confusion of politics and of religion, and the diversion of political force to the maintenance or suppression of doctrines and opinions.77 It is obvious that if the object at which Locke aimed were once attained—if Church and State were separated and universal toleration in matters of doctrine introduced—that the position of Materialism would be also necessarily changed. The earlier hide-andseek fashion in which its doctrines were expounded, and which lasted till late in the eighteenth century, had gradually to disappear. The simple cloak of anonymousness was longest retained; but even this was discarded, as at first the Netherlands, and later the country of Frederick the Great, offered a safe asylum to the freethinkers, until at length the French Eevolution gave the death-blow to the old system.

Al so as regards the idea that the ally mentioned. Here agahi, then, his State should afford the liberty of importance (comp. Note 74) is not so expression in religions opinion, Locke much due to originality as to the had been forestalled by others, among timely and fruitful carrying out of whom Thomas More (in the Utopia, ideas which corresponded to the al 1516) and Spinoza must be speci-tered conditions of society. As to the exceptions he makes to the rule ists and Catholics, comp. Eettner, of toleration with reference to Athe-i. 159 *S.*

Among the English freethinkers who took up and carried further the ideas of Locke, none stands nearer to Materialism than John Toland, who was perhaps the first to conceive the notion of basing a new religious cultus upon a purely Naturalistic, if not Materialistic, doctrine. In his treatise, "Clidophorus," that is, the 'key-bearer,' he refers to the practice of the ancient philosophers to set forth an exoteric and an esoteric teaching, of which the former was intended for the general public, but the latter only for the circle of initiated disciples. Eeferring to this, he interjects, in the thirteenth chapter of the treatise, the following remarks:—

"I have more than once hinted that *the External and Internal Doctrine* are as mucn now in use as ever; tho' the distinction is not so openly and professedly approv'd as among the Antients. This puts me in mind of what I was told by a near relation to the old Lord Shaftesbtjry. The latter, conferring one day with Major Wildman about the many sects of Eeligion in the world, they came to this conclusion at last: that notwithstanding those infinite divisions caus'd by the interest of the priests and the ignorance of the people, All Wise Men Are Of The Same Religion; whereupon a Lady in the room, who seem'd to mind her needle more than their discourse, demanded with some concern what that Eeligion was? To whom the Lord Shaftesbury strait reply'd, Madam, Wise Men Never Tell." Toland approves this proceeding, but thinks that he can suggest a way in which universal truth-speaking may be made possible:—" *Let all men freely speak what they think, without being ever branded or punish'd but for wicked practises, and leaving their speculative opinions to be confuted or approv'd by whoever pleases; then you are sure to hear tlie whole truth, and till then but very scantily, or obscurely, if at all."*

Toland himself has frankly enough expressed his esoteric doctrine in the anonymous "Pantheistikon" (Cosmopolis, 1720). He demands in this treatise the entire laying aside of revelations and of popular beliefs, and the construction of a new religion which agrees with philosophy. His God is the universe; from which everything is born, into which everything returns. His cultus is that of truth, liberty, and health, the three things most highly prized by the wise man. His saints and fathers are the masterspirits and most excellent authors of all times, especially of classical antiquity; but even they form no authority to chain ' the free spirit of mankind.' The president cries in the Sokratic liturgy, 'Swear by no master's word!' and the answer comes back to him from the congregation,' Not even by the word of Sokrates!' For fuller information as to To-of the esoteric doctrine of philosophy, land, especially as to his first work, as the cultus of a secret society of which connects itself closely with illuminati. The initiated may at the Locke, "Christianity not Mysteri-same time give way to a certain exous," 1696, see in Hettner, Litera-tent to the crude ideas of the people, turg. d. 18 Jahrh., i. S. 170 ff. which, as contrasted with them, con'The most striking features' of the sists of children who have not yet 'Sokratic Liturgy'are given hyHett-attained the years of discretion, if ner in the same place, S. 180 ff. only they succeed, through their inHettner has also quite rightly re-fluence in the State and in society, ferred to the connection of English in rendering fanaticism harmless. Deism with Freemasonry. Here, too, These thoughts are expressed chiefly may be indicated the special point, in the appendix, "De Duplici Tan-that Toland treats his cultus of the theistarum Philosophia." The fol Pantheists' distinctly in the sense lowing striking passage from the second chapter of this appendix simum ao perniciosissimum. Viris ("Pantheistikon," Cosmopolis, 1720) principibus et politicis, line animi p. 79 ff.) nmy here find a place:— dispositione imbutis, acceptum re"At cum superstitio semper eadem ferri debet, quidquid eat ubivis hosit vigore, etsi rigore aliquando di-die *religiosac libertatis,* in maximum versa; cumque nemo sapiens eam literarum, commerciorum et civilis penitus ex omnium animis evelleie, concordiae emolumentum. Superquod nullo facto fieri potest, incas-stitiosis aut simulatis superum cultum tentaverit: faciet tamen pro toribus, hirvatis dico homiuibus aut viribus, quod unice faciendum restat; meticulose piis, debentur dissidia, ut dentibus evulsis et resectis ungui-secessiones, mulctae, rapinae, stigbus, non ad lubitum quaquaversum mata, incarcerationes, exilia et noceat hoc monstrorum omnium pes-mortes."

In the "Pantheistikon," however, Toland expresses his views with so much generality, that his Materialism does not appear decided. What he takes from Cicero (Acad. Quaest., i. c. 6, 7) as to the being of nature, the unity of force and matter *(vis* and *materia),* is, in fact, rather Pantheistic than Materialistic; on the other hand, we find a Materialistic theory of nature laid down in two letters to a Spinozist, which are appended to the "Letters to Serena" (London, 1704). The lady who thus gives her name to the letters is Sophie Charlotte, Queen of Prussia, whose friendship with Leibniz is well known, and who had also graciously received Toland (who spent many years in Germany), and listened with interest to his views. The three first letters of the collection, which were actually addressed to Serena, are general in their nature; yet Toland expressly observes in the preface that he has corresponded with the noble lady on other and much more interesting subjects, but that he possesses no fair copy of these letters, and therefore adds the two other letters. The first of these contains a refutation of Spinoza, based on the impossibility of explaining from the Spinozistic system the motion and internal variety of the world and its constituent parts. The second letter handles the kernel of the whole question of Materialism. It might be called 'Kraft und Stoff,' if it were not that we must consider the title it actually bears, 'Motion Essential to Matter,' to be even clearer.

We have repeatedly seen how deeply the old notion of matter as a dead, stark, and passive substance enters into all metaphysical questions. In the face of this notion Materialism is simply true. We are here concerned not-with different equally well-founded standpoints, but with different degrees of scientific knowledge. Although the Materialistic view of the world may need a further explanation, it will, at all events, never lead us backwards. When Toland wrote his letters, men's minds had for more than half a century been used to the atomism of Gassendi; the undulation theory of Huyghens had afforded a deep insight into the life of the smallest particles; and if it was only seventy years later, through Priestley's discovery of oxygen, that the first link was fashioned in the infinite chain of chemical action, nevertheless the life of matter down to its smallest particles was definitely determined from experience. Newton, who is always mentioned by Toland with the utmost respect, had, of course, by his theory of the primitive collision, and the weakness with which he demanded the occasional interference of the Creator in the course of his world-machine, left matter in possession of its passivity; but the thought of attraction as a property of all matter speedily freed itself from the idle patchwork which the theologically narrow ideas of Newton had connected with it. The world of gravitation lived in itself; and it is no wonder that the freethinkers of the eighteenth century, with Voltaire at their head, regarded themselves as the Newtonian natural philosophers. Toland goes on, relying upon indications of Newton's, to maintain that no body is in absolute rest; nay, with an ingenious application of the old English Nominalism, which helped this people to make so great an advance in the philosophy of nature, he explains activity and pas

"Letters to Serena, London, 1704, first book: "Fieri etenim potest ut p. 2or. The passages of the " Prin-nullum revera quiescat corpus," and cipia" there cited (p. 7 and p. 16a of p. 162: "Hactenus exposui motus the 1st ed.), are to be found in the corporura attractorum ad centrum note to the preliminary explanations, immobile, quale tamen vix extat iu and at the beginning of § 1 1 of the rerum nature." sivity, rest and motion, to be purely relative notions, while the eternal inherent activity of matter operates with equal force when, in counteraction to other forces, it maintains a hody in comparative rest, and when it lends it an accelerated motion.

"Every motion is as well a passion in respect of the body that gave it the last determination, as it is an action compared to the body that it determines next; but the turning of these and such words from a relative to an absolute signification has occasioned most of the errors and disputes on this subject." 80 Unhistorical, like the majority of his contemporaries, Toland does not observe that the absolute notions are naturally developed, while the relative notions, on the contrary, are a product of culture and of science. "These determinations of motion in the parts of solid extended matter are what we call the phenomena of nature, and to which we give names or ascribe uses, perfection or imperfection, according as they affect our senses, and cause pain or pleasure to our bodies, contribute to our preservation or destruction; but we do not always denominate them from their real causes or ways of producing one another, as the elasticity, hardness, softness, fluidity, quantity, figures, and relations of particular bodies. On the contrary, we frequently attribute many determinations of motion to no cause at all, as the spontaneous motion of animals; for, however these motions may be accompanied by thought, yet, considered as motions, they have their physical causes, such as a dog's running after a hare, the bulk of the external object acting by its whole force of impulse or attraction on the nerves, which are so disposed with the muscles, joints, and other parts as to produce various motions in the animal machine. And whoever understands in any measure the action of bodies on one another by their immediate contact, or by the imperceptible particles that continually flow from them, and to this knowledge joins that of mechanics, hydrostatics, and anatomy, will be convinced that all tho motions of sitting, standing, lying, rising, running, walking, and such others, have their proper, external, material, and proportionable determinations." Greater clearness cannot be desired. Toland obviously regards thought as a phenomenon which is an inherent accompaniment of the material movements in the nervous system, much as the light which results from a galvanic current. The voluntary motions are motions of matter, which arise in accordance with the same laws that govern all other motions, only in a more complicated apparatus.

Letters to Serena, p. 200 not 100, as in the German edition. —Tb.

When Toland accordingly goes on to intrench himself behind a much more general expression of Newton's, and at length expressly guards against the idea that his system makes the theory of a controlling reason superfluous, we cannot help remembering his distinction between the exoteric and esoteric teaching. The anonymously published "Pantheistikon," which may on that account be very well regarded as esoteric, reverences no transcendental world-spirit of any kind, but only the universe in immutable unity of spirit and matter. Yet so much we may, at any rate, collect from the conclusion of the remarkable letter—that Toland does not, like the ancient Materialists, consider this present world as a merely casual result preceded by innumerable imperfect experiments, but assumes a magnificent purposefulness immutably inherent in the universe. Letters to Serena, pp. 231-233. false, but plausible; it belongs to tho Compare Letters to Serena, pp. same point of the calculation of pro 234-237. Toland here employs, with babilities on tho total misunder regard to the Empedoklean principle standing of which von Hart mann has of evolution, and as far as we can seo based his 'Philosophy of the TJncon quite seriously, the illustration that scious.' Toland, however, in we can just as little explain the de-other respects, by no means sub velopment of a flower or a fly out of scribes to the Epikurean theory, even the in itself objectless concurrence in the most important points. Ha of atoms, as the development of an rejected the atoms and void space,

"Aeneid " or an "Iliad" out of the and with it also the notion of any myriad combinations of the single space at all existing independently of letters. The arjrunent is matter.

Toland is one of those benevolent beings who exhibit to us a great character in the complete harmony of all the sides of human existence. After an eventful life he enjoyed in cheerful calmness of soul the secluded stillness of country life. When scarcely over fifty years of age he was attacked by a disease, which he endured with the calmness of a philosopher. A few days before his death he prepared his epitaph; he took leave of his friends, and fell asleep in untroubled peace of spirit The English reader may be re-1876, a vol.), where indeed Toland ferred also to Mr. Leslie Stephen's seems to be somewhat underrated.

recent "History of English Thought — Tb. in the Eighteenth Century" (Loud.

, END OF VOL. I. PRINTED BY BALLANTYNE, HANSON AND CO.

EDINBURGH AND LONDON

CPSIA information can be obtained at www.ICGtesting.com
Printed in the USA
BVOW09s1110110416

443439BV00028B/43/P